Christian faith in its *wholeness* is the concern of this unusual volume. Professor Gordh seeks to discern and define the "self-consistent character" of historic Christianity and show how it is reflected in all expressions of the faith.

To show Christian faith as a whole, he describes it in three dimensions. First, Christian faith is *a way of looking* at the world and its meaning—at man and his significance. Then, Christian faith is *a set of attitudes*—towards nature, towards oneself, towards others, both in the close relationships of family and friends, and in the larger relationships of racial, economic, and political groups. Third, Christian faith is *a set of expressions.* In ways that are characteristically Christian, men worship (both individually and in church), create art, write books, engage in actions, associate with one another, and use their minds.

Thus, historic Christianity is presented as a faith of individuals, the faith of a church, and as an element in the forming of Western culture.

In dealing with the entire range of Christian concern, the book relates present-day Christianity to the faith of the past. It draws heavily on the Bible, traces the development of creeds in the early church, and treats such works as Dante's *Divine Com-*

(Continued on back flap)

(Continued from front flap)

edy, Kafka's *The Castle*, and Auden's *For the Time Being.*

"The present is recovering a faith which has been partly obscured during the last few centuries," writes Professor Gordh. He intends this work to lead to further study, further recovery, further understanding of the faith, "for no Christian can be exempt from the task of thinking through his faith and its relation to the world in which he lives."

The Author

George Gordh, Ph.D. University of Chicago, is at present Professor of Religion at Hollins College. His articles have appeared in *Review and Expositor*, *Motive*, and *The Journal of Religion.*

CHRISTIAN FAITH AND ITS CULTURAL EXPRESSION

PRENTICE-HALL INTERNATIONAL, INC.
London • Tokyo • Sydney • Paris
PRENTICE-HALL OF CANADA, LTD.
PRENTICE-HALL DE MEXICO, S.A.

CHRISTIAN FAITH AND ITS CULTURAL EXPRESSION

GEORGE GORDH
HOLLINS COLLEGE

PRENTICE-HALL, INC.
ENGLEWOOD CLIFFS, N. J.
1962

Library of Congress Catalog Card No.: 62-13195

Printed in the United States of America

13348-C

TO GWEN

PREFACE

Historic Christianity is here presented as a total faith. It is a vision of the world and its meaning, of man and his significance. It is a set of attitudes toward nature and self, toward others as individuals and in groups. Faith is also a set of expressions in worship and art, in literature and action, in association and thought. All of these together form the wholeness which is historic Christianity.

If the thesis of the book is valid, there is a character in historic Christianity; and this character is apprehended in the vision and reflected in the attitudes of faith. It is that which runs through the various expressions and makes them what they are. It is that which makes it possible to say of them, despite their variety, "These are Christian."

While the book owes much to contemporary scholars, to the reading of works from the past, and to hours spent in discussion with teachers, colleagues, and students, it is, obviously, the work of an individual. This fact involves both advantage and limitation. The author is not a specialist in all the areas discussed. Technical proficiency would have been gained if a group of men had been invited to write a symposium. Unity of perspective, however, would have been forfeited. The author here presents the faith as it makes sense to him. More than this, he speaks of a faith which has taken hold of him, by which he seeks to live. If his holding to the faith is interpreted as a limitation, so be it; the reader is warned. However, he gives his word that the faith as he has known it is ever growing, though sometimes new understanding has come only after struggle and even doubt. Since the book points to the classics of faith and seeks to invite discriminating thought and discussion, perhaps the limitations are not so serious as if the author sought to speak the last word.

When I think of those whose words and works have influenced me most in writing this book, they include the following: Edwin E. Aubrey, Karl Barth, Emil Brunner, William Owen Carver, Nels F. S. Ferré, Bernard M. Loomer, Bernard E. Meland, Reinhold Niebuhr, Anders Nygren, Wilhelm Pauck, Preston T. Roberts, Jr., J. Coert Rylaarsdam, Paul Tillich, Harold W. Tribble, Henry Nelson Wieman, Amos Wilder, and Gustaf Wingren. John R. Everett, President of Hollins College at the time the book was projected, gave helpful counsel. The chapter on the chapel owes a great deal to William L. Addkison and Randolph Frantz, the architects, and to Arthur S. Talmadge, Choirmaster and Professor of Music at Hollins College, as well as to John R. Everett. Many people made significant suggestions with reference to the building; among those whose counsel was particularly relevant to the matters treated in this book are Willard N. James, Vice President; Miss Frances Niederer, Professor of Art; and Edmund B. Wright, organist—all of Hollins College—and to Milton C. Grigg, Consulting Arcithect. Miss Dorothy Doerr, the college librarian, and her staff have been most generous with time and effort; I thank them. I am grateful, too, to Hollins College for granting me a leave so that the work could be carried out. A special word of appreciation is due the administration and faculty of Crozer Theological Seminary where I spent a sabbatical year during which most of the book was written. To the staff of Prentice-Hall, Inc., especially Miss Cora DeVorsey, who has seen the book through production, I am indebted for much valuable assistance. My wife, Gwen Reed Gordh, has been my constant companion in the writing, giving encouragement and making helpful suggestions, typing the manuscript and undertaking innumerable details of its preparation.

No one can write of the faith that is his own, I suppose, without a deep feeling of what he owes to many through whom that faith came to him. For the memory of my father and mother, for churches, ministers, and devoted laymen, for Christian schools, I am deeply grateful.

Ideas have come from many sources. But the way I have used them and put them together is my own, and I must accept responsibility for it. I know that my words do not do justice to the faith they intend to present.

George Gordh

TABLE OF CONTENTS

INTRODUCTORY

THE VISION

INTRODUCTORY

I

THE RECOVERY OF HISTORIC CHRISTIANITY

One of the striking phenomena of the present time is the recovery of historic Christianity. During recent years a flood of books has come upon the market both reflecting and contributing to *The Reawakening of Christian Faith.*[1] The recovery has occurred in the most varied of denominational outlooks and backgrounds. Roman Catholic theologians have examined and re-examined the writings of Saint Thomas Aquinas and other men who have profoundly influenced the faith of the church. Among Protestants there has been a rediscovery of Martin Luther; studies of Calvin and other reformers have appeared in a steady stream. Catholic and Protestant writers have turned to the fathers of the early church to discover what they have said on a variety of subjects. Editions of Christian writings from all the centuries during the life of the church have been produced under a variety of auspices. The prefix *Neo* has been almost worn out—we have had theologies Neo-Thomist and Neo-Scholastic, Neo-Protestant and Neo-Orthodox. We have even had outbreaks of Neo-Naturalism and Neo-Liberalism.

---

[1] Bernard E. Meland, *The Reawakening of Christian Faith* (New York: The Macmillan Company, 1949).

1. THE DISTINCTIVENESS OF THE CHRISTIAN FAITH

Common to the various thinkers of whom we have spoken is the conviction that historic Christianity has something distinctive to say, and that our time is one in which it needs to be said. Indeed, it is the very desperation of the present which in part explains a turning to the past. When the resources about us seem meager, we are apt to look farther afield. And people may well seek for a wisdom that comes to them across the centuries when they feel that what their contemporaries can tell them is not enough. The feeling may indeed be strengthened, if men believe that part of the confusion of the present is due to the severance of life from some of its deepest historic rootages.

The attempt to recover historic Christianity is due in part to the conviction that what has come to be called Christianity among many people is a very poor substitute for the real thing. And yet since the substitute continues to make use of the Christian words, it is easily mistaken for the reality. When there is no great issue at stake, such substitution may not be serious; but there are circumstances under which it can be tragic. The Christian world was appalled when in the name of Christianity the Nazi program of blood and soil received religious sanction. During World War II I was once asked to preach to a group of German prisoners. As I prepared my sermon, I suddenly realized that there were certain words which would have been clearly understood in their Christian sense by American audiences but simply could not be used among a group of men trained as Hitler-youth. I had intended, for example, to speak of "the day" which the Hebrew prophets foretold. Since I was to preach a Christmas sermon, such reference seemed entirely natural. But I came to the shocked realization that I must not say, "*Der Tag.*" The word would not mean what I intended it to convey.

I have used a personal illustration simply to indicate what a great many people came to feel in view of the onslaughts of National Socialism upon the Christian faith. These people came to wonder if we in our time had simply ceased to be aware of the true nature of the faith, if we indeed could tell what was Christian from what only pretended to be. And that wonder drove many to re-examine historic Christianity. Confronted with it they came to feel more than ever that Christian faith did have something to say to our world. For some it was not exactly what they had thought it was.

It is important to see that the recovery is not a wholesale dredging up of the past. Some among our contemporaries do want to recover the past in quite literal form. They want, for example, to hold the faith of the reformers in practically the form it assumed in the sixteenth century. Some feel that the Bible is inerrant in its accounts of scientific and historical matters, and if modern science questions them, so much the worse for science. The greater number of thinkers, however, feel that the past cannot be recovered so simply. Many are rather sophisticated moderns; indeed, sometimes they appear to be considerably more sophisticated than some of their liberal critics. They see the Bible against the backgrounds of history, within the context of ancient cultures. They find in it much that reflects the limited outlooks of men of their time. In many cases, they even regard some of the religious viewpoints of the Bible as being the common religious viewpoints of the primitives—which modern men must frankly reject. But they feel that there is something of abiding and even tremendous significance in the faith of the Bible and in the continuing faith of the Christian people. Just what this is, how it is to be delineated, how it is to be distinguished from that which is to be left in the past—these are problems of great difficulty. We shall be looking at them again and again.

Contemporary thinkers differ, of course, about just what the heart of historic Christianity is. And yet there is a remarkable amount of agreement among them. It is our purpose here to set forth for examination and discussion some of those points where wide agreement appears. The intention is to report what has been said and what is being said today.

2. THE MASSIVENESS OF THE CHRISTIAN FAITH

Christianity cannot be reduced to any brief and simple formula. It seems that this is an affirmation on which there is almost universal agreement. Its distinctiveness cannot be captured in a phrase. Not all writers find it necessary to go to the lengths that Professor Karl Barth of Basel does in order to deal with it. But even those who do not require the quantities of ink used by the Swiss Professor are aware of what one thinker, Professor Herbert H. Farmer of Cambridge, has called "the massive unity" [2] of Christian faith.

Sensitivity to the range and subtlety of faith is held to be imperative if Christianity is to be clearly distinguished from spurious substitutes.

[2] Herbert H. Farmer, *God and Men* (New York: Abingdon Press, 1947), p. 11. Reprinted by permission.

Its massiveness and its distinctiveness are correlatives. An oversimplified Christianity fell prey to the Nazi perversions of which I have spoken. Elsewhere, too, an oversimple version of Christianity has produced captive churches. Currents of life stretching through the centuries since the Renaissance have engulfed the historic faith of the church. Often what is proclaimed from the pulpits is Christian in name only. Simplified Protestantism rendered the conscience of the church insensitive to some of the most fearful brutalities of industrial society and turned a revolutionary prophetism into a thin veneer of respectability over blatantly anti-Christian forms of behavior.

That Christianity should have been simplified was inevitable. After the first flush of enthusiasm produced by the Reformation, learned men sought by prodigious scholarship to guard the insights which had been set forth. In doing so, they changed a living faith into a new set of ideas which must be held—they produced what is generally called by historians of Christian thought "Protestant Orthodoxy." Thinkers representing the various strands of the reformation fought with one another, each holding that his particular brand of thought was the true way of setting forth the heart of the faith. The war of ecclesiastical parties was not restricted to words, however. Germany was devastated from 1618 to 1648 by the marching of armies Protestant and Catholic engaged in the Thirty Years' War. England was soon treated to the spectacle of Protestant against Protestant fighting for the glory of God. It was not surprising that a reaction set in. People were ready to listen to a voice which said, "A plague o' both your houses," [3] and went on to say that the real heart of religion was not to be found in the things about which scholars and soldiers were struggling.

The heart of religion, said some, is so simple that every man in his right mind would agree to it: there is a God, men ought to be good, and God will reward good men here and hereafter. This religion of reason was republished, some said, in a particularly attractive form in Christianity—though the heart of the latter is as old as creation. Men of such views were influential in Europe in the late seventeenth and early eighteenth centuries. In England they were known as Deists, in France they were among "the illumined," and in Germany, among "the clear-minded." They had clarified Christianity and reduced it to that which every rational man could—indeed, must—accept, and even the savage was thought to be rational enough to recognize the religion of nature.

---

[3] William Shakespeare, "Romeo and Juliet," Act III, Sc. 1, *The Works of William Shakespeare* (New York: Oxford University Press, 1938), p. 262.

With the waning of confidence in reason, late in the eighteenth century, this religion appeared to be doomed. However, a stout champion of its tenets appeared, though he provided them with a new base. Immanuel Kant was ready to admit the limitations of reason; but, he urged, the reality of the moral life cannot be doubted. Men are, under some circumstances, called upon to live according to principle; they are confronted by a moral law. And yet, that confrontation is incomprehensible unless we postulate the reality of God, of freedom, and of immortality—the trio of tenets of rationalist religion. Kant was sensitive to some of the subtleties of moral life, however, and he believed that some of the traditional Christian doctrines were ways of speaking of those subtleties. But the doctrines could be treated "within the limits of reason alone,"[4] and their basic reference was to the moral life—which took on a religious character when its demands were regarded as divinely ordained.

At the very time that Kant was writing, however, a groundswell of attitude was sweeping across Europe which was to modify men's views of religion profoundly. Men were developing a new dimension of sensitivity. Feeling, rather than reason, was held to lead to the discovery of the depth of man's being, of the nature in which he lived, of other men of his own time and the past, of the spirit of peoples and nations. The Romantic movement expressed itself in poetry and art, in novel and drama, in collections of folksongs, in social and political theory. It is no wonder that it expressed itself also in the interpretation of religion. The greatest interpreter was a man named Friedrich Schleiermacher, who addressed "the cultured despisers" of religion with the thesis that faith is not something to be believed nor acted; it is something to be felt. To call his seven hundred and fifty page exposition of *The Christian Faith* a simplification appears a bit strange on the surface. And yet, it really was. For he took the traditional statements of belief of the Christian Church and traced them, one by one, back to their rootage in experience. In the process he demonstrated—at least to the satisfaction of himself and many others—that many complexities of expression could be relegated to the past, that many of the ideas connected with religion could be discarded, even though the experiences to which they pointed were in many instances valid.

Thus the past few centuries have seen a series of attempts to set forth a simplified Christianity. Reason, morality, and experience have been proposed as foci around which religion revolves. The distinctiveness and

---

[4] Immanuel Kant, *Religion Within the Limits of Reason Alone*, Theodore M. Greene and Hoyt H. Hudson, trans. (Chicago: The Open Court Publishing Company, 1934), p. 145, and elsewhere.

the massiveness of the faith have been reduced to a minimum or denied altogether.

The efforts at simplification have their value, however. The reaction against them, like most other reactions in history, includes much of what they held to be important. To them is due, in no small measure, a fact which we have noted: that the contemporary recovery of historic faith is no mere dredging up of the past. According to many of our contemporaries the rationalists were right in attacking miracles and magical interpretations of prophecy. They helped to clear the air for a significant rather than a superficial reappropriation of historic faith. And the moralists were right in insisting that faith should issue in responsible action. The social gospel, which issued from Christianity morally interpreted, may have been wrong in some of its theologizing, but it was profoundly right in insisting that Christian faith must be vitally concerned about what happens in economic and political life. And the emphasis on feeling in religion may have sometimes delivered faith to a bathotic sentimentalism. But it was right in pointing out that at some point faith must come to a confrontation with reality which involves the depths of life in its emotional as well as its other dimensions. Men of the past few centuries were right in pointing out that intellect, morality, and feeling are important to the life of faith. In holding that one or another of these could be regarded as a focus around which all else must revolve, however, they appear to many contemporary Christian thinkers to have been mistaken—even disastrously so. The recovery of a faith significant for our time involves the recovery of a massive reality.

3. THE CHARACTER OF CHRISTIAN FAITH

Massiveness, however, is not enough. The whole of historic Christianity cannot be recovered. If the faith is to have something significant to say to our time, it will be because it has something that is recognizably relevant. It must have a character that persists through changes. And our contemporaries are convinced that it does. In their writings such phrases as "from the Christian point of view" and "according to Christian faith" are frequently found.

It may seem strange to press this point. But when it is seen against its historical background, the procedure is understandable. The nineteenth century saw a variety of attempts to define the character of Christianity. And the results exhibited a startling variety. John Henry Newman saw the Christian faith as a developing Catholicism, ever changing, indeed, but ever itself as the faith of Rome.[5] Ludwig Feuerbach held the *Essence of Christianity*—this was the title of his book—to be human love without divine relationships.[6] And in a widely read work which came out about the year 1900, a distinguished liberal Christian named Adolf Harnack asked, *What is Christianity?* and answered that it is the message of "God the Father and the infinite value of the human soul."[7] It is small wonder that, faced with the variety of answers that had been given to the question, a responsible historian like Shirley Jackson Case would conclude that the search for the essence of Christianity is utterly vain.[8] Christianity as he saw it was whatever it was at any given time. Thus to him the search for the character of historic Christianity was a fruitless one.

And yet our contemporaries speak as they do; for them there is a character in Christianity, there are elements which define it. And they are remarkably well agreed on what these are. Granted that the historic faith is massive; it still has a discernible character. And they are agreed for the most part that the character is not to be found in any set of doctrines. Indeed, the point were better stated positively: the character of Christianity is such that no set of doctrines is adequate to express it. They tend, therefore, to speak in such terms as "the Christian point of view." One writer has issued a book entitled *The Christian Perspective*.[9] Emil Brunner has argued repeatedly and in various ways that truth as the Christian understands it is personal encounter; to identify it with doctrines is to distort it—the story is more appropriate than the declarative sentence for its depiction.[10] Anders Nygren has carefully worked out a methodology for discovering the motifs of Christianity which form a structure of meaning at the center of which is a fundamental motif.

---

[5] John H. Newman, *An Essay on the Development of Christian Doctrine* (New York: Longmans, Green and Company, 1949).

[6] Ludwig Feuerbach, *The Essence of Christianity*, George Eliot, trans. (New York: Harper & Brothers, 1957), see p. 339.

[7] Adolf Harnack, *What Is Christianity?* Thomas B. Sanders, trans. (New York: Harper & Brothers, 1957), p. 51; see also pp. 63-70. Reprinted by permission.

[8] Shirley Jackson Case, *The Evolution of Early Christianity* (Chicago: University of Chicago Press, 1914), ch. 2.

[9] Edward T. Ramsdell, *The Christian Perspective* (New York: Abingdon Press, 1950).

[10] Perhaps the most direct statement of the point is given in *The Divine-Human Encounter*, Amandus W. Loos, trans. (Philadelphia: The Westminster Press; London: S. C. M. Press Ltd., 1943).

The motif-structure persists through changing doctrines; these are at most symptoms of its presence.[11] Reinhold Niebuhr has insisted that Christianity is a mythical religion, whose character can be discerned only when one recognizes levels of meaning which lie beyond the possibility of coherent systematization.[12] Thus, in a variety of ways writers of our time describe the heart of the faith in ways that are not primarily doctrinal.

They do not disregard doctrines, however. They find them more important than did the various simplifiers of the faith. Indeed, they take seriously the breadth of concern evinced by the classical Christian theologians. This is part of the massiveness of the faith as they see it. But when they seek to delineate the faith, they speak of a character that is only partly caught in any doctrinal statement.

4. THE SUBJECT OF OUR STUDY

This, then, is our present situation. We live in a time when thoughtful men urge that historic Christianity has something vital to say to us; and that if we are to hear it, we must discern a character in that faith which may have become obscured from us. It is at this point that our own study begins. We are seeking to discover the basic character of Christian faith while we take into account its inherent massiveness. This book suggests two considerations as guides for our effort:

> Christian faith is like a figure in three dimensions; it is a vision, a set of attitudes, and a group of interrelated expressions;
>
> the faith defined by the dimensions receives three sorts of embodiment: in individuals, in church, and in culture.

Whatever else Christianity may be, it is certainly a personal faith. To say this is to say that it is something around which life may be organized, something which can be at the center of life. It is something by which men have lived and for which they have died. It is a fundamental attitude. To this attitude an entire section of this volume is devoted. The

---

[11] The technical aspects of Nygren's methodology appear in works which have not been translated into English. A brief statement is given in the Introduction to *Agape and Eros*, Philip S. Watson, trans. (Philadelphia: The Westminster Press, 1953), pp. 27-49. Nels F. S. Ferré has described the methodology in detail in *Swedish Contributions to Modern Theology* (New York: Harper & Brothers, 1939).

[12] Reinhold Niebuhr, *An Interpretation of Christian Ethics* (New York: Harper & Brothers, 1935), ch. 1.

word *fundamental,* here, must be taken with full seriousness; it denotes that which lies at the foundation of all else. Now this fundamental attitude is clearly the attitude toward God; and yet with it are bound up a whole set of attitudes. These may be distinguished as they appear in the various relationships of life—with things, with oneself, and with others. This fundamental attitude may be compared to the horizontal in a three-dimensional figure; it is that which forms the base line for everything else.

When we seek to define the attitudes of the Christian, however, we find ourselves confronting certain questions: Who is God and what is he like? What kind of world is this? What sort of beings are we? What claims do others have on us? These questions, and others like them, are answered in terms of the ways in which we look at the world and its meaning, at man and his significance. The general answers which Christian faith has given to them constitute the Christian vision; to it the first section of the book is given. It is like the dimension which recedes into the distance, giving a sense of depth to the horizontal line which is drawn against it.

The expressions of faith are like verticals, arising from the horizontal line of fundamental attitude against the background of vision. To them the final section of the book is devoted. If a man's faith is reflected in his attitudes, these in turn will find expression. Rather obviously, his attitudes will be expressed in worship and also in actions. He will express his faith by associating himself with others in a church. If he possesses certain talents, he may also give expression to his faith by creating art or literature, and these will bear a certain character by reason of the faith of their creator. Finally, he will express his faith by thinking about it, by trying to discern its meaning, and its significance for his life.

If we are to see faith as a whole, it is important that we distinguish the expressions from the vision and the attitudes. Otherwise we are likely to reduce its wholeness and seek to make one of its expressions equivalent to faith in its totality. Often faith is viewed as fundamentally ethical, or the whole of religion is traced back to worship. When this is done, the relation between the expressions is obscured, and their mutual relation to the whole of faith is not clearly seen. However, at some given moment one expression may be the focal point for faith, even for the totality of faith. There is a time to worship and a time to act, a time to write poetry and a time to be in church. Faith in its fullness is relevant to all the moments of life. Further, there are differences among human beings such that one of faith's expressions will be more central for one person than it is for another. "There are varieties of gifts," said the Apostle Paul, "but the same Spirit." [13] And yet there is no person, perhaps, who will not, at some time or other, express his faith in most of the ways that are to be described. If the faith is to be kept whole, none may be neglected. While the distinctions are important for analysis, however, they often disappear in life itself. The expressions of faith affect one another, and the expressions help to form the attitudes. Faith is not simply the sum of its parts; but the whole may be seen more clearly if its parts are distinguished and their relation to one another clearly envisaged.

Correlative of personal faith is the faith of the church. To determine which is prior is as difficult as to assign priority to the chicken or the egg. Each contributes to the other. Individual faith arises within the church, and the individual shares with others a faith which thus becomes that of the church. Just as individual faith is a center around which life is organized, so is faith the center around which the life of the church is organized. In it is treasured the vision by which it lives; by it are inculcated those attitudes which determine its very character; from it spring expressions which are the correlates of the expressions of personal faith.

In some cases the social forms of the expressions of faith differ somewhat from the individual. The worship of the congregation includes much that private devotion omits. Usually Christians sing hymns, listen to sermons, break bread and drink wine together. Because of the church there is religious architecture; the needs of congregational worship call liturgies and anthems into being. The church baptizes, solemnizes marriages, buries the dead. Its faith expresses itself in ways that are fitting to the varied experiences of life, and yet the several expressions are related. The wholeness of the church's faith is realized when its vision is so vivid, its attitudes so sure, that their expression becomes a veritable necessity.

With the faith of the church this book has special concern, for the church has been the bearer of the common faith of Christians through the centuries. As we trace out the lineaments of the Christian vision, we shall have to look at significant decisions which were made long ago. As we seek to understand the attitudes of Christians, we shall have to

---

[13] I Corinthians 12:4.*

* Unless otherwise indicated, the scripture quotations in this publication are from the Revised Standard Version of the Bible, copyrighted 1946 and 1952 by the Division of Christian Education, National Council of the Churches of Christ, and are used by permisssion. The notation "K. J. V." will indicate reference to the "King James Version."

attend to trends and tendencies which have been felt in the traditions of the Christian people.

We must, however, take account of the fact that the church has been and now is divided. Christians differ, and their differences cannot be taken lightly. Where it is possible, this book seeks to reflect the faith which is common to the various Christian communions. At times some important divergencies of interpretation are indicated. At certain points the exposition will clearly favor some interpretation of the faith over others because it seems to the author to be more adequate to the fullness of faith than its rivals. Sometimes differences of opinion or practice will be noted as divergent ways of expressing a common faith. Here, as elsewhere, the intention of the book to stimulate discussion is to be taken seriously. One of its objects is to furnish materials for that conversation which is going on actively within the church itself in our time as men of various communions confront one another seeking seriously to discover the fullness of faith.

Because a culture reflects attitudes, because it is infused by vision, it has a religious dimension. And in the history of the West, the attitudes and vision of Christian faith, personal and ecclesiastical, have deeply affected the culture as a whole. Here our concern is not to make a judgment on the extent to which Western culture can be called Christian. However, it seems safe to say, that over a considerable period Christian faith was a determining factor in the ethos of the West. Over the past few centuries powerful forces have been at work which have lessened the influence of Christianity. And now, when our culture appears to be in crisis, when guiding lines are difficult to discern, the question of what the religious center of culture should be is one of momentous concern. To see what the vision and attitudes of historic Christianity have been is to introduce matters relevant for consideration.

Not alone at the level of vision and attitude, however, have Christianity and Western culture been interrelated. When we come to consider the expressions of Christian faith, we shall find that in the early centuries of the church these derived much from the culture into which the faith entered. Christians said their prayers, painted their pictures, worked out their theologies with materials which were, in part, borrowed from their pagan predecessors and contemporaries. We shall see also that Christians have given direct expression to their faith in ways that have contributed to the cultural heritage. Faith has inspired music, influenced political figures, and affected the course of economic history. Further, the vision and attitudes of Christianity, insofar as they have been shared with the culture, have influenced even the expressions of that culture which have no specific religious content. Men of the West have written secular plays, composed secular music, and have tried to set forth principles of government on purely natural and rational grounds. They have done these things partly because their culture was imbued with ideals of Christian faith. Some understanding of that faith is requisite for the understanding of the culture of the West.

5. FAITH AND THOUGHT

Since we are seeking to understand historic Christianity, we must give special attention to efforts at stating men's understanding of their faith through the centuries. We shall have to give particular attention to that expression of the faith which is concerned for understanding—theology. To it an entire chapter will be devoted later, but a few words here are in place. Like the other expressions of faith it takes on both individual and social forms. It appears in the church and is reflected in the culture. Perhaps the simplest clue to its character may be given if we note the nature of thought in any situation. Whatever else we do when we think, we distinguish and relate matters by means of ideas. And theology is the distinguishing and relating of ideas that have to do with a specific religious faith.

Theology serves the church insofar as it defines the church's faith. Much of the time it is in the background, the unconscious assumption of that which is done. But there are occasions when it has seemed important to the church to state just what its faith is. Particularly during the early centuries do we find such statements, and they have been determinative of the whole course of Christian thinking. Sometimes these are credal in character, sometimes affirmations about authorities by which the church will be guided. These statements were forthcoming in part because of the cultural situation in which the church emerged. People were already worshipping, painting, associating, acting, thinking; and it became necessary for Christians to distinguish their own ways of doing these things from the ways in which others did them. At the same time, they related their own ways to those of others; sometimes they found common ground with them. Some ideas and patterns of action were rejected, others accepted; some were modified slightly, others creatively transformed. Those ideas which were held to be incompatible with the faith were called *heresy;* those which were regarded as being in accord with faith were designated as *orthodox.*

The theology of the church would clearly be impossible without the work of individuals. A large group cannot lift out issues, hammer out ideas, state matters with precision. In a sense, of course, every Christian must be a theologian; he has to think about his faith and its implications for his life. But some become theologians of the church because of the contribution they make to the common faith. Among these there are some who are especially concerned with distinguishing the faith, with stating what the Christian faith is. Their work is sometimes called *kerygmatic.* Others enter into conversation with the culture about them, seeking to relate the ideas of Christians to those of others. Sometimes they will consciously employ ideas from the culture for the explication of the faith. It sometimes happens, however, that a man who intends to be a theologian, to contribute to the faith of the church, gives expression to ideas which the church at large regards as out of character with its faith. He becomes, then, even though unwittingly, a heretic. It also happens that a man's ideas are regarded as heretical during his lifetime but later are regarded as compatible with orthodoxy. The task of theology is thus one which is ever going on. New ideas arise within the culture, new problems are encountered.

We must not think, however, that theology is simply responsive, called into being as culture confronts the church. To see it in its fullness is to take account of the fact that the doctrines of the church and the ideas of her theologians have had a formative influence within the culture of the West. Theology, like faith's other expressions, is individual, churchly, and cultural.

But thought remains one expression of faith, and no more. To focus attention too strongly upon it is to distort that which theology itself seeks to understand. Beyond theology is the wholeness of faith. To enter into it is more than to think; it is to act, perhaps to paint or create poetry, to enter into the life of the church, to worship. To think on these things, however, may bring clarity to their execution. And to recall the faith of past centuries is to bring resources for their full expression.

The purpose of this book is to describe that faith—historic Christianity. For the most part, it does not go beyond that point. Thus, in its delineation of Christian thought it takes account of the fact that theology and philosophy have always been in some relation with one another. But it does not set forth one theory of what that relationship ought to be. There have been various theories and there are various theories today. This book does not try to single out one; its concern is to describe what Christianity has to say in its conversation with any philosophy. In its delineation of art the book does not try to deal with any specific theory of art, and then try to relate Christianity to that theory. It seeks rather to describe what faith offers for expression in art. The book does not try to define just what the relationship of faith and culture is. There have been numbers of ways in which the relation of faith to culture has been conceived. This book seeks simply to delineate what the faith is which enters into relation with culture.

The book does not define the relation of Christianity to other faiths, religious and secular, that are abroad in the world today. To do so would involve the delineation of the character of those other faiths. It does deal with ways in which Christians have responded to the faith reflected in the Old Testament and to influences stemming from the life of Greece. And it occasionally will point up the differences between including some emphasis that appears in Christianity and omitting it. But it certainly does not intend to claim that everything which belongs to the character of Christian faith is the exclusive possession of Christians. To decide whether other faiths share it or not means to study those faiths. Conversation between Christianity and other faiths properly goes on in our time. This book intends to clarify what Christian faith might say in such conversation.

I have said that for the most part the purpose of this book does not go beyond description. But it is impossible to avoid some standpoints. The very fact that the book uses language of twentieth century America means that it is written within a certain context of meaning. It uses terms which are heard around a college campus, terms which issue from psychology, sociology, philosophy, and other disciplines. The commonly accepted results of modern Biblical scholarship are assumed. The faith is viewed from the standpoint of the here and the now. The chapter about the building of a college chapel in particular involves reference to the way in which Christian faith receives a very specific expression, one that is related in peculiar ways to the present. But even here notice is taken of the fact that other ages have expressed an enduring faith in other ways. If the Christian faith is anything like what I take it to be, it offers itself for our appropriation here and now, in this present. At the same time, it places a question mark over all that we do and think—even over our appropriation of the faith itself. We are faced then with the difficult problem of delineating that which comes to us in our time and yet transcends our time.

The book is intended for two groups of readers, though the same person might belong to both groups at different times. The groups may be compared to students who come to the examination of a piece of art. One is a student of history and is concerned with a picture because of what it adds to the understanding of the century in which it was painted.

Its artistic merit is a matter of indifference; its aesthetic effect on the student himself does not concern him. He may be moved by it or not. As a student of history he wants to understand a certain century, and the picture helps him do it. Another person is deeply moved by the picture and comes to a study of it in the effort to derive richer and fuller appreciation of it. He studies its colors and contours, he reads about its creator, about trends of artistic production, about symbolisms—indeed, he studies everything he can lay his hands on which deals with the picture. And after his study he looks at it again, still in the mood of one who appreciates. But now his response is richer and fuller than before.

This book offers itself to the one seeking understanding. It seeks to set forth the length and breadth and depth of the faith, to show what are the paths that must be pursued if further understanding is sought. It intends to inform the student of Western culture about the Christian elements which have gone into the forming of that culture. It offers itself also to the person who is concerned about Christianity as a faith by which to live. It offers him materials for understanding the faith so that he may enter into an enriched appropriation of that faith in its wholeness.

FOR STUDY AND DISCUSSION

1. What do you take to be the central affirmations of Chrisian faith? Save your statement. Write another after you have completed your study and compare them.
2. What authorities, if any, does your church recognize? Scriptures? Creeds? Confessions? If it rejects such authorities as these, on what grounds does it do so? (Here, as elsewhere in the materials for study and discussion, the phrase "your church," may be taken to refer to the church to which you belong or some church you choose to study.)
3. If a new church has recently been built in your community, has there been a conscious effort to incorporate or to exclude ancient symbols?
4. Which expressions of faith receive most emphasis in your church? Which are neglected? Why?
5. Is the concern of some churches for the recovery of historic Christianity connected with a desire to evade problems of the present? If so, at what points?

the art [illegible] is a matter of indifference [illegible] effect on the student [illegible] does not concern him. He may be moved by it or not, [illegible] wants to understand a certain century and the [illegible] Another person is deeply moved by the [illegible] to a study of it in the effort to deepen [illegible] and the appreciation of it. He studies [illegible] about its creation, about trends [illegible] He studies [illegible] by the hands [illegible] [illegible] he looks at [illegible] the [illegible] of [illegible] [illegible] before.

[illegible] book [illegible] to the [illegible] seeking [illegible] It seeks to [illegible] and breadth and depth of [illegible] to show what are the paths that must be pursued if further [illegible] It intends to inform the student [illegible] about the [illegible] elements [illegible] into the [illegible] of that [illegible] studies [illegible] also to the person who is concerned about [illegible] [illegible] for [illegible] so that [illegible] an [illegible] appreciation of that which [illegible]

FOR STUDY AND DISCUSSION

1. What [illegible] data [illegible] the [illegible] character of Christianity? [illegible] your statement [illegible] after you have completed [illegible] study and [illegible]

2. What [illegible], if any, does your [illegible] Greek? [illegible] such [illegible] as these [illegible] [illegible] in the material [illegible] the [illegible] [illegible] which [illegible]

3. [illegible]

4. What [illegible]? What are [illegible]?

5. Is the [illegible] connected [illegible] pointed?

THE VISION

II

GOD CREATES

A funeral inscription from the world into which Christianity came reads, "I was not, I became; I am not and I care not."[1] I suppose that the man who ordered it to be chiseled for his grave might be called a person without vision. He was faithless, and his faithlessness reflected itself in his fundamental attitude. To men like him Christians said that life did matter. And part of their message was that it mattered because men came from somewhere: they were creatures of God.

The counterpart of the ancient inscription can be found again in our time. If it is not inscribed on tombstones, it is nonetheless voiced by poets and philosophers.[2] And those who are concerned to recover historic Christianity believe that that faith has something to say to men of our time, that it can impart a vision which will transform attitudes.

As we come to look at historic Christianity, the first dimension which concerns us is that of vision. As this book sees it, the Christian vision has three aspects: it is a vision of

---

[1] S. Angus, *The Environment of Early Christianity* (New York: Charles Scribner's Sons, 1932), p. 104. Reprinted by permission.

[2] See, for example, George Sterling, "Omnium Exeunt in Mysterium," Jessie B. Rittenhouse, ed., *The Second Book of Modern Verse* (Boston: Houghton Mifflin Company, 1920), p. 211.

the basic wholeness of life,
its subsequent brokenness, and
its restoration to wholeness.

Theology refers to the aspects of the vision in terms of doctrines: creation, sin, and redemption. This chapter is concerned with creation, with the Christian conviction about the basic wholeness of life and the world.

1. FROM REDEMPTION TO CREATION

It seems natural that Christian thought should begin with a consideration of the creation of the world. After all, nothing could happen before that! The Bible begins with the story of the fashioning of heaven and earth, and the creeds start with the affirmation that God the father is the creator.

Actually, however, Christian thought starts at another point. Chronologically the faith began as response to Jesus of Nazareth and particularly with the conviction that God had raised him from the dead. Theology starts where the faith has its chronological beginning. The central conviction of Christian faith is that God has revealed himself as redeemer in the midst of human history. After it has said this, it can go on to affirm that the God made known in redemption is also the creator. Christian thought characteristically moves from redemption to creation.

In this it is like Hebrew thought which it mirrors. The faith which produced the Old Testament began with the deliverance of the Hebrew people from oppression and misery in Egypt. Under the leadership of Moses they crossed the Red Sea and made their way to the mountain where they were to enter into covenant relations with their God. Their whole religious outlook was determined by the fact that they regarded the Exodus experience as a mighty act of God delivering his people. A great Old Testament scholar points us to Exodus 20:2 if we are to find something like a definition of Divinity in the Old Testament: "I am the Lord your God, who brought you out of the land of Egypt." [3] The Hebrews were convinced that God was their redeemer.

Centuries later they began to find religious significance in the idea that God was also their creator. From early times they had, no doubt, speculated about the beginnings of the world as other peoples did. But only many hundred years after the Exodus was the idea of creation so

[3] H. Wheeler Robinson, *The Religious Ideas of the Old Testament* (London: Duckworth, 1913), p. 51. The quotation as given here follows R.S.V.

compelling that it called forth the supreme poetry of the first and second chapters of Genesis and the fortieth of Isaiah. Then it was that men became convinced that the God who had redeemed them at the Red Sea could care for them in all circumstances since he was the maker of heaven and earth. Beginning with redemption their thought had made its way to the affirmation of creation.

For Christians the central redemptive event was the coming of Jesus Christ. In him there had been a new and greater Exodus. Their bondage had not been in Egypt, but they had lived in fear and hopelessness and guilt. Now God had given them faith and hope and forgiveness. And they were convinced that it was God himself, the eternal One, who had brought them these things. They knew him as they had not known him before, but this was not because he had suddenly taken on a redemptive character. He had always been the same. The character of God as they had come to know him in Christ was the character he had always possessed, even before the creation of the world. They had not known him before Christ as they could after. But once they had known him in Christ they could say, "This God created the world." The Christian assertion of creation is not simply a declaration that some God made it; it reflects the conviction that a certain kind of God made the world, that God whose redemptive character was disclosed in Christ.

This conviction throws light on some of the ideas we encounter in the New Testament and in the creeds. Early Christians spoke of God as they had known him in Christ as "the Son." Through him they had come to a new relationship with God, they had been adopted into his family, they could call him "my Father." The conviction that God was ever the same meant for them that he had always been Father, though men had never fully realized it. They expressed their conviction by saying that God had an eternal Son. And this meant that this son had existed before the foundation of the world, indeed, that he had participated in its creation. Thus Paul wrote that "in him all things hold together," [4] and the author of the Epistle to the Hebrews spoke of him as "upholding the universe by his word of power." [5] The Gospel of John opened with the magnificent words,

> In the beginning was the Word, and the Word was with God, and the Word was God. He was in the beginning with God; all things were made through him, and without him was not anything made that was made.

---

[4] Colossians 1:17.
[5] Hebrews 1:2, K.J.V.

> And the Word became flesh and dwelt among us, full of grace and truth; we have beheld his glory, glory as of the only Son from the Father.[6]

Some hundreds of years later a council of the church at Nicea declared of the Son that he was "begotten, not made," and that "through him all things were made."[7]

The connection of creation with redemption lies back of much that early Christians meant by the assertion that they believed in "God, the Father Almighty, Maker of heaven and earth."[8] They were convinced, as we have seen, that God had always been redemptive. Looking at the matter in another way, we may see that their conviction implied that God ever remained creative. This is important to see, for we often think of the declaration that God is creator as meaning that once upon a time, long, long ago, he made the world; since then it has run by itself. In the seventeenth and eighteenth centuries, particularly, such an interpretation of creation came into fashion. The Deists, of whom we have spoken, often described the Deity as a sort of celestial clock-maker who made a perfect machine which has been running ever since in good order. Their way of thinking, however, was out of character, so far as historic Christianity is concerned. Christians have not, on the whole, relegated God's creativity to the past. It may be helpful to our understanding of Christian writers, however, to note that many of them have reserved the term *creation* for that which took place at the beginning and have spoken of God's continuing relation to the world in terms of providence. But both are aspects of his creative Reality in its everlasting activity.

The assertion that God the redeemer is also creator has meant for Christians that nothing in his world can finally defeat his redemptive purposes; everything in his world can be made to serve them. "He that spared not his own son," wrote Paul, ". . . shall he not with him also freely give us all things?"[9]

2. PROTECTING A CONVICTION

To us it seems so obvious that creation is a central Christian conviction that it may appear strange that there was ever any question about

---

[6] John 1:1-3, 14.
[7] The Nicene Creed.
[8] The Apostles' Creed.
[9] Romans 8:32, K.J.V.

it. But early Christians were in another situation. Their difficulty about creation grew out of the fact that theirs was a religion of redemption and it soon entered into rivalry with other faiths which were also such religions. During the last centuries of the ancient era there was such widespread disillusionment and despair that it was natural for redemptive faiths to make a strong appeal. One of the problems of the early Christians was that of maintaining the distinctiveness of their own faith in the presence of their rivals. Part of that distinctiveness was bound up with their conviction about creation.

Many of these redemptive faiths had a basically similar outlook; they shared a common religious vision. Its central character was often indicated by a myth. Perhaps we can suggest it by recalling a familiar story. All of us remember the folktale we heard as children about Snow White and Rose Red. One of the sisters was kind to a bear who appeared at the door one night. He turned out, of course, to be a prince who had been bewitched. In response to the kindness of Snow White he resumed his true form and married his rescuer. They lived happily ever after.

The story may well have no connection with the religions of the ancient Near East. But it may, too; for it reflects the view of human life and its problems which was mirrored in them; and this view has persisted, often unnoticed, as an influence in European life and thought. At the very beginning of the Christian era it was embodied in a widespread religious movement known as Gnosticism. In it man is regarded as a spirit, a princely being, perhaps even divine. He is imprisoned in an animal body, a material thing. This is foreign to his real being, for matter in itself is evil. The spiritual part of him longs for release. This may come through his attainment of some hidden knowledge. It expresses itself now in religious ecstasy and at the last in freedom from the body in blessed immortality.

It is not strange that the Gnostics, with their view of the body and of all material things, should have denied that a good God created the world. For them the redeemer and the creator, at least the creator of matter, must be distinguished; they might even be regarded as enemies. The attitude of the Gnostics toward the material also affected their thinking about how men should live. It may well seem strange that they drew two entirely opposite conclusions from the premise that the body is evil. Some said that since it was, it had to be treated harshly. No pleasure should be allowed to it; indeed, it should be actively resisted. Abstinence from food and sex in particular were ways in which the demands of the evil body might be resisted. Others held that since the body was not to participate in redemption anyway, it did not matter what it did. In consequence, they permitted themselves kinds of behavior that allowed the body to have whatever it wanted.

It was not long before some of the Gnostics heard of the redeemer proclaimed by the Christians. Some of them joined Christian churches. And able men among them sought to set forth an exposition of Christian faith in terms of the outlook that seemed natural to them. It was their intention to be theologians who related Christian faith to a philosophy prevalent in their time. They set forth their view as a sort of Christianity for the elite. But the dominant trends in the Christian church were against them. Many felt that what they set forth was out of accord with something central in Christian faith. Gnosticism was declared to be heresy.

If we apply to Gnosticism the terms we are using in this book, we will see it as a total religious faith whose dimensions are interrelated. In rejecting it the early Christians were denying a faith foreign to their own. Their vision was one which saw life in its wholeness first, then in its brokenness and its restoration to wholeness. By contrast, the Gnostics saw life divided, then brought into unhappy unity and finally divided again. Two expressions of their faith, which we have noted, were in keeping with this vision. In the realm of theology they denied the notion of creation by a good god; in the realm of ethics they counselled asceticism or libertinism. For them, as for Christians, vision and expression were aspects of a single whole.

The declaration against Gnosticism was, on its positive side, a declaration in favor of the conviction that creation is an essential aspect of Christian faith. The church set forth this conviction in several ways.

Individual thinkers wrote vigorously in favor of the notion that God the creator is the same God as He who redeems. Some of their writings actually made their way into our New Testament. Thus, the following passage appears in First Timothy:

> Now the Spirit expressly says that in later times some will depart from the faith by giving heed to deceitful spirits and doctrines of demons, through the pretensions of liars whose consciences are seared, who forbid marriage and enjoin abstinence from foods which God created to be received with thanksgiving by those who believe and know the truth. For everything created by God is good, and nothing is to be rejected if it is received with thanksgiving; for then it is consecrated by the word of God and prayer.[10]

---

[10] I Timothy 4:1-5.

Many writings which were not included in the Bible also deal with the notion of creation. During the latter part of the second century a whole series of works appeared from the pens of Christian authors analyzing the views of the heretics in great detail and arguing strenuously that they had departed from the truth.

Early Christians also formulated their affirmation of creation in credal statements, and some of these were officially adopted by church councils. The familiar Apostles' Creed begins with the words, "I believe in God the Father Almighty, maker of heaven and earth." And the creed adopted at the Council of Nicea expands the article to make it even stronger than the simple statement. Indeed, it is interesting that the first creed presented to the Council began with the assertion that God the Father was "maker of all things visible and invisible." During the course of the proceedings the statement was modified by the dropping of one Greek letter so that the creed finally adopted would not imply that even the Son and Spirit were creatures.[11]

The early church also affirmed its faith in creation by the literature which it selected as sacred scripture. As we have seen, some of the writings which became part of the New Testament made explicit reference to false teachers and the need to affirm creation in opposition to them. But perhaps of even greater significance for the course of Christianity was the decision to make the sacred scriptures of the Jews a part of the Christian Bible. We have seen that the notion of creation had become integral to the faith of Israel, even though it followed upon the conviction about redemption. By accepting the Hebrew scriptures into the Christian canon the early church took as its own some great passages that affirm the creation of the world by the redeeming God, and these have marked themselves indelibly on Christian thought and life ever since. Thus in its opening words the Bible of the Christians affirmed that with which the Hebrew Bible had started, the magnificent declaration, "In the beginning God created the heavens and the earth." [12] In the poetry which Israel bequeathed to the Christians were the great stanzas which began, "The heavens declare the glory of God; and the firmament sheweth his handiwork." [13] And Christians, like Jews, have been comforted in their desolate hours by the strengthening words, "Hast thou not known? hast thou not heard, that the everlasting God,

---

[11] Henry M. Gwatkin, *Studies in Arianism* (Cambridge: Deighton, Bell and Co., 1882), p. 45.

[12] Genesis 1:1.

[13] Psalms 19:1, K.J.V.

CREATOR AND CREATURE The Almighty humbles Job by reminding him of the greatness and glory of creation. "*When the morning Stars sang together.*" Plate from the "Book of Job." William Blake (Courtesy of The Metropolitan Museum of Art. Gift of Edward Bement, 1917)

the Lord, the Creator of the ends of the earth, fainteth not, neither is weary?" [14]

The affirmation of creation has been woven into the texture of Christian faith by thinkers, creeds, and scriptures.

3. DOES IT MATTER HOW?

The early Christians were profoundly convinced that God had created the world. But their creeds did not mention how he did it, nor did the theologians bother themselves much about the matter. From time to time through the centuries thinkers tried to trace out the way of things. Indeed, some of the pioneers of modern science were Christians seeking to set forth "the work of the six days."

The impact of the theory of evolution upon the nineteenth century brought the how of the creative work into prominence. Reactions were many; two extremes are of particular interest to us. There were, on the

[14] Isaiah 40:28, K.J.V.

one hand, those who felt that the Biblical account must be held to at all costs. When the writer of Genesis said that plants were made "yielding seed according to their own kinds," [15] he was excluding any evolutionary interpretation of the origin of species. Generally speaking the denial of biological evolution has been a cornerstone of the thought of Christians who call themselves "Fundamentalists." To them the literal accuracy of the Bible is part of the heart of Christian faith.

Another view was expounded by many who felt that what was important in Christianity was not bound up with the literal accuracy of the Bible. They sought to relate Christian faith to what they believed to be the well authenticated theories of scientists. Indeed, they felt that the discovery of evolution had made possible a whole new apprehension of the true meaning of the Bible and of Christian faith. Evolution, they said, was God's grand strategy through the ages. By it he had brought forth ever higher forms of life, and he was continuing his creative work in the historic life of mankind. The Bible shows men reaching ever enlarging conceptions of God, and it points to a hope that some time in the future his kingdom will be realized on this earth. Through the toil of the centuries God has been leading his people toward it. And with the optimism engendered by new discoveries in science and new hopes for society, so-called religious liberals looked for the coming of God's kingdom soon, the final objective of the evolutionary process. In a hymn with stirring rhythm one of them wrote,

> These things shall be,—a loftier race
> Than e'er the world hath known shall rise
> With flame of freedom in their souls,
> And light of knowledge in their eyes.[16]

Thus did the evolutionary theory evoke contradictory reactions among Christians. To some it was a threat to the very heart of the faith, to others a key to the discovery of some of that faith's long kept secrets.

Contemporary theologians who are concerned for the recovery of historic Christianity tend to disagree with both of the positions we have noted. The optimism of the liberals, they feel, is not in accord with the actualities of human life nor with the heart of Christian faith. It is doubtful that any real moral or religious progress is discernible in human history. The brutalities of contemporary economic and political life and the unbelievable barbarities of contemporary warfare do not seem to

---

[15] Genesis 1:12.

[16] John A. Symonds, "These Things Shall Be,—A Loftier Race," Henry H. Tweedy, ed., *Christian Worship and Praise,* no. 563.

indicate that modern man is in any significant sense superior to even his caveman ancestors. And a closer look at the Bible makes it questionable if that book is committed to a view of history in which man gets increasingly better until he becomes a perfected child of God. The kingdom may, indeed, bring to consummation that which is good in human life, but it also breaks into history in judgment upon the evil which is always there.

The fundamentalist view, however, which sees in the first chapter of Genesis a literal description of the creation of the world, is fairly generally rejected too. Contemporary Christian thinkers are usually ready to accept the widely recognized results of recent biblical scholarship. It is now a commonplace that there are actually two accounts of creation in the early part of Genesis. That which begins with the second part of the fourth verse of the second chapter starts with the creation of man. In an attempt to overcome man's loneliness, God then makes the animals. But since none of these is a companion suitable for man, God makes of Adam's rib the woman who is to be bone of his bone and flesh of his flesh. The other account, written much later and with more sophistication, is the familiar first chapter together with the opening verses of the second, telling of the successive creation of various things during a period of six days. This account has traces of a myth of Babylonian origin which lies behind many references to creation which are scattered throughout the Old Testament, particularly in the poetical books. Thus when the Psalmist says to God,

> Thou dost rule the raging of the sea;
> when its waves rise, thou stillest them.
> Thou didst crush Rahab like a carcass,[17]

he is referring to the ancient story of creation which was acted out in ritual fashion in the Babylonian New Year's festivals. The high God, Marduk, had, at the beginning of time, slain the monster of the deep, Tiamat; and out of her carcass he had made a place for the world. The myth was general in the Near East, and it would have been a miracle if the Hebrews had not been affected by it. What is remarkable about their reflection of it, however, is the manner in which it is transformed so that it fits into the vision of the world of which we have been speaking. God is the high and holy one who inhabits eternity; he is the ruler from beginning to end.

We come back to the vision again. Even when the Hebrews took over

[17] Psalms 89:9-10.

materials from the myths of their contemporaries, they changed them in ways that brought them into consistency with that which was expressed in the total life of faith. They did not believe in creation because it was set forth in dramatic fashion at the beginning of their sacred book. What it meant was written into their laws; it determined the character of their worship; and it was the inspiration of much of their poetry. They seem to have been willing to enshrine several accounts of the *how* of creation in their sacred literature. The *what* was suffused throughout their faith.

4. WHAT CREATION MEANS

If there has been some diversity of opinion among Christians concerning the way in which the world was created, there has been remarkable uniformity in their thinking about what creation means. Amidst the greatest variety of expressions of theology and worship certain notions have persisted within the history of Christianity which are directly connected with the assertion that God is the creator of heaven and earth. One of these has come before us already—that of the close connection of creation and redemption. Two others recur again and again, and their relation to each other is also of the substance of what Christians have meant by creation. Both are implicit in the passage we have noted from the first letter to Timothy.

The author notes that false teachers will come who will command abstinence from certain foods and will forbid people to marry. The author rejects their viewpoint. For him no line can be drawn through the center of reality such that everything above it—the spiritual—is good, and everything below it—the material—is evil. No, "everything created by God is good." [18] Here is the first aspect of the assertion of creation.

Side by side with it goes the other. That which is good is to be received with gratitude. Its source is God. Though created things are good, they are not divine. In a magnificent passage in the *Confessions,* Augustine tells of going out and asking all sorts of things to tell him of God. Again and again they say, "We are not He." Then, he says, "I asked the heavens, the sun, the moon, the stars, and they answered: 'Neither are we God whom you seek.' And I said to all the things that throng about the gateway of the senses: 'Tell me of my God, since you are not He.

[18] I Timothy 4:4.

Tell me something of Him.' And they cried out in a great voice: 'He made us.' "[19]

The notion that things are good and yet are not divine creates the tension which Christian thought has ever noted as being involved in the assertion of creation. The very goodness of things may lead man to forget God. On the other hand the very pre-eminence of God may lead a man to indifference to the creation and thus to the disregard of God's gifts. As we shall see, this tension is of great significance for the Christian notion of sin. In itself, however, it is simply given; it is part of the goodness of the created situation. "For everything created by God is good, and nothing is to be rejected if it is received with thanksgiving."[20]

5. MAN, THE SELF-CONSCIOUS CREATURE

Among the creatures coming within the range of our experience, only one can say, "I am a creature." That is man. And his ability to say this makes him unique within the created order. The religions and philosophies of the world have recognized his uniqueness, and they have attributed it to various causes. Christian faith, too, has given recognition to it. Most often in speaking of it, it has echoed words of the Old Testament: man is made "in the image of God."[21]

The preeminence of man within creation has been a constant theme in Christian thought and life. The Genesis story describes God as saying, "Let us make man in our image, after our likeness; and let them have dominion over the fish of the sea, and over the birds of the air, and over the cattle, and over all the earth, and over every creeping thing that creeps upon the earth."[22] The Psalmist contrasted the smallness of man with the grandeur of the heavens, only to add, "Thou hast made him little less than God, and dost crown him with glory and honor."[23] In familiar words Jesus spoke of the tender care of the heavenly Father for the birds and said, "You are of more value than many sparrows."[24] Man alone is able to say, "I am a creature."

In saying it, he uses the first person pronoun; he says, "I." And this

---

[19] *The Confessions of Saint Augustine,* translated by F. J. Sheed (Copyright 1942, Sheed and Ward, Inc., New York), p. 177. (X, vi). Reprinted by permission.

[20] I Timothy 4:4.

[21] Genesis 1:27.

[22] Genesis 1:26.

[23] Psalms 8:5.

[24] Matthew 10:31.

THE CREATION OF MAN A Renaissance artist interprets the wonder of the creative act and the grandeur of the human creature. From the ceiling of the Sistine Chapel in Rome. Michelangelo (Alinari Photo)

means that he is a self and is aware that he is a self. He can act and can accept responsibility for his actions. He can act in a way that is self-determined. Perhaps this is the best way to phrase the assertion that man is free, for the word "freedom" is used in many senses. It is a convenient word, however, and it will be helpful for us to use it. And we note here that we shall usually mean by it just this—that man can act in a self-determined way. This Christians have said again and again, and in many ways. When astrologists in the early centuries of the Christian era were proclaiming that man's life was determined by the stars, Christian theologians insisted that they were wrong. And when some modern scientists said that man's life was determined in such ways that his selfhood became an illusion, Christians resisted their view. It is important to note, however, that the Christian assertion of self-determination does not deny that man is in many ways the product of forces which play upon him. Indeed, the Christian faith itself would be meaningless if human life were completely indeterminate. It does, however, insist upon such a measure of self-determination as will make responsibility a meaningful matter. The Christian assertion is not necessarily the equivalent of any specific philosophic position; there are some who hold that a Christian assertion of self-determination is perfectly compatible with a philosophic determinism; others hold that such is not the case. These are problems which concern theologians when they seek to relate Christian faith and philosophy. Our concern here is simply to record a continuing Christian conviction about the self-determining character of the human creature.

Not only is man a self; he is aware of being one. To say this is to affirm that he has a mind, and this is assumed in the Christian faith. Adam names the animals,[25] and he can understand a commandment given him by God. The prophet Hosea bewails the fact that his people are destroyed "for lack of knowledge."[26] And in Proverbs, Wisdom calls men to listen to her.[27] Jesus commands men to love God with all their minds,[28] and Paul feels that worship with the feelings alone is incomplete: "I will sing with the spirit and I will sing with the mind also."[29] No council ever met to determine whether man was rational, but the Bishops at Chalcedon defined in part what they meant by calling Jesus a human being by saying that he was "of reasonable soul and body."[30]

Realization of the importance of the mind has been of great significance in Christian faith; but in itself it bears no specific character. What is characteristic of Christians' assertions about it seems to be a reflection of Hebrew ways of thinking inherited from the Old Testament. The mind is not, as, for example, the Gnostics said, a divine spark which has fallen into an alien body. It is one aspect of man's totality and it qualifies all of his relationships. Because of man's mind everything he is and does can have meaning. And because he is a total self, his mind is involved in everything he does and undergoes.

The selfhood of man expresses itself for its own sake. Like the God whose image he bears, man is creative. This is woven into the texture of Christian thinking all the way through. Man at his creation is told to conquer the world and subdue it. He is described as singing songs, keeping herds, making things of brass. When he builds a tabernacle or temple for his God, he uses all kinds of skill to make that which will

[25] Genesis 2:19f.
[26] Hosea 4:6.
[27] Proverbs 8:32.
[28] Matthew 22:37.
[29] I Corinthians 14:15.
[30] The Creed of Chalcedon.

have beauty and will be the proper habitat of glory. Because man is creative, history is possible. Human life is not simply a cycle of repeated revolutions. It begins somewhere and goes somewhere else. Indeed, because man is creative, the faith is not a set of timeless ideas. Here we find a Christian reason for asserting that the life of faith is a changing, ever renewed reality.

Man is able to utter pronouns other than the first person singular. He can say, "we" and "you." And his ability to do so is also part of his created nature. He is made for life with other selves, and his own selfhood cannot realize its being in isolation. Sociality is as essential as individuality to him. The second creation story in Genesis tells in delightful fashion of God's declaration, "It is not good" for man to "be alone." [31] Recognizing this, God makes a woman as a companion for him. The first creation story simply says, "So God created man in his own image," "male and female created he them." [32] When Jesus enunciates the great commandments, love for neighbor follows upon love to God. Man was so made that love for his fellow is part of the law of his being. "No man is an island." [33]

Man singular or men plural are creatures. Man can say, "I am a creature." And in so doing he means, in part, that in his totality he is good. No line runs through the center of his being dividing him into good spirit and evil matter. He is not divine spirit which has fallen into the evil prison house of the body. And yet he is not the good. He is a derived being, and he knows it. The tension which we have noted as being involved in the Christian assertion of creation has its most poignant expression in the human situation. With his freedom and his creativity, his self-hood, man is a being of dignity. And yet he can never assert himself as the end of his own being. He is hemmed in. The story of creation tells of commandments he has received from God. Relatedness to God is essential to him. He must live by trusting the divine Reality. And yet that Reality is not easy to find nor to trust.

In the tension between himself and his Creator lie the tremendous possibilities for significant freedom, marvellous creativity, heroic sociality. And in it lie the possibilities of fearful degradation. Man is made so that sin is a possibility. But in his essential being he is such that it is not a necessity. Essentially he is good. And to be free, creative, and social is good, too.

---

[31] Genesis 2:18.

[32] Genesis 1:27, K.J.V.

[33] John Donne, *Devotions* (Ann Arbor: The University of Michigan Press, 1959), p. 108.

READINGS

From the Bible

1. Among the poetic celebrations of creation are Genesis 1, Isaiah 40, Psalms 8, 24, and Job 38-40.

2. The significance of creation for human responsibility is set forth in Romans 1.

3. Problems arising from the presence of evils in God's world are presented in Ecclesiastes, Habakkuk, and Job.

From Historic Christianity

1. Tertullian, *Against Marcion,* Book I. A forthright Christian father of the second century points out the implications of denying the conviction that this world is God's creation.

2. John Calvin, *Institutes,* III, x, sets forth his attitude toward "The Right Use of the Present Life and its Supports."

3. Thomas Aquinas, *Summa Theologica,* Part I, questions 90-102, describes the first man and his endowments.

FOR STUDY AND DISCUSSION

1. Is there any relationship between the Christian affirmation of creation and scientific accounts of how the world came into being?
2. The question, "Is this a good world?" has haunted Christians through the centuries. A contemporary poet confronts it in Archibald MacLeish, *J. B.* (Boston: Houghton, Mifflin Company, 1956).

3. Some thinkers have suggested that God is limited; is this notion compatible with the affirmations of Christian faith?
4. Evaluate Bernard E. Meland's suggestion that the notion of the creative is a link between modern thought and Christianity. *The Reawakening of Christian Faith*, pp. 87 ff.
5. Does the traditional idea of a Devil have any meaning for contemporary Christianity? If so, what? If so, why did God create the Devil?

III

MAN REBELS

In the second act of T. S. Eliot's *The Cocktail Party* a character named Celia is pictured in consultation with a psychiatrist. When she has completed the description of the first symptom of her illness, the psychiatrist asks her about the second. "That's stranger still," she replies,

> It sounds ridiculous—but the only word for it
> That I can find, is a sense of sin.[1]

She is surprised at herself for analyzing her symptom as she does because she has had, as she puts it, a pretty conventional upbringing.

> . . . anything wrong, from our point of view,
> Was either bad form, or was psychological.[2]

Now she finds that the only word that does justice to what she has done is drawn from traditions which she had thought were utterly outdated.

Celia is, of course, typical of many in our time. They have regarded the notion of sin as a vestige of an outgrown manner of life and thought. And yet they have been brought up short by the feeling that some of their own actions and those of others call for a description as sin. Among

---

[1] T. S. Eliot, *The Cocktail Party* (New York: Harcourt, Brace & World, 1950), p. 134. Reprinted by permission.

[2] *Ibid.*, p. 136.

those of our time who have rediscovered the idea of sin are the theologians themselves. The theologies of the eighteenth and nineteenth centuries were not particularly sensitive to it. Those influenced by the age of reason treated sin as intellectual mistake; those influenced by ideas of evolution treated it as atavism. But the experience of a century in which the most civilized people have been guilty of the most barbarous behavior has been a rude shock. Thinkers of our time are ready to listen again to what historic Christianity has to say about sin.

1. REJECTION OF REDEMPTIVE LOVE

The great creeds do not define sin. However, they draw, so to speak, a frame around it so that its general outlines are fixed even though some of its details are not sharply delineated. Thus by their emphasis on redemption they draw attention to the conviction that men need to be redeemed from something. And in the light of declarations concerning other subjects, this something can be understood as sin.

The adoption of the books we know as the New Testament as part of their sacred scriptures was of the greatest significance for the fixing of the conception of sin among Christians. These books, as we have seen, are centrally concerned to witness to the reality of God's redemptive act in Christ. And much of what they say of sin focuses just here: sin is the rejection of God's redemptive love. In the light of this idea we can understand the horror of the early Christians at the rejection of Jesus. He was, to them, the very incarnation of redemptive love, and the worst that men could do was to do away with him. Men have "crucified the Lord of glory," wrote the Apostle Paul.[3] It was, from the viewpoint of the Christians, an act of base ingratitude. Indeed, man's hatred at being grateful is at the very heart of sin. Old Lear was voicing Christian conviction in his heart-rending words on ingratitude, "the marble-hearted fiend."[4]

However, redemptive love is not simply an attribute of God in the eyes of New Testament writers; it is also the rule for those who respond to him. At the climax of a passage describing the attitudes and actions of those who would be children of the kingdom Jesus said,

> Love your enemies, and do good, and lend, expecting nothing in return; and your reward will be great, and you will be sons of the Most

[3] I Corinthians 2:8.
[4] William Shakespeare, *Works,* p. 893, "King Lear," Act I, Sc. IV.

> High; for he is kind to the ungrateful and the selfish. Be merciful, even as your Father is merciful.[5]

In these words the redemptive love of God is taken as the norm for human conduct. Thus a second aspect of sin as viewed from the standpoint of redemption comes to light: it is the refusal to make redemptive love the spirit of one's life.

The Old Testament has much to say that is similar in character to that which we have noted, and the choice of the sacred scriptures of the Jews as part of the scriptures of the Christians has done much to enrich Christian thinking about sin. As we have seen, the Hebrews looked at life from the standpoint of redemption, and much that is written of sin in the Old Testament reflected that viewpoint. The book of Deuteronomy, for example, may be noted as having a great deal to say. It was written, most scholars hold, to remind the people of Israel of the events of the Exodus and of the great figure of Moses at a time when they were turning to paganism and idolatry. It was written as if Moses himself were speaking to the people whom he had led from Egypt, who were soon to enter the land of promise. The people are told that they have been rescued from Egypt out of the sheer love of God; he has chosen them for inscrutable reasons of his own. And soon he will give them "a good land, a land of brooks of water, of fountains and springs, flowing forth in valleys and hills, a land of wheat and barley, of vines and fig trees and pomegranates, a land of olive trees and honey, a land in which you will eat bread without scarcity, in which you will lack nothing, a land whose stones are iron, and out of whose hills you can dig copper." [6] When they enter that land they must not forget God. Their temptation will be to think that their own might and skill have gotten it for them. If they do so, they will be turning away from the redemptive love which has taken them out of the misery of slavery, through the years in the wilderness, and into the land of milk and honey. Their sin will be the rejection of redemptive love. Thus Hebrew writers pictured sin in terms which were similar to those of Christians who wrote centuries later.

There were other ideas of sin in the Old Testament too, however; and some of these have been a problem for Christians. One is of particular concern to us. We have seen that in the Old Testament the ideas of God as redeemer and creator are central. But along with these in much of the Old Testament goes the idea that God is a lawgiver. He sets forth

---

[5] Luke 6:35f.

[6] Deuteronomy 8:7-9.

his requirements, some of which are moral and others ritual in character. And he requires obedience. To those who obey him he offers rewards; those who disobey he punishes. The definition of sin which follows from this conception of God is, then: sin is disobedience to the revealed laws of God.

The tension between the views of sin which arise from the conception of God as redeemer and those which stem from the thought of him as lawgiver appear in the Old Testament itself. It is of central importance in such books as Job and Habakkuk. And the tension has been present in the history of Christianity too. Indeed, it was the occasion of one of the most serious crises in the primitive church. The earliest Christians were Jews, and many of them felt that the sense of God as redeemer which they encountered in Jesus was not incompatible with the notion of God as lawgiver which was part of their ancestral heritage too. Paul believed that the notion of God as redeemer had to be absolutely central and that the idea of him as lawgiver had to be absorbed, so to speak, into it. He felt that there had been two strands in the religion of ancient Israel. For the one, whose hero was Abraham, God had been a redeemer whose love for men was based on his own nature. For the other, whose hero was Moses, God was a lawgiver. The first was the enduring strand which had been continued, indeed fulfilled, in Christianity. The other was temporary. It was a provisional faith which pointed toward the other. It was, in his own terms, "our schoolmaster to bring us unto Christ." [7] When it was superseded, it had to be set aside. In his view the attempt to keep it as part of the larger faith always vitiates the latter. Thus sin defined in terms of lawbreaking is badly defined, dangerously so. For the man who keeps the law may reject redemptive love, and thus be betrayed into sin. Here surely is an echo of that which had already appeared in the teaching of Jesus, who put the point in an unforgettable story.

> Two men went up into the temple to pray, one a Pharisee and the other a tax collector. The Pharisee stood and prayed thus with himself, 'God, I thank thee that I am not like other men, extortioners, unjust, adulterers, or even like this tax collector. I fast twice a week, I give tithes of all that I get.' But the tax collector, standing far off, would not even lift up his eyes to heaven, but beat his breast, saying, 'God, be merciful to me a sinner!' I tell you, this man went down to his house justified rather than the other; for every one who exalts himself will be humbled, but he who humbles himself will be exalted.[8]

---

[7] Galatians, 3:24, K.J.V.

[8] Luke 18:10-14.

For both Jesus and Paul sin at its heart is the rejection of redemptive love.

For both of them there is something to which they sometimes refer as law. It is the character of the redemptive love of God, the character which is to be reflected in the attitudes of men. "The law of the Spirit of life in Christ Jesus," said Paul, "has set me free from the law of sin and death." [9] And Jesus is willing to answer the questioner who wishes to know the content of the commandments: "You shall love the Lord your God with all your heart, and with all your soul, and with all your mind. This is the great and first commandment. And a second is like it, You shall love your neighbor as yourself. On these two commandments depend all the law and the prophets." [10] But this law can hardly be equated with other things called laws. It disregards desserts and gives freely to the undeserving. It ever breaks through moralities and moral pretensions. Hence those contemporaries who repeatedly tell us that the Christian view of sin is not "moralistic" appear to be right. The heart of sin is not to be found in disobedience to any command that can be capsuled into a moral pronouncement.

The placing of sin in the closest relation to redemption gave a deepened sense of sin to the Christian community. For some it was as if sin had never really been known before. The Fourth Gospel describes Jesus as saying to those who oppose him, "If I had not come . . . , they would not have sin." [11] He was a light coming into the world. And when the light came, the shadows became even darker than they had been. The utter outpouring of redemptive love was the occasion for the disclosure of the deepest depths of sin.

2. DEFIANCE OF THE CREATOR

The emphasis of the creeds on redemption has significant implications for the notion of sin, as we have seen. By itself, however, it does not clearly delineate what man is redeemed from. On this matter the assertion of creation is of signal importance. And those who formulated the creeds were aware of this. Their contemporaries who denied the idea of creation defined sin in ways which were consistent with that denial. And the rejection of their viewpoint by the early Christian community was, in no small measure, due to the conviction that their ideas of sin were not consonant with the genius of Christian faith.

---

[9] Romans 8:2.
[10] Matthew 22:37-40.
[11] John 15:22.

REBELLION AND JUDGMENT For the Renaissance artist the grandeur of man persists even through sin and punishment. From the ceiling of the Sistine Chapel in Rome. Michelangelo (Alinari Photo)

Two views of sin, in particular, tend to emerge with the denial of creation. These were present in the early centuries of the Christian era and have appeared in various places in the religious history of mankind. The first identifies sin with finitude. It holds that anything finite is, in a sense, evil; man, aware of his finitude, is a veritable concentration of evil. The way to get rid of sin, then, is to hate all finite things. The way to get rid of the specifically human sin is to hate oneself. Against this view of sin the doctrine of creation has guarded Christianity. Theologians have often seen sin as being tied up in a peculiar way with selfishness. But they have been careful not to identify selfishness with selfhood. Individuality itself is not evil. The prayer which begins, "Almighty and everlasting God, who hatest nothing that thou hast made," [12] goes with a current that runs deep in the stream of historic Christianity. Self-denial there may be, but self-hatred, No!

---

[12] *The Book of Common Prayer* (New York: The Church Pension Fund, 1945), p. 124.

A second view of sin which is rejected by the assertion of creation is that which identifies it specifically with the love of the material. As we have seen, the Christian declaration of faith in creation was in part directed against those who divided spirit from matter in such a way that they called the one good and the other evil. Now Christian faith has never denied the commonly observable fact that material things or impulses of the body may occasion evil behavior. But this is not because these things are evil in themselves. There may be situations in which denial of the wants of the body is essential to our well-being and to our proper relation to God and each other. But again denial is not hatred. We have seen that the writer of First Timothy warns his readers against those who counsel abstinence from foods and forbid marriage—on the grounds that these are sinful because they are concessions to the material side of life. Whoever believes that "everything created by God is good" [13] will reject a definition of sin which is based on a division of life into good spirit and evil matter.

If Christians have rejected the identification of creatureliness and sin, they have nonetheless noted the ease with which man in the creaturely situation is tempted. The first human creatures are also the first sinners. And the early pages of the Bible are full of the violence and malice of primitive mankind. We have already noted that there are difficulties in the human situation as such, difficulties which are not in themselves evil, but which make a direction toward evil an easy one to take. Man must live by trusting, and God does not seem near. It is surely simpler for him to trust something in the world around him or himself, for after all he has been given a self with tremendous powers. And just this, say Christian thinkers, is what man has done since the beginning of time. He has replaced the trustworthy Reality with things untrustworthy. And this is sin.

He has misplaced his trust precisely because of the condition of the world in which he is placed. God looked upon the things which he had made, and lo, they were very good. And man, too, looking upon them saw them to be good. Here Paul's analysis in the first chapter of Romans is classic. Though God's divinity and wisdom were discernible in the world he had made, man chose to worship creatures. And, writes Paul with tragic realism, "God gave them up" to all sorts of evil.[14] A difficulty resulting from living in a good world is the occasion it offers for the temptation to pride in the specific religious sense: that is, it can lead to

---

[13] I Timothy 4:4.
[14] Romans 1:24.

a confusion of the creature with the Creator. And since man is a creature of unique powers, his world worship usually issues in self-worship. Indeed, even the choice of the creature over the Creator as an object of worship is in itself a form of self-adulation. It is the assertion that man has the right to determine what the object of his worship shall be.

Indeed, the Bible most often thinks of sin in terms of personal defiance. And this is in keeping with the view of man which we have noted. Man is a totality, a whole; he is a self-determining being. Here lies the possibility of that which is sin, for only a free being who has an awareness of what it means to defy the Creator can be termed a sinner.

It is significant, too, that the Bible links the original pair in their committing of sin. As we have seen, sociality is of the very essence of man, and men are together in their sinning. Indeed, in early Israel we have the story of Achan who held back part of what should have been devoted to God after the capture of Jericho. When his evil deed was discovered, his whole family was doomed with him.[15] Later in the history of Israel the prophet Ezekiel repudiated the idea of corporate guilt; "the soul that sinneth," he wrote, "it shall die."[16] His view is at the other extreme from that presented in the Achan story. A full view of the relation of sin to the poles of individuality and sociality must take the claims of both into account. To this matter we shall return in another context. It is enough at this point to note that Christian faith has been aware throughout its history of the social dimensions of man's sin.

Sin, then, is a departure from the creative intent. It is defiance of the Creator; it is trust in the untrustworthy; it is choice of the creature over the Creator as object of worship. It lurks like a serpent in the lovely garden of man's original innocence.[17] But it is always an intruder. Of this Christian faith has been convinced. To be finite is not, in itself, to be evil. To have a body is not to be a thing half good. "Everything created by God is good."[18]

3. VIOLATION OF THE HOLY

We have seen that there are important implications for the idea of sin in the credal assertions concerning God as creator and redeemer. It may seem fatuous to add that there are implications, too, in the simple

---

[15] Joshua 7.
[16] Ezekiel 18:20, K.J.V.
[17] Genesis 3.
[18] I Timothy 4:4.

phrase, "I believe in God." It is by no means certain that the creed makers were consciously affirming these implications, for the word *God* had connotations for them and their contemporaries which did not need to be spelled out. Indeed, in using it they were relating Christian faith to the religious life of mankind as they knew it rather than distinguishing it from other faiths. Like some, but not all, of their contemporaries early Christians believed in God. And those among whom they lived understood at least part of what they meant by the term.

The connotations which are of concern to us here cluster around the notion that when men speak of a god they mean a being who is holy. This idea was common among the ancients. But when, during the past few centuries, men became preoccupied with rational and moral interpretations of religion, they tended to forget this. More recently the notion of holiness has come to the fore again, and some understanding of it has contributed significantly to the recovery of the historic faith.

The word *holy* is not easy to define. It refers to that quality which inspires a response of awe. Indeed, a modern classic on the subject describes it as that which is mysterious, tremendous, and fascinating.[19] We are confronted with it in great religious poetry. The Psalms are full of it. Look for a moment at the twenty-ninth:

> Ascribe to the Lord, O heavenly beings,
> ascribe to the Lord glory and strength.
> Ascribe to the Lord the glory of his name;
> worship the Lord in holy array.
> The voice of the Lord is upon the waters;
> the God of glory thunders,
> the Lord, upon many waters.
> The voice of the Lord is powerful,
> the voice of the Lord is full of majesty.[20]

Here, and in the verses which follow, it seems that some great storm has aroused in the spirit of the poet a sense of that awe which is at the heart of the sense of the holy. Great art and architecture are always suffused with it, and it is central in the experience of worship.

The sense of sin which is the correlative of the awareness of God as a holy reality is, of course, the sense of being unholy. The word "unclean" is used repeatedly in religious literature for this. We can see it

---

[19] Rudolf Otto, *The Idea of the Holy*, John W. Harvey, trans. (London: Oxford University Press, 1923), pp. 12-42. Used by permission.
[20] Psalms 29:1-4.

in many passages in the Bible. A series of chapters in which image after image calls attention to the majesty of the Deity is found near the end of the book of Job. At their close the man who has listened says,

> I had heard of thee by the hearing of the ear,
>   but now my eye sees thee;
> therefore I despise myself,
>   and repent in dust and ashes.[21]

At the beginning of the book of the Revelation appears a vision of the glorified Christ. Having seen it the writer says, "I fell at his feet as though dead." [22] And Simon Peter, aware of the presence of a holy Reality in Jesus of Nazareth, cries out, "Depart from me, for I am a sinful man, O Lord." [23] Here is guilt in its purely religious sense. Before the holy Reality man is aware of his own unholiness.

It is important to see that men have identified their gods as holy even when they have not thought of them as particularly moral. Thus sin as violation of the demands of a holy reality often has been completely divorced from what we generally think of as morality. The Old Testament tells the story of a man who touched the ark of the covenant, to keep it from falling, and was killed for his rash action.[24] It also relates an incident in which Saul, the king of Israel, pronounces a curse on anyone who eats on a certain day. His son Jonathan, unaware of his father's words, does eat a little honey, and the army is defeated because a curse has been violated.[25] Jonathan has committed sin without knowing what he is doing. We may, then, speak of "sin," in its general religious sense, as violation of the holy. This is its character no matter how the holy is further defined.

This broadly religious use of the word appears to be central in the words of Celia in T. S. Eliot's play. Having spoken of her sense of sin, she tries to explain what she intends by it. "I don't mean sin in the ordinary sense," she says. And when she is asked about the ordinary sense, she replies,

> Well . . . I suppose it's being immoral—
> And I don't feel as if I was immoral:
> In fact, aren't the people one thinks of as immoral

---

[21] Job 42:5f.
[22] Revelation 1:17.
[23] Luke 5:8.
[24] II Samuel 6:7.
[25] I Samuel 14:24-46.

> Just the people who we say have no moral sense?
> I've never noticed that immorality
> Was accompanied by a sense of sin: . . .[26]

After a bit she speaks this way,

> It's not the feeling of anything I've ever *done*,
> Which I might get away from, or of anything in me
> I could get rid of—but of emptiness, of failure
> Towards someone, or something, outside of myself;
> And I feel I must . . . *atone*—is that the word?[27]

Against the background of currents of thought noted, we can understand the significance of Celia's words. The "ordinary sense" of the word sin is that which appears when religion is thought of primarily as morality: sin, then, is simply immorality. This Celia rejects, returning to a more primitive conception, one that she hardly knows how to describe since her whole education has served to obscure it. This conception is one of sin as "against someone or something," that which in our terms has been called "a holy Reality."

In Christian faith, however, sin which is simply violation of the holy rarely, if ever, appears; for Christianity emerged against a background of Judaism in which the holiness of God had been firmly associated with his redemptive and creative character. The creeds affirm belief in God and go immediately to the description of him as "creator of heaven and earth" and of his activity in the redemption of the world. Violation of the holy is one aspect, a very important one, in a complex experience. It is that which imparts the sense of horror into the rejection of redemptive love and defiance against the Creator.

While the notion of sin as unholiness relates it to the religious life of mankind, it also helps to distinguish the Christian conception of sin from other ideas often confused with it. Herein lies, perhaps, its greatest importance. As we have seen, the idea of sin as rejection of redemptive love differentiates it from moralistic conceptions. The definition of sin which emerges from its connection with the idea of holiness further emphasizes this differentiation. Sin, as Celia points out, is not immorality. And sin is not simply divergence from the rational ideal, as it is sometimes defined by those who divide spirit and matter. It is a specifically religious category. It is linked to the notion that God, whatever else he may be, is the "high and lofty one, who inhabits eternity, whose name is Holy."[28]

---

[26] T. S. Eliot, *The Cocktail Party*, p. 135.
[27] *Ibid.*, p. 136f.
[28] Isaiah 57:15.

4. PERVERSION OF THE CREATURE

The major elements in a conception of sin which has received repeated statement during the course of the Christian centuries are now before us. Sin is rejection of redemptive love; it is the self-determined act of defiance against the Creator on the part of a creature made good; it is violation of the holiness of God. Through these several statements runs a single thread, and we shall follow it through the rest of this chapter. When man sins, he is perverse; and the effect of sin is to make him perverse.

In the first place, his relation to God is perverted. He is intended to be God's creature responding to his maker with love and reverence. He is intended to accept the conditions of his creaturehood, conditions which actually make for his own fulfillment. But in defiance he turns to another than God and makes of it his deity. Thus his relation to God is transformed. And his experience of God undergoes a transformation too. In his perverted condition he no longer knows God as the love which creates and sustains him. He now experiences God as a wrath which torments him. He sees him as the giver of a law which he has broken. He knows him as the one in whose presence he feels guilt. He does not cease to be in relation with God, for God still exists. Man in sin exchanges the love of God for his wrath. God cannot be escaped; one must know him one way or another. Sin is perverted relation to him.

Sin also perverts the man himself. The aspects of his createdness do not disappear; but they are changed. Of his freedom we shall speak in the following section. Of his creativity it can be said that it is changed so that the energies which might normally go into creative expression now vent themselves in meaningless and destructive ways. Man's sociality is so changed that he turns on other people in hatred or dissociates himself from them and becomes an isolate, unable to experience the upbuilding effects of their companionship. The goodness of his creaturehood is disregarded: it is overprized so that man makes an end of himself and seeks only his own power and enjoyment, or he becomes sated with life and loses the zest of living. In all of these the relation to God is a dimension which adds tragic depth to their perversion. One of the most penetrating sections of Augustine's *Confessions* is one in which he analyzes his motives in the boyhood prank of robbing a pear tree. He comes to the conclusion that the basis of the thrill of robbing the tree was the desire to be like God—in the wrong way. He had wanted to be omnipotent, and he had gone about it by throwing off the restraints which had been imposed on him. All sin, he concludes, is perverse imitation of God.[29] Thus, we might say, sin is the perversion of the creature from what he should be into something else.

What is perverted is the very being of the sinner; this lies in the assertion that man is one and that his acts are self-determined. Christian faith has generally rejected ideas of sin which find its essence in acts which are committed. The source of the acts is perverted. "A sinner," says Emil Brunner, "is not a human being who has sinned a certain number of times; he is a human being who sins whatever he is doing." [30] Here the whole matter of motive becomes central. Man has been described in Christian writings as having a heart turned in upon itself, *cor incurvatus in se*. Thus he may act in ways that seem outwardly very good, but if his acts come from the wrong disposition, they are evil. Out of this emphasis on the background of action has come one of the most common distinctions in Christian writings: between the sinful nature and the acts. The perverted being is often called a sinful nature. This is expressed, for example, in the confession of sin in the Lutheran liturgy,

> "We poor sinners," say the congregation and minister, "confess unto thee, that we are by nature sinful and unclean." [31]

Now it is important to see here that the nature to which the confession refers is not that given by God. Man is by first nature good. But having sinned, he has so perverted his nature that he has received, so to speak, a second nature; it is this which is sinful and unclean.

So universal is the perversion of men that Christian faith has generally spoken of it as "original sin." The notion has been expressed in terms of a taint which came upon the race at the sin of the first human beings, Adam and Eve. It has often been thought of as being passed on in the blood stream, particularly when Christians were influenced by ideas from other sources which tended to regard the flesh as evil. The words, "In sin did my mother conceive me," [32] taken from the Psalms have been a proof text supporting such a view. Many writers of our own time reject any biological conception of original sin, but feel that it stems from the recognition of something that must be taken seriously. It under-

---

[29] *The Confessions of Saint Augustine,* translated by F. J. Sheed, pp. 28f. (II, vi).

[30] Emil Brunner, *The Mediator,* Olive Wyon, trans. (Philadelphia: The Westminster Press, 1947; London: Lutterworth Press, 1947), p. 142. Reprinted by permission.

[31] *Service Book and Hymnal of the Lutheran Church in America* (Minneapolis: Augsburg Publishing House, *et al.,* 1958), p. 1. Reprinted by permission.

[32] Psalm 51:5.

lines the notion that sin is universal, that it is superpersonal; that is, sin is not simply a single, chosen action on the part of the individual. He comes into a world which has sin reflected in its every aspect. His family, his community, his nation are what they are in part because of the perverseness of men. And this perverseness gets into him, too. No one escapes it. Individual acts of sin come out of this perverseness, though into them something of self-determination enters, too. Thus the distinction is made between original and actual sin. And a tragic fact about the history of mankind is this: original sin is actualized in everyone at some time.

And yet it is actualized in such a way that it is the self-determined act of a creature made good. This is simply part of the dreadful truth about us as men.

5. BONDAGE

The relations of sin and freedom have been the source of some of the thorniest problems in the history of Christian thought. Convictions appeared to be required which were difficult, if not impossible, to reconcile with each other. It is not our purpose here to try to resolve the difficulties. Rather we are concerned to report the persistent themes which have run through Christian thought on the subject.

The perversion of freedom in the act of sin is itself a puzzle. Obviously from the Christian point of view, sin is an act of a self-determining being. But why should he do, in freedom, that which is not for his true good? The ideal picture of man fresh from the hand of God is given in the Genesis story of Adam. For centuries Christians had no reason to doubt its historical accuracy and they took it as a literal description of our first parents. Many in our time have given up such an idea, but feel nonetheless that the story can be taken as a significant symbol of certain convictions. Why should Adam choose to disobey God? Part of the answer, no doubt, is in the remark that he saw the fruit to be good. We have already seen that a good creation presents man with a temptation. And yet he knows that it is not truly good, for God has commanded him not to eat it. Somewhere in the story must come a decision which is just that: Adam chooses because he chooses. His act is, in a significant sense, self-determined. It arises out of the mystery of freedom. Without that freedom there can be no sin. And yet by that freedom he chooses what a free being ought not choose, something that deprives him of the good of life.

The perversion of freedom which results from sin is even more perplexing. Once sin has entered the world, it spreads its perversion throughout the fabric of mankind. Traditionally this idea has been expressed in the notion of original sin, which we have already noted. But sin becomes actualized in a self-determining act, else it is not sin. But the Christian observation of life is such that it has always been held that no one actually does escape from actualizing sin. "There is none righteous, no, not one." [33] Here is the source of the tragic sense which haunts the writings of the great prophets of Israel. They live in a period when doom is about to fall upon their people. And they believe that the doom to come is the righteous judgment of God. They call on the people to change their ways. And yet they know that the people will not change. In our time Reinhold Niebuhr has expressed the matter in the formula that sin is inevitable "but not in such a way as to fit into the category of natural necessity." [34] If it were necessary, it would not be the act of man's self-determination. And yet no one, in actuality, does escape sinning. Sometimes in the history of Christianity the inevitability of sin has been expressed in ways that made it tantamount to necessity. But then the conviction of man's freedom and responsibility is forfeited. Man always sins, but it is man who does the sinning: this has been the abiding conviction of the Christian faith.

Perhaps the most dangerous result of the perversion of freedom through sin is just this: man's sense of self-determination engenders the illusion that he can free himself from sin. It is an illusion because the perversion which is sin destroys freedom from sin. Dante pictures Satan embedded in the very center of the earth, at the bottom of the pit of hell. There he beats his huge wings eternally—eternally because the very beating stirs up winds which freeze the ice in which he is held fast ever more solidly.[35] His efforts to free himself increase his bondage. The poet has here portrayed another enduring conviction of Christians: men's efforts at self-salvation are always self-defeating—hence the suspicion of identifying sin with immorality. For one of the ways in which men seek to overcome sin is by morality. But a morality which grows out of the effort to escape self-centeredness always results in more self-centeredness. It results in what Augustine called "splendid vices." [36] Another of the

---

[33] Romans 3:10, K.J.V.

[34] Reinhold Niebuhr, *The Nature and Destiny of Man* (New York: Charles Scribner's Sons, 1953), I, 263. Reprinted by permission.

[35] Dante, *The Divine Comedy*, "Inferno," Canto 34.

[36] Augustine, *City of God* (XIX, xxv) as cited by Alfred Weber, *History of Philosophy*, Frank Thilly, trans. (New York: Charles Scribner's Sons, 1896), p. 198.

ways in which men have sought to escape sin is through religion. But self-centered religion is always perverse religion and it is defeated at the very start. Luther plumbed the depths of the effort of man to get right with God by the way of religion. In his agony he discovered that even in God man seeks himself.[37]

Man seeking by his freedom to find freedom has no chance. At the last he will cry after Paul, "Wretched man that I am! Who will deliver me from this body of death?"[38] Christian faith has also echoed Paul's answer. To that we shall turn in the next chapter.

READINGS

From the Bible

1. The classic story of the beginning of sin is given in Genesis 3. Other stories of the evil of early men and its consequences are found in the ensuing chapters.

2. Stories involving various aspects of sin are found in the following passages: Joshua 7, II Samuel 6:1-9, I Samuel 14:24-52.

3. Personal expressions of the sense of sin are given in Psalms 32 and 51.

4. The prophets sometimes paint a dismal picture of their peoples' sinfulness, as in Jeremiah 5, Amos 1-2, Isaiah 1.

5. Paul takes up the theme of sin in various places: as in Romans 1, 6, 7; Galatians 4.

From Historic Christianity

1. Dante Alighieri, *The Divine Comedy*. "Inferno" and "Purgatorio" deal with sin and its effects on people. Analyses of types of sin are given in "Inferno," canto 11, and "Purgatorio," cantos 17 and 18.

---

[37] Edgar M. Carlson, *The Reinterpretation of Luther* (Philadelphia: The Westminster Press, 1948), p. 51.

[38] Romans 7:24.

2. John Milton, *Paradise Lost*, tells "of Man's First Disobedience" in Books 9-11.

3. Blaise Pascal, *Pensées*, Section 2, is a series of thoughts about "The Misery of Man without God."

FOR STUDY AND DISCUSSION

1. Sin is an outworn idea; it is no longer useful. Other ideas are far more helpful for our time.
2. We should never make the judgment that someone else is a sinner, though we may appropriately make such judgment about ourselves.
3. Study the chapter on "The Christian Conception of Sin" in Reinhold Niebuhr, *An Interpretation of Christian Ethics*.
4. Are there actions which would be sinful under any circumstances?
5. Study an act of penitence (such as a service for Ash Wednesday) in a Service Book.

IV

GOD REDEEMS

The Greek philosopher Epicurus taught his followers that the good of life consists in the pleasure which comes when the mind is free from confusion and the body from pain. And since he felt that much of men's mental anguish issues from erroneous religious ideas, he proceeded to set them straight on theological matters. The gods, he taught, are perfectly blessed, and since they are content to think on things heavenly, men need be in no fear of them.

A few centuries later the early Christians were proclaiming a view of God that was markedly different from this. Blessed he surely was, but not unmoved by the miseries of men. Indeed, he had come into human life, shared men's lot, enduring even their deepest woe. So doing, he had brought them freedom. Those who responded to him would not discover the good of life in freedom of the mind from confusion or of the body from pain. They might even be called upon to reflect the love of their God by giving their minds over to anguish and their bodies to crosses. Yet in so doing they would enter into fellowship with God himself and have a share in his blessedness.

With their vision of his redemptive love this chapter is concerned.

1. THE REDEEMING GOD

Several aspects of the Christian affirmations about redemption come to light in a simple analogy drawn from everyday life. Sometimes it happens that we come to know someone rather well. We have watched him in many situations and feel that we know how he will react under any circumstances. But we are not sure. Then a crisis comes; and under pressure he does exactly what we had expected him to do. Now, at last, we feel that we know what he is really like. We know that we can count on him under any conditions. We know what manner of man he is.

In some such way the early Christians responded to the life of Jesus and the events surrounding it. The experiences they had had during his life and after it had shown them, they believed, what God was really like. In a crisis he had acted in such a way that they knew what manner of being he was. And they were sure that they could count on him under any conditions.

God, they said, had visited and redeemed his people. He had made himself known to them as pure redemptive love. No longer need they seek to make their way to him by uncertain speculations. No longer need they search for him in hidden wisdoms proclaimed by proud men. No longer, indeed, need they try to make expiation for their moral failures, try, by morality or religion, to find release from their bondage. He had come to them, and they had been found by him.

The analogy points up the fact that early Christian faith was centered in God and in a conviction of what he was like. This is what lies behind the high claims made for Jesus. We must see the matter thus, or we will be led astray by questions about how a mere man, even a very challenging one, could become, under the impact of the minds of theologians, a God. The Christians were always concerned about God; and Jesus was important because through him they had come to know what God was like.

In the early creeds they simply spoke of Jesus as God's only son. But such a statement as this turned out to be inadequate to convey what they meant. They saw in the sonship of Jesus, to be sure, an intimate relation of a man with his Maker. But there was, they believed, something in him which might be called sonship of God in another way. Of this they spoke in terms of a reality within God himself, an eternal Son. This Son was the image of God, his Word, his Wisdom.

Early in the fourth century a quarrel in the city of Alexandria brought about the definition which has been repeated by many Christians ever since. A man named Arius set forth the idea that there were, so to speak, two levels in the Deity. There was an eternal God, distant and blessed, somewhat after the fashion of the untroubled gods of Epicurus. There was, in addition, a Word of God, a second Divinity, generated from the first. This Deity had been associated with his Father in the creation of the world, and it was he who came to men in Jesus of Nazareth. However, there were those in the church who felt that to accept the position of Arius was to betray the church into a pagan polytheism, and eventually a council of three hundred and nineteen bishops met at Nicea in the year 325. There, after discussion, the overwhelming majority affirmed their faith in

> one Lord Jesus Christ, the Son of God, begotten of the Father, only begotten, that is, of the substance of the Father, God of God, Light of Light, true God of true God, begotten not made, being of one substance with the Father, through whom all things were made, things in heaven and things on the earth.[1]

Their use of the notion of substances introduces a note which is different from the thought forms of the earliest Christians. But within the idea-patterns of the time, the bishops were reaffirming in the strongest way possible the primitive conviction that in Jesus he who acted was the eternal God himself and that he had disclosed his redemptive character.

The final selection of the books of the New Testament was completed at about this time. Their choice, as we have seen, was an action intended to distinguish the true faith from counterfeits. And in choosing just the books they did, the early Christians affirmed their response to the message that God had so acted in Christ as to make known what he was like. Standing first were four books describing deeds of Jesus. To many moderns they appear at first as biographies. But, as many have pointed out, they cannot be so understood. They were written by men convinced that the words and actions of Jesus were a disclosure of the reality of God. At the beginning of Mark's gospel stands the declaration of a voice from heaven at the baptism of Jesus: "Thou art my beloved Son."[2] Matthew and Luke speak of his divinity in the very days before his birth. And John starts by speaking of a Word, eternally with God, who "became flesh and dwelt among us" with a "glory as of the only Son from the Father."[3] The epistles of the New Testament speak the same way.

---

[1] The Nicene Creed.
[2] Mark 1:11.
[3] John 1:14.

CHRIST AS RULER OF THE WORLD The enthroned Christ, surrounded by the stars, confronts the worshipper from the apse of a twelfth century church. *Christ in Majesty.* Catalonian fresco from the Church of Santa Maria de Mur. (Courtesy of the Museum of Fine Arts, Boston)

For Paul, Christ is "the power of God and the wisdom of God." [4] He quotes, as it seems, an early Christian hymn which says of Christ,

> though he was in the form of God, [he] did not count equality with God a thing to be grasped, but emptied himself, taking the form of a servant.[5]

And the Apocalypse sees him under many images—lion, lamb, man with hair like wool, eyes like fire, feet like bronze and a voice like the sound of many waters. Through them all runs the theme of the redeemer, who says, "I died and behold I am alive forevermore, and I have the keys of Death and Hades." [6]

---

[4] I Corinthians 1:24.
[5] Philippians 2:6f.
[6] Revelation 1:18.

By incorporating the sacred scriptures of the Jews into their Bible the early Christians proclaimed their acceptance of the idea that God had revealed himself redemptively in the religious history of Israel before he had made himself known decisively in Christ. Thus the Old Testament was for them—and has been for Christians ever since—a book which gave a great sweeping background for the Christian proclamation. In the analogy which has been suggested for God's redemptive action it has been noted that sometimes we are at a stage in our relations with another person when we feel that we know him fairly well; and yet we are waiting for a situation in which he will disclose his nature unmistakably. Just so did the Christians think of the writers of the Old Testament—as men who knew much of God but were waiting for his decisive disclosure. Before the Exodus, said the ancient story, God had come to Moses saying,

> I have seen the affliction of my people who are in Egypt, and have heard their cry because of their taskmasters; I know their sufferings, and I have come down to deliver them.[7]

He was no God aloof like the deities of Epicurus; he identified himself with human woe. And he acted in history redeeming his people. But the redemptive self-disclosures to Israel were not enough, said the Christians. Indeed, the Israelites knew this themselves. They were looking for a time when God would establish his will among the nations, when there would be righteousness and peace on the earth. They were looking for a messianic age. And the one through whom the age would come they called the messiah. That age, said the early Christians, had dawned with the coming of Jesus. The decisive redemptive self-disclosure of God had begun.

2. GOD AND MAN

Thus by credal definition and by choice of scriptures did the Christians of the first few centuries affirm their conviction that it was none other than the eternal God, the High and Holy One, who had disclosed his redemptive character to them. We turn our attention now to the act of disclosure itself. It will be helpful, perhaps, to examine it under three aspects. In doing so we shall follow the manner in which it has frequently been treated in the writings of theologians.

The first part of the Christian affirmation is this: that God made him-

---

[7] Exodus 3:7f.

self known in the life and career of a man named Jesus from the Galilean village of Nazareth. Thought concerning this aspect of the faith is usually referred to as "the doctrine of the person of Christ."

The earliest Christians, being Jews, interpreted what Jesus meant to them in terms with which they were familiar. Some of these were drawn from the specific currents of Judaism of their time, others from the broader backgrounds of their sacred scriptures of which we have been speaking. Those scriptures contained the dream of a messianic age. Now, said the Christians, that age had started. God's kingdom was breaking into history; and, as one writer has pointed out, it brought Jesus with it.[8] The early Christians went through the Jewish scriptures with the greatest avidity, seeking for passages which would support their claim that Jesus was the looked-for Messiah. Thus many of the things which he did were interpreted by them as specific fulfilments of prophecies made long ago. In him, said the Christians, God had acted in a way that confirmed what the men of the Old Testament had expected of him. There was one point, however, on which there was particular difficulty. As we have seen, the Jews had looked upon God as lawgiver as well as redeemer. And sometimes these two aspects of his being appeared to be in conflict. The early Christians were particularly impressed by the way in which Jesus seemed to set aside legal prescription when it stood in the way of redemptive action. And Paul felt that the idea of God as lawgiver must be set aside completely if his redemptive nature was to be seen in its true light. He it was who gave a solution of the problem that has been generally accepted by Christians ever since: the legal enactments of the Jews were a provisional revelation of God, helpful to sustain weak men. Now that men were brought into a relationship of sonship with a redemptive father, the law could be set aside. Thus, even the law was part of the redemptive action of God, one of a series of actions in the Old Testament which constituted—to use a phrase common in contemporary theology—a history of salvation culminating in the coming of Christ.

That coming was set forth in writings which the early Christians chose as scripture, the New Testament. Its writers interpreted the life of Jesus partly in terms drawn from their Hebrew heritage. As the one in whom the messianic age had started he received the title "The Christ." This term is simply the Greek equivalent of the word "Messiah" in Hebrew. Both refer to the act of anointing by which a king is set apart as the

---

[8] Rudolf Otto, *The Kingdom of God and the Son of Man*, Floyd V. Filson and Bertram L. Woolf, trans. (Grand Rapids: Zondervan Publishing House, 1938), p. 80.

agent of God. Some New Testament writers also used terms from their hellenistic backgrounds to make clear to their contemporaries their own convictions about Jesus. Thus Paul, writing for people to whom the term "Lord" had special meaning, told them that Jesus was Lord.[9] Whatever their specific terms of interpretation, the New Testament writers were agreed that in Jesus God had acted in decisive fashion. And they were agreed, too, in stressing the genuinely human aspect of that disclosure. The gospels pictured Jesus as a man, one who "increased in wisdom and in stature, and in favor with God and man." [10] They spoke of his temptations, of his prayers, of his joys and sorrows, of his final sufferings and death. And the other writings of the New Testament in their own ways spoke of a "man Christ Jesus." [11]

As the Christian movement spread beyond Palestine, the process of interpreting Jesus went on. Even certain books of the New Testament spoke of him in terms that had broader import than those of the specifically Jewish community. Theologians arose who related the ideas inherent in the Christian affirmations to ideas abroad in the culture of the time. At the same time they used terms taken from that culture to distinguish their views from those of others. There were two tendencies of thought that they were particularly careful to avoid. Some people were so concerned to assert that it was the eternal God who had really acted in the man Jesus that they reduced the latter to a mere puppet; others were so concerned to assert the reality of the humanity of Jesus that they were in danger of making his relation to God a rather adventitious matter. The church went through several centuries of struggle before a statement was formulated which seemed to make clear what it wanted to say. At a council meeting at Chalcedon in 451 the following formula was adopted: "one and the same Christ, Son, Lord, Only-begotten recognized in two natures, without confusion, without change, without division, without separation." [12] The key words here are the terms "person" and "nature." It is held that there is one person: the divine-human Lord, and two natures: one divine, the other human. The terms themselves were taken from the legal and philosophical language of the day. Through them the men of the church were seeking to protect the Christian affirmation as they understood it.

In speaking of the divine nature, they were referring to God's redemptive self-disclosure. Behind them lay the decision of Nicea which we

---

[9] I Corinthians 8:5f.
[10] Luke 2:52.
[11] I Timothy 2:5.
[12] The Creed of Chalcedon.

have already noted: as divine the Christ was of one substance with the Father. In speaking of the human nature, they were referring to Jesus, the man of Nazareth.

The tenacity with which the early church clung to the reality of that manhood is interesting to watch. Before and after Chalcedon there were many who were willing to let it go. One facet after another of human personality was denied to the Christ, and in each case the theologians of the church gave answer: the redemptive self-disclosure of God is made in a real human being. Already in the days of the New Testament there were those who denied that Jesus had a human body. They looked at incarnation after the fashion we see in the *Iliad.* At one point in furious fighting, Hector suddenly sees his brother Deiphobos standing beside him. He takes hope only to find that in the next moment his brother is gone.[13] He realizes that Athena has tricked him; she has come in the appearance of a man. He was not a real human being. Against such an

---

[13] The incident occurs in Book 22, lines 224-305.

THE REALITY OF THE INCARNATION The Christ brings glory into the midst of man's common life. *Christ with the sick around him, receiving little children* (The "Hundred Guilder" Print). Rembrandt van Ryn (Courtesy of the National Gallery of Art, Washington, D.C., Rosenwald Collection)

interpretation of the incarnation are directed such passages as that which appears in the first epistle of John: "That which was from the beginning, which we have heard, which we have seen with our eyes, which we have looked upon and touched with our hands . . ." [14] And likewise the oldest creeds assert firmly that "Jesus Christ was born . . . suffered . . . died." His was a true body, his a real suffering. A century or two later a bishop of the church (one of those unintentional heretics of whom we have spoken) set forth the notion that Jesus had a human body and life, to be sure; but, he held, the divine Word had replaced his human mind. The bishop's name was Apollinaris, and his position has ever since been called "Apollinarianism." Against him many replies were made, the heart of which is suggested, perhaps, by the statement of one thinker: if Christ is not wholly man, then we are not wholly redeemed by him.[15] Later, indeed after Chalcedon, the struggle on behalf of the humanity of Jesus entered its final phase, one which is probably closer to our comprehension than questions about bodies or minds. An emperor discussing the matter, in an effort to secure peace within his domains, denied the reality of a third facet of Christ's personality: he insisted that there was only one will in him, the divine. Again, theologians came to the defense of the full humanity of Jesus. At a council in Constantinople in 681 the bishops affirmed that the view of the church was that Jesus had a truly human will—though this was always in obedience to the divine will. Thus it was that various men denied to Jesus some aspect of human personality—body, mind, or will—only to be answered in terms that secured the Christian affirmation that the redemptive act of God was accomplished in a human being, with a body that could suffer, with a mind of his own, with a will expressing genuine self-determination.

The position was a difficult one. To many it seemed that the very glory of God demanded a diminution of Jesus. But Christians, convinced that God had truly come down to them, that he had fully shared in human life, were not willing to sacrifice their convictions even though they were left with a puzzle that has defied logic throughout the centuries.

When we turn to the gospels, which tell us just about all that we know about the man Jesus, we gain some understanding of why men connected him with the idea of the redemptive character of God. It is

---

[14] I John 1:1.

[15] Gregory of Nazianzus, "To Cledonius against Apollinaris (Epistle 101)" in Edward P. Hardy, Jr., and Cyril C. Richardson, ed., *Christology of the Later Fathers* (Philadelphia: The Westminster Press; London: S. C. M. Press, Ltd., 1954), pp. 218f.

true, of course, that these books were written by men who believed him to be the Messiah, and that scholars differ widely in their judgments regarding their historicity. But it is hard to escape the impression that the man Jesus taught his followers in unforgettable ways that God is a redemptive reality, like a shepherd who seeks a lost sheep, a woman who sweeps the house until she finds a lost coin, a father who welcomes home a wandering son. Further, Jesus' own attitude toward others reflected a redemptive spirit. He ate with publicans and sinners, because the sick need the physician. Indeed, on occasion he could proclaim the forgiveness of God in such a way that he gave the impression that he was acquainted with the workings of the divine mind. To those who knew him, at least to some of them, he seemed, in very truth, to be bringing the forgiving love of God into the midst of their human life. In him the Shepherd himself was going out to find the sheep which was lost. The Epicurean view of God was wrong; he had visited and redeemed his people.

3. GOD FOR MAN

The gospels pictured the career of Jesus as moving inexorably toward his death. And this death they interpreted as the ultimate expression of his redemptive concern as a human being. But they saw it also as one part of the redemptive action of the eternal God. Here we have come to the second phase of God's redemptive self-disclosure, as it has been viewed by Christians. Theological tradition has usually spoken of it as central in the "doctrine of the work of Christ." To speak in this way is not to deny that the life of Jesus is part of his work; indeed, his self-determined obedience to the will of God has been a constant theme of theologians. However, his death is, so to speak, the most critical moment in the crisis; it is the extreme expression of willing obedience. "Greater love hath no man than this, that a man lay down his life for his friends." [16]

The work of Christ has been viewed throughout the history of the church as that of atonement; it stands at the center of that redemptive action of God by which he restores rebellious men to fellowship with himself. Two who were separated, God and man, have now become at-one. We may recall that when Celia in *The Cocktail Party* by T. S. Eliot was trying to make clear to her doctor what she meant by sin,

[16] John 15:13.

she remarked that it was something, she felt, that she had to atone for.[17] In traditional Christianity this is just what sin would make her feel that she must do; and it was this that sin made it impossible for her to accomplish. We have seen that Christians have regarded sin as something that renders ineffectual man's efforts to free himself from it. The Christian affirmation is that God himself has done what man cannot. In Christ he has brought men into that fellowship with himself for which they were made.

The New Testament is suffused with this conviction, and yet it is never developed into an explicit theory. The gospel writers were convinced that Jesus himself saw his death as a means by which God was reaching out to bring men to fellowship with himself. "The Son of man came," he said, "not to be ministered unto, but to minister, and to give his life a ransom for many." [18] And in the last hours before his death he gave his disciples a cup with the words, "Drink of it, all of you; for this is my blood of the covenant." [19] Paul sees the death of Christ as an utter pouring out of God's love for man which forever makes it unnecessary for man to seek to save himself. And it is as a futile attempt at self-salvation that he views the law by which he himself had sought to live. Thus, he says, "God has done what the law, weakened by the flesh, could not do: sending his own Son in the likeness of sinful flesh and for sin, he condemned sin in the flesh." [20] The writer to the Hebrews pictures Christ as the perfect high priest who presents the perfect offering—himself—in the perfect sanctuary—heaven itself.[21] And the book of the Revelation describes a song sung by the blessed in praise of the lamb that was slain for the remission of sins.[22]

The figure of the lamb, used here and elsewhere in the New Testament, is drawn from the sacred scriptures of Israel. The choice of those scriptures by the Christian church made available throughout the centuries much of the imagery by which Christians have described their understanding of the death of Christ. Two themes have been of special significance. In the first place, the lamb has a place in the sacrificial systems of Israel. The death of an animal had a part in those acts in which the fellowship of men with God was celebrated or in which it was restored when it had been broken by human acts. Christians com-

---

[17] T. S. Eliot, *The Cocktail Party,* p. 137.
[18] Mark 10:45, K.J.V.
[19] Matthew 26:27f.
[20] Romans 8:3.
[21] Hebrews, chapters 6-10.
[22] Revelation 5:6-10.

pared the death of Christ to an animal sacrifice, insisting that it ended the necessity for such sacrifices. It did this because in it God himself had taken the initiative, he had provided the sacrificial victim, he had done that which was necessary to bring men into fellowship with himself. Because he had made his redemptive love evident in a decisive way, men need no longer undertake actions by which they themselves seek to make atonement for the evil they have done. In the second place the figure of the lamb appears in the fifty-third chapter of Isaiah, and Christians from earliest time connected this chapter with their understanding of Jesus. The chapter describes a servant of God, obedient to his divine master, who suffers and dies undeservedly. In some way that the writer does not explain, his sufferings and death bring about the redemption of others:

> All we like sheep have gone astray;
> we have turned every one to his own way;
> And the Lord has laid on him
> the iniquity of us all.[23]

Christians saw in Jesus the obedient servant who died an undeserved death. And they believed that God used that death for the redemption of men. So it was that Christians saw in the laws of the Jews and in the dreams of their prophets a profound awareness of the Redeemer God.

The creeds, like the books of the Bible, set forth no clear-cut theory of the atonement. They do, however, reflect the conviction of Christians that the death of Jesus is central in their faith. Thus the apostles' creed specifically mentions—as among those things which Christians believe—that Jesus Christ "suffered under Pontius Pilate, was crucified, dead, and buried." The creed of Nicea refers explicitly to redemption in its article about Jesus Christ, "who for us men and for our salvation was made flesh and was made man."

Back of the words of creed and scripture is the figure of a lonely man dying on a cross. He has spoken of the redemptive love of God and he has exhibited the redemptive spirit in his life. Now he prays, "Father, forgive them; for they know not what they do." [24] To the human spirit here expressed, Christians have said, corresponds the divine Spirit. Indeed, there is a veritable disclosure of God here. God has shown himself redemptively—forgivingly—in such a way that full account is taken of

[23] Isaiah 53:6.
[24] Luke 23:34.

CHRIST CRUCIFIED A twentieth century artist interprets the agony of the cross. *Beneath a Forgotten Crucifix.* Georges Rouault (Courtesy of Collection, The Museum of Modern Art, New York, Gift of the artist)

the horror of sin and the reality of the Divine Wrath. The recurrent phrase in Christian writings is "Christ died for us." In him God treated human sin and guilt as though they were his own; and he treated men as if his own goodness belonged to them. The theme of substitution has been frequently found in theories of the atonement. Sometimes it has been set forth as if God were basically a righteous Reality from whom a loving Christ wrested a grudging redemption for men. To put it so is to turn the whole Christian outlook upside down. God takes the initiative in redemption; it springs from his love. But since sin and wrath are to be taken seriously, the act of redemption is no easy one. The Christ, fully realizing the dereliction of spirit that humans can suffer, cries out, "My God, my God, why hast thou forsaken me?"[25] His death is the complete repudiation of the Epicurean conception of Divinity. In Christ God has entered the uttermost depths of human experience.

[25] Matthew 27:46.

4. THE VICTORY OF THE REDEEMING GOD

The recurrence of Easter throughout the centuries is witness to the continuing conviction of Christians that the death of Jesus was not the defeat of God. The climax of the redemptive self-disclosure of God in Jesus Christ took place in his resurrection. The early church centered on that as its focus. Without that his person was meaningless and his work incomplete.

So full of the joy of the resurrection is the New Testament that there is no room for detailed doctrine. Indeed, such doctrine would seem an impertinence. Of the fact they were certain; of its general meaning they were sure; for its explication they felt little need. As a matter of fact, they were not agreed fully about what had happened. Paul wrote that in the resurrection the body which rises is not that which has been buried; "it is sown a physical body, it is raised a spiritual body."[26] John described the risen Christ as a being who passes through closed doors, who said to an adoring woman, "Do not hold me."[27] All the accounts agree that Jesus did not simply resume his normal life among people. He rather appeared from time to time, and only to those who did or might believe.

It seems that in the matter of the resurrection, as with the notion of creation, Christians have differed on how it happened, but have been firmly convinced that it did. Even historians of a sceptical turn of mind find it difficult to explain the emergence of early Christianity without the resurrection. The creeds simply state it without embellishment. "The third day he arose from the dead," says the Apostles' Creed, and the Nicene follows it almost verbally. Christian art and literature and worship have reflected it repeatedly. That one of the earliest hymns still in constant use by the Christian people should be one inspired by the resurrection is no accident:

> The day of Resurrection,
> Earth, tell it out abroad.[28]

Again, the choice of the Hebrew scriptures as the Old Testament of the Christian church brought a breadth of background to the Christian

---

[26] I Corinthians 15:44.
[27] John 20:17, and see verse 19.
[28] John of Damascus, "The Day of Resurrection," John N. Neale, trans., Henry H. Tweedy, ed., *Christian Worship and Praise*, no. 322.

affirmations. The redemptive event of the Exodus had been a sort of resurrection, a victory of God over enemies, over dereliction and despair. The experience of the destruction of Jerusalem and its temple, and of its people made captive came later. To them this was often spoken of in the language of death. But in the land of Babylon a prophet named Ezekiel was sent to look at a valley full of dry bones. At the word of his God he prophesied to the bones and they began to form themselves into bodies which finally took on life.[29] It was a symbol of what the Lord intended to do for his people. And in Babylon came a word to an unknown prophet,

> Comfort, comfort my people, says your God, . . .
> In the wildnerness prepare the way of the Lord,
> make straight in the desert a highway for our God. . . .
> And the glory of the Lord shall be revealed,
> and all flesh shall see it together.[30]

The Hebrews were convinced of the redemptive power and intent of their God, and they had seen it exerted more than once. Now, said the Christians, it had been disclosed again, this time in decisive fashion.

The meaning of the resurrection for the Christian vision can, perhaps, be suggested by relating it to the themes of which we have spoken in this chapter. The resurrection was, of course, the reversal of Jesus' death; it was its inseparable complement. God might enter into the depths of human life, but unless by so doing he could also redeem, his sympathy was helpless. One image that occurs several times in the New Testament brings in certain picturesque ideas which were common at the time. Man is represented as being in the possession of certain superhuman powers that are inimical to him, among them sin and death. These powers have brought about the defeat of Jesus and in it they are temporarily triumphant. But in the resurrection they, in turn, are defeated.[31] Man is released from their sway and able to live victoriously. Even where such imagery is not present the theme is set forth. God in Christ suffers wrath and evil; he truly enters into human life in its depths. But he is not finally held by evil. He emerges victorious, and in so doing procures a victory for man too. "We were reconciled to God by the death of his son," writes Paul, and "we shall be saved by his life." [32]

The resurrection also vindicates the man Christ Jesus. The earliest

---

[29] Ezekiel 37:1-14.
[30] Isaiah 40:1, 3, 5.
[31] Colossians 2:15.
[32] Romans 5:10, K.J.V.

Christian preaching as it is represented in Acts speaks of the resurrection as the way in which God proclaims the Messiahship of Jesus.[33] In the risen Christ God is continuing the redemptive action he began in his life and death. And that continuation takes Jesus into it. This is a vindication of the goodness of the creature, the proclamation that God is for, not against, man.

The resurrection is also the climactic disclosure of the redemptive character of God. Here he proclaims himself as the "Father almighty" for he has met and conquered all of man's enemies. Hence the redemptive disclosure throws its light back on the proclamation of creation once more. He who created cannot be defeated by that which disturbs his creation. And the disclosure which had been made in the life and death of Jesus is here seen to its conclusion. Here God is set forth as triumphant redemptive love.

And here, finally, the Christian vision makes contact with the viewpoint of Epicurus. God is blessed at the last. Peace and joy are his. And men, too, can know peace and joy. But they know it not by imitating the indifferent bliss of an untroubled divinity. They know it by entering into the life of God as it is shared with human beings for the sake of their salvation. Paul prays that he might know Christ, "the fellowship of his sufferings," and "the power of his resurrection."[34] In his prayer the Christian vision is presented in miniature, as the experience of man following the history of God. In the resurrection God did that which was necessary to bring his world back together again, having entered fully into its dividedness and taken upon himself the results of the division. Thus he had made possible a new creation. How this comes about is the theme of the following chapter.

READINGS

From the Bible

1. The redemptive act of God in the Exodus is described in Exodus 15; it is the theme of numbers of Psalms such as 78, 105, 106; it is recalled by the prophet in Hosea 11.

---

[33] Acts 2 and 3.
[34] Philippians 3:10f, K.J.V.

2. The redemptive activity of God in restoring the exiles to their homeland is celebrated in Isaiah 40-55.

3. The redemptive spirit of God wrestles with a reluctant prophet in the book of Jonah.

4. The redemptive activity of God in Christ is celebrated throughout the New Testament. A few notable passages are Luke 1,2,15; John 1; Romans 3,4,5,8; I Corinthians 1; II Corinthians 5; Philippians 2; Colossians 1; Hebrews 7-9.

From Historic Christianity

1. Athanasius, *Of the Incarnation of the Word of God.* Here the hero of Nicea gives his version of the human predicament and the manner in which God deals with it.

2. Anselm, *Cur Deus Homo?* A Medieval thinker sets forth reasons for the incarnation and atonement.

3. Søren Kierkegaard, *Philosophical Fragments,* David F. Swenson, trans. (Princeton: Princeton University Press, 1946), chapter 2, "God as Teacher and Saviour: an Essay of the Imagination." Here a modern thinker gives a version of what might be called "the divine predicament" and the manner in which God deals with it.

FOR STUDY AND DISCUSSION

1. How does the manner in which Jesus Christ has been presented to you in your church compare with the affirmations of the early church?
2. Did Jesus really "grow in wisdom"?
3. Is Jesus necessary for Christianity? Why can't we have the idea of redemption without him?
4. Is the notion that the Christ "bore" the sins of others immoral, as some have suggested?
5. Examine some hymns about Jesus or some pictures of him from different periods. Note how they reflect their times. Which seem adequate, which inadequate? Why?

V

MAN RESPONDS

At the close of the chapter about sin we left man bound with unbreakable bonds. His creaturehood had been perverted so that his self-determination could not express itself in ways that were truly free. And his position was rendered the worse because he sought to free himself by trusting powers which could not deliver him. By religion and morality he gave expression to his false faiths. And yet those forces from which he hoped to receive help had simply made his bondage the more secure.

However, Christian faith proclaims the possibility that a trust will arise in man by which he can be delivered. So it has happened in the past, and so it may happen again. This trust is his very own, and it makes possible a renewal of the self-determination that is one aspect of his true being. But it is not trust in himself; it cannot be, for such trust he has found to be vain. Hence the very arising of trust is possible by reason of an action not his own.

Such trust arises, says Christian faith, in an experience of being loved. Confrontation with a Reality which loves him utterly makes it possible for a man to relinquish his false faiths and turn to a trustable Reality. The pledge that the Reality is trustable and loves him utterly has been given, according to Christians, in Jesus Christ. In him God has poured out his love in an act of absolute self-giving. Here, according to the analogy of the preceding chapter, God has so disclosed his character that men ever after can know what he is like.

1. THE ACT OF MAN: REPENTANCE AND FAITH

The act in which man turns to God is his own; and yet it is possible by reason of the divine love. Thus there is a double action—divine and human at once. The history of Christianity records the difficulties which men have encountered in dealing with its two aspects. A pendulum has swung back and forth through the centuries. At times theologians have so emphasized the divine aspect of the action that they have reduced man to a puppet dangling from strings held by the hands of God. When they traced the implications of their position, it appeared to some of them that God from the beginning of time had chosen some whom he would open to his love and others whom he would leave closed up in their false securities. Such thinkers were trying to secure the affirmation of which mention has been made: a faith which rescues man from bondage cannot be faith in himself; it must come from God. At other times, men have emphasized man's part in the experience; they have been clear about his self-determination in the double action. But they have been in danger of making man's release his own action and thus delivering him to the task of securing salvation by his own effort.

When theologians have focused attention upon the human aspect of the action, they have noted that a resolution has been required in accepting trust in the divine Reality and denying trust in the others. For the most part this has been referred to as *faith* or as *believing*. It is an active thing, an expression of self-determination. It is a whole-souled laying hold on the forgiving love of God which has been made known in Christ. Along with it goes the willingness to accept responsibility for one's involvement in past rebelliousness and its consequences.

> The fault, dear Brutus, is not in our stars,
> But in ourselves, that we are underlings.[1]

For this aspect of the action the usual term within the traditional Christian vocabulary has been *repentance*. It involves sorrow and dismay, willingness to face the seriousness of sinful action, to be aware of the wrath of God, to admit one's rejection of proffered love, to confess one's false

---

[1] William Shakespeare, "Julius Caesar," Act I, Sc. 2, *Works*, p. 584.

faiths, to shudder at one's violation of the holy. The two, repentance and faith, are inseparable. Neither is possible without the other.

Christians have been agreed that a self-determining turning to God is an integral part of the life of faith. But they have differed in the manner in which they have conceived it. Some have felt that the event must be one of a rather dramatic sort with deep emotional accompaniments. Others have felt that while such conversions do take place on occasion, for those who are nurtured in Christian families and have been reared in close connection with the church, the experience may come quietly, and perhaps even imperceptibly. For the most part Christians have agreed, however, that it is important at some time in life to make one's self-determined affirmation of trust in God a matter of public declaration. They have also agreed that there must be recurring in the Christian life acts of deliberate trust in which the person repudiates his false faiths and the actions to which they lead and affirms his adherence to God. Thus repentance and faith are integral aspects of life throughout its entire course.

The act of responding to the divine love is human; it arises out of the self-determination of the individual. It also has another human aspect. Normally, at least, it arises through contact with a human community, the church. It can come in this way because the church, whatever else it is, is a group of people whose existence as a community is traced to the divine love. They have treasured through the centuries the memory of the act in which God's redemptive love was rendered visible. They are those who say, "We love, because he first loved us." [2] The love they have known is divine, yet they remain human beings. But even as human beings they have a love to offer through which a man may find faith, a faith of his own which is, at the same time, a work of God.

2. THE ACTION OF GOD: THE HOLY SPIRIT

When Christians have focused attention on the divine aspect of the action which occurs when trust arises in the human being, they have often spoken of it as a work of the Holy Spirit. In so doing they have followed the custom of the earliest believers who were Jews and who made use of terms inherited from their ancestral religion. The terms *Holy Spirit, Spirit of the Lord,* and others of similar import often appear on the pages of the Old Testament. One scholar has suggested that the

[2] I John 4:19.

phrase "God in action" gives a good account of their meaning.[3] In the stage of Hebrew religion which embodies many primitive characteristics the spirit is conceived as a reality which causes ecstatic utterance or behavior. When it comes on a man, he may receive superhuman strength, as in the case of Samson, or he may dance or utter strange words.[4] Later

SYMBOLS OF FORGIVENESS An ebony cross hangs on a reredos embodying the figures of cross, bread, and cup. Jessie Ball duPont Chapel, Hollins College, Frantz and Addkison, Architects. Cross designed by architects and made by Armento Metal Arts Company, Buffalo. (Deyerle Studios, Roanoke)

the Spirit was identified as giving skill and sensitivity to those who had prepared the fine materials which were intended for the tabernacle in the wilderness.[5] In writings embodying hopes for the future the Spirit was conceived as being connected in a special way with the person of the Messiah and with the coming of the messianic age.[6]

The last conception, in particular, was associated in the minds of

---

[3] Harold W. Tribble, in lectures given at Southern Baptist Theological Seminary, 1936-37. Used by permission.

[4] Judges 15:14.

[5] Exodus 35:30.

[6] Isaiah 61:1.

Christians with the figure of Jesus. His baptism was accompanied by the apparition of a dove which was identified as the Spirit.[7] When he preached in Nazareth at the very beginning of his career, he appropriated to himself words that had been written by Isaiah:

> The Spirit of the Lord is upon me,
> because he has annointed me to preach good news to the poor.
> He has sent me to proclaim release to the captives
> and recovering of sight to the blind,
> to set at liberty those who are oppressed,
> to proclaim the acceptable year of the Lord.[8]

John voiced the common conviction of early Christians when he said of Jesus that the Spirit was given to him without measure.[9] The Spirit and the Messiah were inseparably related.

After the death of Jesus, however, a new era of the Spirit's activity began. The book of Acts relates that at the time of the feast of Pentecost the disciples were gathered together in prayer when a strange thing happened. With the sound of a mighty rushing wind the Spirit came upon the assembled men and attached itself to them as flames of fire. Peter interpreted the event as fulfilment of a prophecy:

> And in the last days it shall be, God declares,
> that I will pour out my Spirit upon all flesh,
> and your sons and your daughters shall prophesy,
> and your young men shall see visions,
> and your old men shall dream dreams.[10]

Christians have usually referred to Pentecost as the birthdate of the church. In terms of the first century, it was the time when the Spirit which had been upon Jesus came upon his followers and made them a messianic people.

There are constant references to the Spirit throughout the New Testament. It continues the activity of God which had begun in Jesus; indeed the Spirit is the Reality through which what God had done in Christ becomes present for the believer. Sometimes it is identified with the living Christ, who is thought of as a veritable presence, active in human life. Thus Paul speaks of the Spirit, or the Spirit of Christ, or simply of Christ with reference to the same activities; once he explicitly says, "The

---

[7] Mark 1:10.
[8] Luke 4:18f.
[9] John 3:34.
[10] Acts 2:17.

Lord"—that is, Christ—"is the Spirit." [11] Sometimes, as in the early history of the Hebrews, the effect of the Spirit in the life of man is to induce ecstatic utterance or behavior. Peter at Pentecost points out that the men on whom the Spirit has fallen are not intoxicated. "Speaking with tongues" seems to have been frequently associated with inspiration by the Spirit. But the more permanent and significant effects of the Spirit's action are the creating of faith and the activation of love. In a passage which is classic Paul lists the fruit of the Spirit, "love, joy, peace, patience, kindness, goodness, faithfulness, gentleness, self-control." [12]

There were no dramatic controversies about the Spirit in the early church similar to those which called forth repeated attempts at credal definition in the case of the meaning of Jesus. The early creeds, including that called the Apostles', were content with the simple affirmation that Christians believed in the Holy Spirit. After Nicea there were some who wished to deny to the Spirit the dignity which had been accorded the Son. In response to them there was incorporated into the Nicene creed an article about the Spirit which appears in the form in which that creed is now spoken in many churches. Having affirmed belief in the Father and the Son, the statement continues with affirmation of faith

> in the Holy Spirit, the Lord, and Giver of Life, Who proceedeth from the Father and the Son; Who with the Father and the Son together is worshipped and glorified; who spake by the prophets.

Thus full divinity is accorded the Spirit.

Christian affirmations about the Spirit have relevance for the vision we are considering at several important points; three will come before us. In the first place, the Spirit is connected with God's activity in history. Thus it was in the Old Testament, and thus it continues in the New. The point is important, if only for reasons of usage. In the literature and philosophy of the West the word spirit has been frequently associated with an ethereal reality, exercising gentle force; in the Bible Spirit is active and mighty, though sometimes gentle too. Also in the West spirit has often been identified with timeless, spiritual substance, and contrasted with matter. In the Bible Spirit is active, and sometimes uses material beings as its vehicles. In the New Testament the Spirit is associated particularly with the historical events surrounding the life of Jesus. By the Spirit the meaning of his life is disclosed to his contemporaries, and through the Spirit he becomes present to those who live after

---

[11] II Corinthians 3:17.
[12] Galatians 5:22f.

him. It is by the Spirit that the redemptive action of Christ is carried on; the Spirit's work is part of the work of Christ of which we spoke in the preceding chapter. By the Spirit the disclosure of God in Christ becomes a disclosure to someone. Until this happens the disclosure is not complete.

Further, the Spirit is connected in a special way with the church. Of this there will be occasion to speak at another point. Here many of the controversies about the Spirit have arisen. The church is human; yet it is a creation of the divine Spirit. Hence there is, in a sense, a continuation of the sort of divine activity which we have in Jesus. According to the language of early Christianity, there were two natures present in him, one divine, the other human. The divine used the human as its instrument of self-disclosure. Now if the church is the continuation of the incarnation,[13] similar language would seem appropriate for describing it. Again a reality with two natures—one divine, the other human—is the instrument of the divine self-disclosure. It is clear from the New Testament that the church is not a group of perfected people; it is human, yes, all-too-human. And yet it is connected with the divine; the Holy Spirit works in and through it. The Apostles' Creed and those which follow it make certain affirmations about God. But they also make affirmations about some things that are human. They speak of Jesus, who was born, suffered, and died. They also speak of the Church, the communion of saints. For all its frailty the church is touched with the divine in such manner that it is regarded as an essential element in the faith of Christians. This is due to its relation to the Spirit.

A third aspect of the Spirit's work which is significant for the Christian vision brings us back to that which was discussed in the first section of this chapter, the arising of faith within the spirit of man. The Christian conviction is that faith is a creation of the Spirit. "By grace are ye saved through faith; and that not of yourselves; it is the gift of God." [14] The initiative in redemption is with God; it is he who restores the world to himself. And he does so by making his love known to man in a way that brings about man's response. When man becomes aware of a trustable Reality he is enabled to relinquish his faith in those not trustable. The repentance which goes with faith is thus also the Spirit's doing. Faith makes penitence possible. Man cannot face the seriousness of sin without being assured of the possibility of forgiveness. God's love comes first, then the penitence which recognizes the sins which have separated man from that love. It is the experience of being loved that brings man's

---

[13] I Corinthians 12, Romans 12:3-8.

[14] Ephesians 2:8, K.J.V.

sins before him and gives him the courage to face them. To say these things about the divine action, however, is not to forget what has already been said about the human. Grace and faith go together.

In the Apostles' creed four phrases are closely joined; they belong together. In them Christians declare their faith in "the Holy Spirit, the Holy Catholic Church, the communion of saints, the forgiveness of sins."

3. THE NEW CREATURE

The action of God by which trust was aroused in the life of man was looked upon by the early Christians as a restoration of life to its primeval unity. The unification which looked toward the future had its reference to the past also. Here again the close connection which Christians traced between redemption and creation was important. Early they came to speak of the Spirit who created trust as a person, and in asserting his full divinity they were tracing his acts to the everlasting God. Indeed, they said that he was that same Spirit which the opening chapter of the Bible had described as brooding over the waters before the creation of the world.[15] They also, as we have seen, thought of God as he had been made known in Christ as a person. He, too, had existed before the foundation of the world. He was, said the early Christians, that Word through which God spoke the world into being or the Wisdom by which he had planned it.[16] And the God to whom they were related by the Spirit, whose forgiving love had been made known in Christ, was "The Father Almighty, Maker of heaven and earth." And yet there were not three Gods; they were not polytheists. The word "person" which they used had to be qualified carefully so that no such interpretations could arise. There was "ever One God, world without end." [17]

The various intellectual problems connected with the doctrine of the Trinity need not, however, detain us here. It comes before us simply as one of the ways in which the early Christians expressed their convictions about the world and its meaning, those convictions which came together in the Christian vision. They were convinced that forgiveness had brought them into right relationships with the Reality to whom they were finally responsible, the one who was the source of their being, the one who mattered most in all things. By acting toward the early Christians as their Redeemer, God had brought them to himself as their Creator.

---

[15] Genesis 1:2.
[16] John 1:1ff. and I Corinthians 1:24.
[17] *The Book of Common Prayer,* p. 32.

They were also brought into a new relationship with the world which was his creation. All things in it could be recognized as good, to be received in gratitude. Theirs was not, however, any facile optimism. There were still many ambiguities in life; the world presented them with hostilities and apparent evils. There were creatures who had rebelled against God and who had also stirred up troubles against his people. But Christians were persuaded, as Paul put it, "that neither death, nor life, nor angels, nor principalities, nor things present, nor things to come, nor powers, nor height, nor depth, nor anything else in all creation, will be able to separate us from the love of God in Christ Jesus our Lord." [18]

Forgiveness also brought them back to the unity which was theirs by virtue of their origin. "If any man be in Christ," said Paul, "he is a new creature." [19] Man returns to that which was the creative intent for him. A new creature is a true creature. Those elements in him which had been perverted by his rebellion were restored, in a measure at least, and could receive their rightful expression.

God's forgiving love had come in a way that did not destroy man's self-determination; it was not forced upon him. He could reject it—else it were not love. And yet when man responded to it, he discovered his selfhood in a new way. No longer need he be at enmity with himself, no longer need there be self-hatred. He was loved by the Eternal and man could be at peace with himself. His mind, then, might operate with a measure of clarity it had not known before. The perversions and biases which were the product of his self-preoccupation need no longer infect his thinking. Secure in the center of his being, he could exercise the intellectual powers which God had placed in him in ways that were wholesome and normal.

Forgiveness also released a love for others. So long as man was not at peace with himself, he was unable to give himself to them. So long as he was not sure of being loved, he had to try desperately to love himself. He might in his efforts to do so try to obey the law which said that he must love his neighbor. A man might have done very fine things for others; but the motive of concern for them was lacking. Even the things he did for them were done to satisfy himself. With the assurance of love release from self-preoccupation could come. The sociality which belonged to the created nature of man could express itself. Man could love his neighbor in reality, truly seeking the other's good. Thus there was a chain leading from God's love for him, through his trust in God,

---

[18] Romans 8:38f.

[19] II Corinthians 5:17, K.J.V.

to his love for others. As one early Christian writer put it, "Faith [is] the beginning and love the end" of the Christian life.[20]

Man's creativity, then, could be both self-expression and communication. At peace with himself he could create with the intent to do something for others at the same time as he was externalizing that which was within himself. In his total being there was peace. Man had a new center for his life. Trust had brought him to a relation to God, himself, and others which was right because it was normal. It was natural because it was the expression of his very nature.

4. THE LIMITATIONS THAT REMAIN

The love of God making its way into the life of man can, then, make of him a new creature; but he remains a creature. Therefore trust remains the appropriate way in which his relation to God is expressed. Man is still limited in wisdom, he is short of perfect moral strength, he is lacking in perfectness of devotion. Hence he cannot trust himself; he must live by faith.

Further, the anxieties of man's creatural situation ever impel him toward trustlessness. He turns his faith again toward himself, toward various objects about him. He finds the things of the world good and neglects the God who made them. The patterns of habit which have developed from faithlessness continue to exert their force in his life. As Christians have sometimes put it, the old nature survives along with the new—that is, the sinful nature continues to make itself felt in the life. In another time it was customary among some to speak of occasional lapses of Christians from the life of faith as backslidings.

The faithlessness of others also affects the lives of those who know the meaning of trust. Sometimes there is active opposition to the good on a grand scale. Emperors require worship, states become tyrannous, entrenched evil insists on its way. In various ways the brokenness of life asserts itself; the wholeness has not fully established itself. Hence, in the words of Paul, "we walk by faith, not by sight." [21]

There is, therefore, a place for discipline in the Christian life. There will be occasion to speak of this at greater length in other contexts. It is enough to say here that the discipline cannot be such as to lead to self-

---

[20] Ignatius, "Letter to the Ephesians," 14:1, in Cyril C. Richardson, trans. and ed., *Early Christian Fathers* (Philadelphia: The Westminster Press; London: S. C. M. Press, Ltd., 1953), p. 91. Reprinted by permission.

[21] II Corinthians 5:7.

reliance. Then trust would be misplaced again. And yet, as some sensitive Christians have pointed out, it is possible for the very experience of faith to lead to a self-exaltation which brings about faith's denial.[22] Here is a Christian counterpart of the notion of *hybris,* of religious pride, which plays a great part in Greek tragedy. The hero, thinking he is more than human, commits an act which brings the proper vengeance of the gods down upon himself and others. So it may be with faith—faith which began as faith in God can turn into faith in oneself. The disciplines appropriate to faith are those which make the person open to the ever-forgiving love of God.

The limitations which the creatural situation imposes upon men, however, are not restrictions on the freedom of God. It has been the continuing conviction of Christians, as it was of the Hebrews before them, that God's redemptive and creative activity could not be bound. Hence every situation was one in which that activity could operate. The attitude of the prophets toward the fall of Jerusalem is a case in point. Ezekiel, for example, saw the fall coming and gave his people no hope that it could be averted. Like other prophets he saw it as the act of God's righteous judgment. But once the city had fallen he spoke words of encouragement to his people; he proclaimed hope. God who had judged his people would redeem them.[23] Paul, in a familiar passage, tells of a thorn in the flesh which God had given him as a rebuke to his pride. He asked that it be removed. It was not. Instead, he was told by God, "My grace is sufficient for you, for my power is made perfect in weakness."[24] The history of Christianity is full of stories of people who tasted in full the bitterness that life can bring, but were able to trust God to bring something creative and redemptive out of their sufferings. They reminded themselves of the death of a rejected man on a cross whose sorrows, they believed, had been used by God for the redemption of his world.

5. FULFILLMENT

Nowhere are the limitations of our finitude more baffling than in our confrontation with our own death and with questions about the end of the world and of human history. Here "we see through a glass, darkly."[25]

---

[22] Jacob Boehme, *The Way to Christ,* John J. Stoudt, trans. (New York: Harper & Brothers, 1947), p. 51.

[23] See Fleming James, *Personalities of the Old Testament* (New York: Charles Scribner's Sons, 1951), p. 346.

[24] II Corinthians 12:9.

[25] I Corinthians 13:12, K.J.V.

Some Christians have spoken of these matters with great confidence; elaborate charts have been prepared purporting to disclose the succession of events leading to the consummation of all things. Many theologians who have been unwilling to set down divine time tables have, nevertheless, set forth opinions of a very definite sort about conditions beyond the grave. But thinkers of our time are, for the most part, rather reticent about such matters. They may affirm their faith, but hold that all that they say must be understood as symbolic. Here the trust of which we have been speaking throughout this chapter seems the appropriate attitude. To God can be entrusted our living and our dying, though we cannot know just how he will care for us.

For all this, the matter is of prime importance, even for present living. At the close of his classic treatment of resurrection in the fifteenth chapter of First Corinthians Paul writes in a very practical manner of the implications of what he has said for the conduct of the Christian:

> Therefore, my beloved brethren, be steadfast, immovable, always abounding in the work of the Lord, knowing that in the Lord your labor is not in vain.[26]

The early Christians were looking toward the end of things. Jesus who had recently left them was to return; then there would be judgment, and God's kingdom of love and righteousness would be established. Waiting for it some of them sold their possessions to join with others in a life of worship and mutual concern that would soon be over. Looking toward it they celebrated the supper in which they "shew the Lord's death till he come." [27] And in the confident expectation of his imminent return they endured persecution and painful death. The end-time had begun; the kingdom was already partly present. Soon it would arrive in its fullness.

The Old Testament which they made their own contained some references which confirmed their faith. Most of that book, however, was rather indifferent to things which lay beyond this earth. Perhaps the prevalence of cults of the dead among the Canaanites in Palestine led Israelites to disregard such things. The word which is sometimes translated "hell" in older versions of the Bible should not be taken to mean what Christians have traditionally meant by the term. Better is the simple transliteration of the Hebrew, "Sheol," as it is given in most modern translations. It refers to a shadowy existence at best; little joy is there.

---

[26] I Corinthians 15:58.

[27] I Corinthians 11:26, K.J.V.

After death there is little to look forward to. The Hebrew concern for life in history and for God's redemptive actions in it left them little energy for speculations about what might lie beyond. At a few points the Old Testament does break forth into confident hope.[28]

The New Testament speaks with confidence, but with little attempt at explicit statement. The book of the Revelation is full of mysterious pictures of the end time; much of what it says about human history can be referred to events near the turn of the first century.

The early creeds expressed the conviction of the New Testament Christians concerning the return of Jesus. He was looked for "to judge the living and the dead." How literally these words are to be taken has been a matter on which Christians have differed. At the least, they point to the conviction that the redemptive love which was disclosed in Jesus is the standard by which men are ultimately judged.

The Apostles' Creed also speaks of belief in "the resurrection of the body and the life everlasting." Here there is definite concern to set forth that which distinguishes Christian faith from alternative points of view. There is repudiation of the vision of the world which the early Christians encountered in Gnosticism. Man was no being whose good soul was imprisoned in an evil body; whose redemption was release of that soul. He was a creature good in his totality; and the redemptive concern of God included his whole being. The salvation of his soul was not enough. Perhaps the fifteenth chapter of First Corinthians should be noted in connection with the conviction of the creed. Paul is firmly convinced of the resurrection of the body. But he also holds that the body that is to be raised is not the same as that which is sown. God will give a body as pleases him, he says.[29] What kind of body might be appropriate for heavenly life Paul does not attempt to say. Here trust is sufficient; but it does not pretend to be sight.

A term which does not appear in the creed is of such constant recurrence in Christian thought about the end that some attention must be given to it. The words "Kingdom of God" have been used since the very beginnings of the church, and before that, to point to what God will bring about. It has referred, for the most part, to the manner in which God will bring to pass the consummation of human history. It has stressed the social dimension of redemption. Views of its relation to

---

[28] E. g., Daniel 12:2.
[29] I Corinthians 15:38, K.J.V.

history have been various. Some have thought of it, as we have seen, as the end of the evolutionary process,

> One far off divine event
> To which the whole creation moves.[30]

Others have held that the world would grow progressively worse until God would break in, destroy his enemies, and set up his kingdom. Others have held a so-called "dialectical" view: the kingdom stands for that which God will bring about at the end of history, taking up into itself all that is good and eliminating all that should not be. Thus the kingdom is both the redemption of and the judgment upon human history.[31]

While Christians have agreed in affirming their faith in the fulfillment of God's redemptive purposes, they have held a variety of opinions about the fate of individuals. Some have held that what has been said in the tradition about the survival of bodily death and the end of human history must be taken metaphorically. It is a symbol pointing to the character of God's creative and redemptive actions in the present. It is of the greatest significance, for it points to an ultimate meaning for human life and history. For the most part, however, Christians have held that there was some more tangible meaning in the affirmations which have been made. Some have held that only those who have made explicit profession of faith in Christ or in some prescribed set of doctrines together with those Old Testament characters who longed for the Messiah would enjoy a blissful existence forever. The holiness and righteousness of God in reaction to the seriousness of sin made it necessary that all others endure everlasting torment. Others have softened the position somewhat by including among the believers in Christ all those who shared his spirit no matter where or when they may have lived. Some have held that for certain people there was a period of purging beyond this life when they underwent such disciplines as would prepare them to be the kind of people who would be capable of enjoying the bliss of fellowship with God.

Recurrent in the history of the church has been another view; it appeared in the writings of a thinker named Origen in the beginning of the third century and has been held by some ever since. It holds that the love of God must eventually prevail over all men, that his redemption cannot be limited. His true enemies are also those of mankind—sin,

---

[30] Alfred, Lord Tennyson, "In Memoriam," *Works,* II, 310.
[31] Reinhold Niebuhr, *The Nature and Destiny of Man,* II, 299ff.

hatred, suffering, sorrow, and death. These he will overcome and bring to himself all those who have been hurt by them. Some words of the New Testament appear to support such a view. "In Christ," wrote Paul, "shall all be made alive."[32] Its opponents usually point out that it does not take seriously the awfulness of sin or the dignity of the divine majesty.

In much that has been said and is still said about the life to come there seem to be notions that are at variance with the Christian vision in its totality. That vision attributes redemption to God, but often heaven is spoken of as if it were the reward for human goodness. That vision speaks of a motive of love which should flow through all human action; but fear of hell and desire for heavenly pleasure are sometimes presented as motives of a purely selfish sort. Here as scarcely anywhere else in Christian thought and action, it seems, is there a tendency to separate what is said from its context in the totality of the Christian outlook.

Perhaps, then, a concluding word might point to those elements of the Christian vision which should be remembered in all that is said on the subject of the life everlasting. Thus we might bring into review some of those matters which we have been treating.

> God's creation is good, and in his redemption he brings to fulfillment the good he has begun.
> God acts in history, and in his redemption he brings that action to completion.
> Man is a totality, and God's redemptive purpose includes his whole being.
> Man is social, and in his redemption God will fulfill his life in society.
> Man has rebelled, and God's forgiveness is the basis of his happy relationship with his creator.
> Man is self-determining, and his redemption comes about as he finds true freedom in his love of God and his neighbor.
> Redemption is God's act into which man enters.

READINGS

From the Bible

1. The response of faith is central in many passages, as John 3, Romans 3, 8; Galatians, Philippians, Habakkuk.

---

[32] I Corinthians 15:22.

2. Questions about death and new life are treated in I Corinthians 15.

3. Pictures of the final actions of God are given in II Peter, Jude, and Revelation 21-22.

From Historic Christianity

1. Martin Luther, *Christian Liberty*, describes what man needs to be redeemed from, what he is redeemed to, and the means by which he is redeemed.

2. Dante, *The Divine Comedy*, "Paradiso," celebrates the realization of redemption.

3. Fyodor Dostoyevski, *The Brothers Karamazov*. "The Grand Inquisitor" points up the significance of love and freedom for redemption.

FOR STUDY AND DISCUSSION

1. Is the notion that man needs saving insulting to him?
2. Does the idea of predestination have any significance for today, or is it sheer nonsense?
3. Should the phrase "the resurrection of the body" be dropped from creeds spoken in a contemporary church?
4. Have the notions of heaven and hell been so abused that they should be abolished? Is the idea of purgatory valid?
5. Study an order for a funeral service or a musical setting of a *Requiem Mass*.

THE ATTITUDES

VI

MAN AND NATURE

William Temple, the late archbishop of Canterbury, once said that Christianity was "the most avowedly materialist of all the great religions." [1]

The response of many Christians to his statement is one of immediate denial. It is so obvious to them that religion in general and Christianity in particular are matters of the spirit that to speak of them as materialistic is a contradiction in terms. When some of their fellow believers voice in the name of their faith opinions about economic or racial or political matters, they feel that the action is inappropriate. Religion for them has to do with spiritual and not with material things.

Others might respond to the late Archbishop's statement—if they ever heard it—with a shrug of the shoulders. They, too, feel that religion is a spiritual thing. For this reason they have abandoned it. They are frankly preoccupied with the securing of material things or the satisfaction of bodily wants, and they do not want to be placed under any restraints. The prevalence of their attitude in contemporary America is

[1] William Temple, *Nature, Man and God* (London: Macmillan & Co., Limited, 1940), p. 478. Reprinted by permission.

among the factors which have led a renowned sociologist, Pitirim Sorokin, to speak of ours as "a sensate culture." [2]

Both of the groups which have been described had their counterparts in the early centuries of the Christian era. The reasoning that lay behind their viewpoints was, in some cases, somewhat different. However, one of the central concerns of early Christian writers and creed makers was to distinguish the Christian message from their points of view. And it is just here that some of our contemporaries feel that a recovery of historic Christianity is significant for our time. Cultural trends reaching back over several centuries have separated us from a central attitude in primitive Christianity, that expressed in the words of William Temple.

The attitude toward nature—this is our first concern as we move from the consideration of the Christian vision to the treatment of attitudes explicit in it. We are now to look at a second dimension of faith: the fundamental attitude that is reflected in the several relationships of life. Things subhuman may well be divided into two classifications. Each of us has a subhuman aspect, what we usually call our body. And around us are all sorts of things that do not behave in the ways we associate with distinctively human actions. Some of these are material, in the common usage of the term; others are living beings. To all of these realities the terms *nature* and *subhuman* apply as they will be used here. They refer to a realm of "things" which may be contrasted with the realm of history in which human decisions are of central significance.

1. WHAT THE BIBLE SAYS

There are some great passages in which the biblical writers have set forth in picturesque fashion their convictions about creation, sin, and redemption. They have become literary classics, laying hold on the imaginations of men through the centuries and influencing their thought and feeling in subtle ways. It is significant that in many of these attention is accorded to nature.

In the story of the six days with which the Old Testament begins, the creation—of sun and moon and stars, of land and sea, of birds and creeping things and beasts of the earth—is related with a repeated refrain making commentary on what has been described: "And God saw that it was good." [3] In the other creation story God makes dust from the earth, breathes into it a living soul, and makes it a man.

---

[2] Pitirim Sorokin, *Social and Cultural Dynamics* (Boston: Porter Sargent Publisher, 1957), pp. 699ff. Used by permission.

[3] Genesis 1:10.

Man's first habitat is described as a garden of great beauty with plants responsive to the work of their caretaker. Eve is tempted by a subtle subhuman, a serpent, who promises that she may be like God—knowing good and evil—if she disobeys the divine commandment. Involved in the temptation is the fact that her physical appetite craves a material thing; "the woman saw that the tree was good for food, and that it was a delight to the eyes." [4]

In the eleventh chapter of Isaiah the prophet describes conditions which will prevail at some time in the future when a shoot will come forth from the stump of Jesse. Animal life will be transformed along with human.

> The wolf shall dwell with the lamb,
> and the leopard shall lie down with the kid,
> and the calf and the lion and the fatling together,
> and a little child shall lead them.

[4] Genesis 3:6.

REDEMPTION OF NATURE An American Quaker depicts a redeemed world, with peace reigning over animals and men. *The Peaceable Kingdom.* Edward Hicks (Courtesy of the Abby Aldrich Rockefeller Folk Art Collection, Williamsburg, Virginia)

The cow and the bear shall feed;
their young shall lie down together;
and the lion shall eat straw like the ox.
The sucking child shall play over the hole of the asp,
and the weaned child shall put his hand on the adder's den.
They shall not hurt or destroy
in all my holy mountain;
for the earth shall be full of the knowledge of the Lord
as the waters cover the sea.[5]

These passages give poetic expression to ideas which appear frequently on the pages of the Old Testament. The attitudes they express were reflected in the moral codes as well as the ritual observances of the Hebrews. Indeed, they helped to form the total character of their life.

Much of what appears in the Old Testament concerning nature reflects the reaction of the Israelites to the religion prevalent in the land of Canaan when they came into it. We read often of the Baals and Ashtaroth which were worshipped in the land and tempted the Hebrews to forsake their ancestral faith. These were simply the local expressions of a form of religion that was widespread in the ancient world. Baal was the male, Astarte the female—together they represented the powers of fertility. It is not surprising that peoples who depended on the soil for their very life should have sought to keep on good terms with deities of the earth. Throughout the Near East were variants of a myth of the deity who dies in the autumn, is mourned through the winter, and is revived by the efforts of another deity as the spring comes on. Connected with the myths were rites of imitative magic; sexual acts were given ritual significance and were supposed to encourage the gods to give fertility to fields and animals. Prophetic voices among the Hebrews were raised in horror at the choice of fertility gods over the Lord who had brought his people from Egypt and who had insisted on moral conduct in their relations with one another. However, the prophets did not deny the relation of God to nature; they proclaimed that the Lord who had worked redemptively in their history was also the giver of the goods of nature; he was the creator of the earth. The struggle between Baalism and the worship of Israel's Lord reaches dramatic climax in the story of Elijah on Mount Carmel.[6] There it is established that the Baals do not control the falling of the rain. Israel's God is the Lord of nature as well as history.

Those who look to the Old Testament for poetic celebration of the

[5] Isaiah 11:6-9.
[6] I Kings 18:20-40.

CHURCH AND NATURE The Motto of Hollins College, "I will lift up mine eyes," appears with the college seal on the Chapel and suggests the hills which surround the school. Jessie Ball duPont Chapel, Hollins College. Frantz and Addkison, Architects (Deyerle Studios, Roanoke)

wonders of nature will find a few magnificent passages, but not many. The Hebrews were so deeply concerned about avoiding the preoccupation with nature expressed in the worship of the gods of fertility that they did not often speak of the glories of the world. For the most part their poetry spoke of God's actions in human history. Here and there they expressed the thought that nature was good because it came from the hand of God; and yet they were ever reminded that he alone was worthy of worship.

Attitudes expressed in the New Testament are similar to those we have encountered in the Old. Creation is assumed; occasionally it is stressed, as in the passage previously cited in which the writer, referring specifically to questions about food and marriage, insists that "everything created by God is good." [7]

In his epistle to the Romans Paul specifically connects human sin with worship of the sub-human in a way that suggests the reaction of the Hebrew prophets to Baalism. The world itself, he says, is such that it reflects the divine power. But men turned from the Creator and diverted their worship to "images resembling mortal man or birds or animals or reptiles." Because of this, he goes on, "God gave them up" to all sorts of vices.[8] He lists many which were familiar in the world of his time. Thus Paul connects moral depravity in part with man's choosing the worship of nature in place of devotion to its everlasting Creator.

The world itself, however, is not evil; to the open eye of good men it does speak of God. Paul reveals his profound sympathy with nature

---

[7] I Timothy 4:4.
[8] Romans 1:23, 26.

on occasion. In another passage in the same epistle to the Romans he speaks of the eager longing of the whole creation for redemption. Now it is "subjected to futility," it is "groaning in travail," but eventually it "will be set free from its bondage to decay and obtain the glorious liberty of the children of God." [9]

The gospels picture the Redeemer as a man with a genuine feeling for nature. Lilies and sparrows and lambs are in his stories, though he knows that men are of greater value. He is tempted to make a concern for bread of paramount importance for a moment of his life, but in his reply to the tempter he does not deny the importance of food: "Man shall not live by bread alone." [10] By contrast to stern and self-denying John the Baptist he appears to some of his contemporaries as a "gluttonous" man and "a wine-bibber." [11] His concern for the good of men's bodies is expressed in numerous acts of healing.

The final chapters of the New Testament are a vision of the fulfillment of redemption. The city of God comes down out of heaven. A river of life is there, and along its banks are trees whose leaves are for the healing of the nations.[12] From its beginning to its end the Bible is sensitive to the world of nature.

2. THE CONVICTION OF THE CREEDS

The credal statements of the early church were, as we have seen, developed, in part, by reason of the struggle with Gnosticism. A pivotal point in the quarrel was the very thing with which we are concerned in this chapter. Christians and Gnostics differed in their attitude to what we have called the sub-human or nature. It was specifically matter that the Gnostics would not admit as the creation of the supreme God. A good deity could not be contaminated by contact with an evil reality.

The movement called Gnosticism was a complex one, and the influences that went into its making were diverse. With most of these we are not concerned. However, one of the influences which played upon it has been of such great significance for the history of Christianity, as well as the entire cultural life of the West, that we must give it some attention. It is one which stemmed from Greece. Again, we are not concerned to trace all Greek influences in the West; we are giving atten-

---

[9] Romans 8:19-25.
[10] Luke 4:4.
[11] Matthew 11:19, see K.J.V.
[12] See especially Revelation 22:1-2.

tion solely to one strand which received classic expression in the writings of Plato.

Two attitudes toward matter appear in his writings. They are closely related and sometimes merge into each other. Indeed, they are variations on a single theme. However, their implications are in some instances quite diverse. Hence they need to be distinguished.

According to the first attitude matter is in some real sense evil. It is, as Plato said, a many-headed monster which must be overcome by a tremendous struggle.[13] The material drags man downward, imprisons him, keeps him from reaching his true good; it must be actively resisted. It may be helpful to our understanding of this attitude if we treat it in terms of the triad of notions that we have used to describe the Christian vision: creation, sin, redemption. Matter is that which resists creation and must be overcome. In the case of man his creation is in itself a fall. His soul has come down from its true home to inhabit an alien body, its prison house. Redemption is release from the material. Hence Socrates can face death unafraid. Throughout his life, he says to his friends who sorrow at this impending demise, he has been giving himself to the life of the mind, seeking to free himself from the demands of his body. Now he is to be fully free.[14]

The second attitude toward matter is one which regards it as neutral. Sometimes resistant to good—here is contact with the preceding view—it can be brought under the sway of reason. Then it participates in something that is, in a measure, good. In terms of the triad of ideas we have been discussing, creation is the achievement of something truly good as reason brings material things into a condition of harmony. In the dialogue called "The Timaeus," Plato describes the creation of the world as the work of a craftsman who brings order to things by molding them in accordance with eternal patterns. This is the attitude reflected in Greek sculpture where the perfection of the human form receives magnificent expression and in architecture where stone takes on the shapes dictated by geometric genius. Sin is the resistance of matter to the harmonizing reason, redemption the overcoming of that resistance in the achievement of harmony of line in art, of harmony of action in fineness of moral conduct, of harmony of society in the ideal state.

The two attitudes cannot be sharply distinguished at all points. But the fact that Platonism expressed itself in both of them explains to some

---

[13] Plato, *The Republic of Plato*, Francis M. Cornford, trans. (New York: Oxford University Press, 1945), p. 317.

[14] Plato, *Phaedo*, F. J. Church, trans. (New York: The Liberal Arts Press, 1951), p. 9 (IX).

extent its enduring influence. The optimism of the Renaissance looked to the Greeks for models of beauty of form, for that harmonizing of the material that would bring its potential goodness to reality. The pessimism of the days surrounding the emergence of early Christianity led many, including the Gnostics, to find in teaching derived from Plato a reason for looking with hostility upon the material world.

To say that early Christians or their successors have reacted in flat denial or full acceptance of either or both of the attitudes described would be to oversimplify the account of the way things have gone. Actually Christians have generally found themselves in partial agreement and in partial disagreement with them.

Early credal statements are clear reactions to certain elements in the Platonic attitudes which reflected themselves in Gnosticism. The early Christians, as we have seen, stood firmly on the affirmation that the whole world was God's creation. Recalcitrant elements there might be in the cosmos, but this was not because they were inherently evil. In spite of the fact that the creation story in Genesis speaks as if there were something in existence before God created the heavens and the earth, early Christians insisted that it was essential to their faith to hold that God created from nothing. Since theologians enjoy using foreign terms, it is probably just as well to become acquainted with one here. The early Christians, they say, believed in *Creatio ex nihilo*, creation out of nothing.

Against the Gnostics the Christians further asserted that Jesus Christ "was born, suffered under Pontius Pilate, was crucified, dead, and buried." They said these words in part as a rejection of a view called "docetic," which holds that the body of Jesus was simply an apparition. Christians, however, insisted that Jesus had a real body. This meant that a body was not in itself evil, and in having one the redeemer was not contaminated. To be physical was not in itself to be sinful.

The early Christians also affirmed their faith in "the resurrection of the body." They usually interpreted their words in a way that was similar to the outlook we have encountered in the apostle Paul. The body in the world to come, they felt, must differ somehow from that which we inhabit here. But redemption did not mean the release of a good soul from an evil body. And the fulfillment of life was held to be of such a character that the goodness of the material was not to be denied.

3. A SUMMARY STATEMENT

It may be helpful at this point to state rather simply the attitudes toward sub-human realities which are implicit in the Christian vision.

Thus we may bring into some sort of unity the various affirmations to which we have accorded attention. For purposes of convenience the word "thing" will be used in the statement; it is intended in a very broad sense, to refer to actualities and forces of many kinds—food and drink, sex drives, vitalities of various sorts. The key idea in the statement is this: a thing can be a focal point. It can be a focal point for the creative action of God and for our apprehension of it. It can be a focal point in which sinful impulses may find a center. It can be a focal point through which the redemptive activity of God can operate. Let us look briefly at each of these ideas.

Because things can be focal points for the creative activity of God, they can become occasions for the specific apprehension of his goodness. Perhaps the most recurrent worship pattern within Christendom, sometimes continuing when other patterns have been abandoned, is the simple word of thanksgiving offered at the meal table. All creation is good, and created things can show forth their goodness in ways that appeal instantly to the imagination. However in their goodness they can be a specific focal point for the tension we have already noted, the tension of man living in a world made good. The very goodness of things tempts man to sin by neglecting the Creator who made them.

Preoccupation with things involves the rejection of redemptive love and defiance of the Creator. Failing to recognize the sacredness of the work of his hands, it offends his holiness. Perversion of the creature ensues because man becomes like that he worships; to bow before the subhuman is to experience the judgment of God in the dehumanization of man. And preoccupation with things finally leads to a trust in untrustworthy objects. Things have a fatal fascination because they can be manipulated and controlled; it is far more comforting to man to trust that which he can control than that to which he must give himself in trust, not knowing what the outcome will be. Preoccupation with things is bondage; and other things cannot release one from such bondage. The man bound by things may find himself moving from one idol to another in a hopeless quest.

Neglect of things is also sin against their Maker. Dante encountered in one of the deeper levels of hell those who had done violence to God "by scorning nature and her bounty." [15] Here, again, is rejection of redemptive love and disregard of the Creator. No sanctity is seen in objects of nature, no tracing of the giver's goodness is found in them. Such neglect is often met with in the history of religion, because of the

---

[15] Dante, *The Divine Comedy*, "Inferno," (XI, 48).

sinful possibilities involved in preoccupation with them. But the very effort to find freedom results in bondage. Man is not released from the lure of things so long as he is forced to deny them. Indeed, things sometimes take their vengeance upon him and bring him into deeper bondage; thus the pure spirituality of the Gnostics sometimes betrayed them into libertinism. Perversion of the creature results because he has to deny part of himself and of the world which is meant to sustain him. A purely spiritual man is never quite normal from the Christian point of view.

Things can be focal points for God's redemptive actions, however. The most dramatic symbols for this conviction are the waters of baptism, the bread and wine of the communion service, which have been intimately connected with Christian faith from its earliest days.

Things are also part of the totality which is the object of God's redemptive concern. Men are not to be saved from them but with them.

4. NATURE WITHIN US: THE BODY

The nineteenth and twentieth centuries have heard Sigmund Freud and Karl Marx bitterly attack Christianity, in no small measure because of its alleged neglect of concern for the body. Freud called attention to the imperious claims of sex, and he disparaged religion which counselled repressions which might lead to neuroses. Marx called attention to the need of men for food, for basal economic wants, and he assailed the churches for their indifference to men's bodily requirements and their disregard of the importance of the economic factor in human history. Religion which turned men's attention solely to spiritual matters and to a world beyond this was, to him, "the opiate of the people." [16]

Contemporary theologians are inclined to think that the charges made by Freud and Marx were partly true. They feel that during the nineteenth century attitudes had developed toward both sex and the significance of the economic factor in life which were out of character with the heritage of historic Christianity. The church had felt the influence of forces within the culture which had tended toward a devaluation of the body that was not authentically Christian. To some of these forces reference has already been made, and we can here note some of their effects upon the attitude toward the body. Where emphasis on reason had captured

---

[16] Often quoted, e.g. Mandell M. Bober, *Karl Marx's Interpretation of History* (Cambridge: Harvard University Press, 1950), p. 122. Reference is to Marx and Engels, *Gesamtausgabe*, Part I, Vol. 5, p. 607.

men's religious imagination, the disparagement of the significance of vital forces in life and history was natural. Where religion became equated with morality, an attitude of legal prescription surrounded the entire area of bodily activity. Prudishness and self-righteousness were equated with religious rightness. A deep sense of the sanctity of the body itself was surrendered to a sense of the sacredness of moral codes. Where religion was primarily connected with religious experience, the place of the body was neglected. After all, it was what happened in the spiritual realm that was all important!

If modern Christianity has sometimes yielded to forces which tended to undervalue the body, it has also had to resist forces which have overvalued it. The Renaissance brought with it a spirit which gloried in the physical. Sometimes this cast aside the Greek heritage with its counsel of prudence as well as the Christian with its word concerning responsibility to God. Gargantua and Pantagruel are its proponents. Its motto hangs over the order they founded: "Do what you want." [17] This century has seen a great people bowing down to gods of blood and soil, determining ethical decisions on the basis of race, glorifying the vitalities of life.

Historic Christianity disagrees with Freud and Marx as well as with those whom they criticized, with those who overvalue and those who undervalue the body. It sees the body as a focal point for God's creative action, for man's rebellion, and for God's redeeming work. For it, the body is good because it is God's creation; it is a part of the totality which is man and is involved with him in all that he does. But its very goodness can make it a focal point of temptation. Man can sin by giving in to a body which wants what it wants when it wants it. He can also sin by disregarding the fact that his body makes demands on him. He may court abnormality by seeking to be a purely "spiritual" being. Redeemed he will know freedom from control by the body. He may suffer fearful pain, be the victim of an incurable disease, but live creatively and redemptively by the grace of God. And yet his very freedom from domination by the body is compatible with a positive attitude toward it. He can rightly concern himself that men become healthy and that they have enough to eat. He may be puzzled as he says in the ancient words of the creed, "I believe in the resurrection of the body," but it can mean at least that the physical life participates in man's redemption here and now. Christian faith says to him, "If you belong to your body, you are enslaved to a

---

[17] François Rabelais, *Oeuvres de François Rabelais* (Paris: Honoré et Edouard Champion, 1913), II, 430.

wrong master; your faith has been misplaced. But your body can belong to you, for 'all things are yours, . . . and you are Christ's; and Christ is God's.'"[18]

5. NATURE AROUND US

In its attitude toward nature western Christianity has not always reflected the spirit of the words, "And God saw everything that he had made, and behold, it was very good."[19] But the conviction contained in them has brought it back again and again to itself. That conviction has affected the entire spirit of Western culture. Perhaps there is no more winsome expression of it than that which is found in the life of Saint Francis of Assisi. As a young man he turned his back on the wealth that was his as the son of a prosperous merchant and announced his decision to be wed to lady poverty. In devotion to her he called nothing his own. The spirit of his life was put into a phrase he was heard to utter repeatedly during a night spent in prayer—"My God, My God."[20] But his intense preoccupation with God did not lead him to despise God's creatures. The familiar verses of the *Canticle to the Sun,* which can be found in any hymnal, remind us of his friendship with brother sun and moon, wind and earth, and even brother death. His sermon to the birds is full of charm:

> Much are you bound to God, birds, my sisters, and everywhere and always must you praise him for the free flight you everywhere have; for the double and triple covering, for the painted and decorated robe; for the food prepared without your labor; for the song taught you by the Creator . . .[21]

If the birds were able to understand, they were reminded of that attitude which is consonant with the Christian affirmation of creation: God's gifts are to be received with gratitude to the giver.

Saint Francis lived within the context of the wholeness of historic Christianity. As the modern world moved away from a sense for that wholeness, it departed from some of the attitudes toward nature that belonged to it. And yet, even as it moved away, it brought with it parts from the earlier whole.

---

[18] I Corinthians 3:21ff.

[19] Genesis 1:31.

[20] *The Little Flowers of Saint Francis,* Ch. ii.

[21] As given by Henry Adams in *Mont-Saint-Michel and Chartres* (Boston: Houghton Mifflin Company, 1904), p. 339. Reprinted by permission.

The Christian affirmation that the world is good continued to exercise its influence over men's imaginations. It was in part the inspiration of poetry, art, and music which were sensitive to the significance of the subhuman. But sometimes men divorced their appreciation of nature from its place in a total faith which included more. Sometimes in rather fierce fashion they deified nature itself; in love with its beauties and harmonies, or awed by its grandeurs they felt no need for deity beyond it. Often they made nature the clue to all reality, neglecting the line between the human and the subhuman. Thus God was a clockmaker who had wound up a mechanical universe; he was the force who moved within the stars and pressed the animals toward higher levels of life. That he was, as Christian faith asserted, the one who gave meaning to personal decision, to man's intellectual and moral powers, to life in history—this was obscured. That he revealed himself redemptively seemed unimportant. Men needed no church, no companionship but nature's in their life with God.

The Christian conviction that man was the summit of creation, that he was intended to subdue the world, also continued to influence men in the modern world. In part it was the inspiration of a continuing sensitivity to the primacy of man over nature. And yet, detached from its historic rootages, it sometimes betrayed men into a disregard of their subhuman surroundings. Emphasis on the intellectual powers of man and upon the significance of civilization tended to make men indifferent to the natural surroundings in which they lived. A focusing of attention on the importance of morality tended to give attention to relations with persons at the expense of relations with things. And yet, so far as there was a sense of reverence for the divine, some restraint was placed on man with reference to his treatment of things. Where that sense failed, the commandment to subdue the subhuman was perverted into the effort to exploit it. Things ceased to have any sacred quality whatever. Man simply used them; nature was plundered.

Consideration of these currents of attitude yields us some understanding of the broad relationships between science and Christian faith. It is important to note that the emergence of science occurred within a culture which was deeply imbued with the spirit of that faith. That Western culture also included attitudes inherited from the Greeks was, of course, also an important factor in its development. It is true, indeed, that science encountered an otherworldliness among many Christians, a suspicion of innovation, and a preoccupation with the miraculous that inhibited its growth. And yet the affirmation that this is a good world related to a dependable Reality was a tremendous force in its favor. Many of the earliest scientists were tracing "the work of the six days" of creation, and they thought of their investigations as dedicated efforts, seeking to discover God's ways and make them known to men. A culture in which the world is regarded as evil, where only by flight from it can there be salvation, or one which designates matter as evil from which the good soul must be released is not likely to be hospitable to science. Some of the most significant attitudes which fostered the development of science came into the culture of the West from its Hebraeo-Christian heritage.

As a sense for the wholeness of that heritage began to weaken, attitudes toward nature which belonged to it lost their place within its totality. Science responded to those currents of attitude which emphasized parts of the Christian outlook and neglected others; it also contributed to the forces which were severing the ties of men with their religious heritage. At times there was a veritable warfare between science and theology. The eighteenth century saw a prolonged struggle about the possibility of miracles and the nineteenth century witnessed a battle about biological evolution. Perhaps of more significance than these, however, were the tensions between science and religion that lay in the area of meanings. The amazing success of science in dealing with natural phenomena focused attention on these and encouraged men to think of them as giving the clue to the whole of reality. Thus the relations of subhuman realities were taken as a pattern for all sorts of relationships, and the distinctively human characteristics which had been so important for faith were regarded as unessential. Man was regarded by many as a product of forces which determined him with such completeness that to speak of any margin of self-determination seemed nonsense. That there was anything in him which suggested a relationship to the divine was regarded as outworn superstition. Even where men did not carry their thoughts to conclusions as extreme as these, the importance of science was such that a religion of nature crowded out the concern of one which emphasized the significance of personal decision and historical existence.

It may seem strange that the same science which seemed to point men toward nature for their link with the divine should have contributed to the attitude which found no sacred depth in her. And yet this has happened. For some the very preoccupation with the quantitative aspect of things has lessened their appreciation of their qualitative properties.[22] Color, sound, and beauty have been relegated to a status having no es-

---

[22] Alfred North Whitehead, *Science and the Modern World* (New York: The Macmillan Company, 1948).

sential place in the world. Further, the sense of control over things which science has fostered has sometimes given men a sense of emancipation from control by God. The tools by which men have exploited nature have been put into their hands—often, surely, without such intention—by the scientists. Modern machinery has facilitated the robbing of forests, the denuding of hillsides, the rending of rocks.

And yet science may help remind men of the wholeness of their faith, and it has often done so. It has underlined the ancient conviction that the world is good; indeed, it helped to bring this conviction to the attention of Christians who had neglected it. Nature responded to the probings of men by yielding treasures of beauty and wonder. The universe was seen to be greater and more awe-inspiring than men had dreamed. Science also called upon men for the utmost integrity of intellectual effort. It threw into relief that in man which sees the truth as something which must not be compromised. It also rebuked man's pretensions, made him aware of his limitations, of the smallness of his knowing and his being. Reminding him that he must ever be ready to admit himself wrong in the light of new evidence, it would not allow him to take himself too seriously; all that he asserted must be open to the examination and even the criticism of the world. And the same science that taught men to exploit the world taught them to conserve its treasures and enhance them. It brought deserts to blossom and showed men how to harbor the soil so that it could produce in abundance. It enlarged the ways in which a redemptive love for people in the wholeness of their beings could be expressed. Painstaking research disclosed the causes of diseases which men through the centuries had simply endured. Men's expectations about health and life were revolutionized.

The advent of the atomic age pressed insistently for renewed thought about the relations of men and nature, of the significance of man's control of the subhuman, of his responsibilities with reference to his fellows. For many it called for a new consideration of the problems to which historic Christianity had ever directed their attention: of the meaning of the world, of the significance of man. Christian faith sees man entering a world of things already created and pronounced good. It sees him charged with solemn responsibility with reference to these things: they must not control him, and he must not exploit them. It sees his rebellion against his Maker reflected in his treatment of the world around him and in its response to him. It sees God's redemptive act transforming him and with him his attitude toward all of creation.

Though the vision of a redeemed nature appears in the Bible and has had a place in classical Christian theologies, it is hard to say what

Bill Hedrich,
Hedrich-Blessing, Chicago

James J. Dion

Bill Hedrich,
Hedrich-Blessing, Chicago

Gerald Gard, Grand Rapids, Michigan

NATURE IN CONTEMPORARY CHURCH ARCHITECTURE Flooding sunlight, growing plants, and a quiet pool remind worshippers of the world which God made good. First Methodist Church, Midland, Michigan. Alden B. Dow, Architect.

we can make of it in our time. As we have noted elsewhere, the very fact that here and now we walk by faith and not by sight makes us chary of offering pronouncements on matters beyond our sphere of experience. But Christian faith is eternally haunted by the fact that the seer of Patmos saw more than a new heaven. His vision included a new earth, too.

READINGS

From the Bible

1. Celebrations of the glories of nature can be found in Psalms 8, 19, 29, 33, 104 and in Job 38-40.

2. The affirmation of the goodness of nature is set forth throughout Genesis 1 and in I Timothy 4:1-5.

3. The effects of sin on nature are described in Romans 8:19-25.

4. The redemption of nature is pictured in Isaiah 11 and Revelation 21-22.

From Historic Christianity

1. *The Little Flowers* of Saint Francis contain numerous echoes of the Saint's utter dedication to God and of his appreciation of God's world.

2. Alfred, Lord Tennyson's "In Memoriam" is a poetic revery of a nineteenth century Christian seeking assurance that nature is good.

3. Thomas Aquinas, *Against the Gentiles,* book IV, ch. 97, records his conception of redeemed nature.

FOR STUDY AND DISCUSSION

1. Do science and religion deal with completely different subject matters?
2. Is the question of miracles of any significance for contemporary Christianity?
3. Study the sermon entitled " 'Nature, also, Mourns for a Lost Good' " in Paul Tillich, *Shaking of the Foundations* (New York: Charles Scribner's Sons, 1950), pp. 76-87.
4. Examine each of these sentences: Nature adds nothing, subtracts nothing, so far as faith is concerned—Christ is all. My most profound religious experiences have come from communing with nature, and I need nothing else for my faith.
5. Leaf through a hymnal and note the hymns which speak most persuasively to you. Are they about nature?

VII

MAN'S RELATION TO HIMSELF

In Goethe's *Faust* the hero at one point cries out in great bitterness that two souls dwell within his breast.[1] Likewise in Plato's *Phaedrus* a description appears of the human spirit as a charioteer desperately seeking to control two horses intent on going in opposite directions.[2] Thus the modern German poet, epitomizing in his hero some of the dominant moods of the Renaissance, sees his tragedy against the backdrop of a view of life which finds restlessness and eternal growth as good. Plato, on the other hand, the rational Greek, sees the soul seeking to find peace in the contemplation of eternal harmonies. Despite their differences, however, the poet and the philosopher see what many sensitive men have observed: that man is a being who has relations with himself. Therein lies the clue to much that is tragic and also the clue to much that is great in human nature.

---

[1] Johann Wolfgang Goethe, *Faust,* in the scene "Vor dem Thor;" the passage is found in Philip Wayne's translation (Hammondsworth: Penguin Books, 1949), p. 67.

[2] Plato, "Phaedrus," *The Works of Plato,* Benjamin Jowett, trans. (New York: The Dial Press, n.d.) III, 430ff.

Our own time has been peculiarly sensitive to man's relation to himself. People have been intrigued by the title *Man Against Himself*[3] and have bought a book in which they expect to find a mirror of their own condition, and perhaps some help in speaking to it. Self-hatred is a concept frequently met. And psychologists and pastors alike often describe the basic human problem as that of self-acceptance.

When we turn to classical statements of historic Christianity to seek there the delineation of an attitude of man toward himself which is consonant with the Christian vision, we may be disappointed at first. Little is said that explicitly deals with the matter. No credal formulation neatly sets the orthodox view of Christians against the views of Gnostics, Arians, or Apollinarians. A quick run through a concordance of the Bible for references to *self* turns up, for the most part, completely commonplace instances. Typical is David's word to Jonathan in First Samuel 20:5, "let me go that I may hide myself in the field."[4]

A few passages, however, are significant. Job responds to the revelation of the greatness and glory of God in the familiar words,

> I had heard of thee by the hearing of the ear,
> but now my eye sees thee;
> therefore I despise myself,
> and repent in dust and ashes.[5]

Jesus utters the troublesome words,

> If any man would come after me, let him deny himself and take up his cross and follow me.[6]

We may also be reminded of the words of Paul,

> I do not do the good I want, but the evil I do not want is what I do.[7]

These passages are obviously filled with meaning. And it does not require much imagination to see that they are related closely to many matters of importance for the Christian vision and attitude. Though the Bible and the creeds say little explicitly about man's relation to himself, they say a few words directly that are of great significance and they imply a great deal more.

---

[3] Karl Menninger, *Man against Himself* (New York: Harcourt, Brace & World, Inc., 1956).

[4] I Samuel 20:5.

[5] Job 42:5,6.

[6] Mark 8:34.

[7] Romans 7:19.

1. SPIRIT AND FLESH

For all their differences, Goethe and Plato agree in their general view of the differences between the forces which seek to carry the human spirit in divergent directions. They use the familiar analogy drawn from geometry to indicate their meaning. One force seeks to take the soul up, another tries to drag it down. The upward force is the spiritual; the downward is the physical. By contrast, Paul, in speaking of the two forces within him speaks of both of them by the pronoun of the first person singular. "I do not do the good I want." [8] One *I* accepts responsibility for what the other *I* does, feels guilt because of it and seeks forgiveness because of it. There are two forces within him, but they cannot be distinguished as the spiritual and the physical. Goethe and Plato on the one hand and Paul on the other agree that a central problem in human life is constituted by man's ability to be related to himself, but they disagree about the way in which they view the relationship.

The fact that the Christian writer does use the word "flesh" to refer to the impulses of one of his selves does complicate matters; at first it appears that he is simply in agreement with the Greek and modern writers. But a closer look at his vocabulary, and that of other Hebrew and Christian writers will, perhaps, help us to an understanding of his point of view. The words *flesh* and *spirit* require some clarification.

Common sense observation discloses something that primitive men must have discovered long before history began: man has at least two aspects. Obviously he has a body which is in a certain place. Almost as obviously he has another part by which he can dream of things distant, think of times long gone, imagine courses of action for the future. In some way this other part escapes some of the limitations which are imposed on the body. Some of the Greeks made a philosophy of the distinction we have noted. They identified the immaterial with the soul and found its center in the reason. And they said that the divine was immaterial and rational too. Hence, they traced a kinship between man's mind and the eternal. The body was time and space bound, and, as we have seen, constituted a problem for the soul. The two horses of Plato's charioteer were the divergent forces of body and spirit. The divine reality by its goodness sought to attract the divine in man to itself, but the body acted as a recalcitrant or even a hostile force. Thus from this point of view man against himself was defined as body against mind.

---

[8] *Ibid.*

Biblical and Christian writers sometimes express themselves in a way that reflects the common-sense observation we have pointed out. Thus man is first formed from dust; then God breathes into his nostrils the breath of life and he becomes a living soul.[9] In a passage that may well reflect Greek influences as well as the Genesis story the book of Ecclesiastes speaks of what takes place at death: "the dust returns to the earth as it was, and the spirit returns to God who gave it." [10]

More often, however, Biblical writers and those who reflect their views use the terms *spirit* and *flesh* in a rather different way. Here the contrast is between the divine and the human. The very parallelism of Hebrew poetry becomes a vehicle for its expression in a couplet from the prophet Isaiah:

> The Egyptians are men, and not God;
> and their horses are flesh, and not spirit.[11]

Flesh is the whole sphere of human and earthly realities, spirit the sphere of divine actuality. Within man there is a corresponding distinction: in him spirit is that which is responsive to God, flesh is that which is simply human and weak or that which is actively hostile to God. And yet spirit and flesh are not distinguishable parts of him, as if he were a composite creature. A look at some words of Paul in his letter to the Galatians may help us to understand the matter more clearly. He begins with a sentence which by itself could easily be taken for a bit of Greek philosophy,

> Walk by the Spirit, and do not gratify the desires of the flesh. For the desires of the flesh are against the Spirit, and the desires of the Spirit are against the flesh; for these are opposed to each other.[12]

As he goes on, however, we can see that Spirit and flesh cannot be defined as mind and body:

> the works of the flesh are plain: immorality, impurity, licentiousness, idolatry, sorcery, enmity, strife, jealousy, anger, selfishness, dissension, party spirit, envy, drunkenness, carousing, and the like.[13]

A few of these are expressions of bodily impulses, and any Greek would regard them as "desires of the flesh." But it is hard to see how idolatry, party spirit, and envy can be put into this category; these will be called "fleshly" only by a person who understands the word "spiritual" in a

[9] Genesis 2:7.
[10] Ecclesiastes 12:7.
[11] Isaiah 31:3.
[12] Galatians 5:16f.
[13] Galatians 5:19ff.

special sense. And Paul does so. A clue to his understanding can be gained from the list of the fruits of the Spirit which he contrasts with the works of the flesh:

> love, joy, peace, patience, kindness, goodness,
> faithfulness, gentleness, self-control.[14]

These are not simply rational; they spring, as Paul views life, as gifts of the free love of God making its way into human life against the forces which oppose it. From the point of view of this contrast man against himself is either the part responsive to God seeking mastery over his other self, or the part that rebels against God trying to secure mastery over the other part of him. Hence Paul identifies himself with the *I* who does the things his other *I* does not approve; and he identifies himself, too, with the *I* which passes judgment on the acts of the other.

Sometimes the two usages of flesh and spirit coincide. The reason for this has been noted in the preceding chapter: the body can be a focal point for sinful impulses. Here is a reason for the element of truth Christian writers have often seen in the Greek point of view; it is also the reason for a feeling on the part of some that the Christian viewpoint sees more deeply into human life than does the Greek. From the point of view of Christian faith the sins of the body are never simply bodily; they are also spiritual. The self is involved in them. When a man's body sins, he sins; no sin can be described as simply "carnal." Hence the horror of Paul at the thought of a man's going to a house of prostitution:

> Do you not know that your bodies are members of Christ? Shall I therefore take the members of Christ and make them members of a prostitute? Never! Do you not know that he who joins himself to a prostitute becomes one body with her? For, as it is written, "the two shall become one."

The converse, however, is also true. So intimately is body connected with spirit that a man's relation with God is a total relationship. "He who is united to the Lord becomes one spirit with him."[15] A man's body may become a focal point for that in him which is at enmity against God; it can be *flesh* in the religious sense. It can also be part of that which is at one with the Lord; it can be *spirit* in this sense. An early Christian writer saw the point involved in the dual conceptions of flesh and spirit as he wrote to some of his friends, "even what you do in the flesh is spiritual."[16]

---

[14] Galatians 5:22f.
[15] I Corinthians 6:15ff.
[16] Ignatius, "To the Ephesians" (8:2), *The Apostolic Fathers,* Edgar J. Goodspeed, trans. (New York: Harper & Brothers, 1950), p. 209. Reprinted by permission.

2. MAN AGAINST HIMSELF

"The flesh lusteth against the Spirit, and the Spirit against the flesh."[17] Here, Greek and Christian agree, is a statement of the source of life's anguish. But the Christian is likely to read the statement differently from the way in which the Greek does for reasons we have seen. He finds the anguish of life in man's action against himself. Here is but another expression of a Christian conviction, already noted, that man's deepest difficulty is to be defined as sin. To that notion a chapter has already been devoted. Its several aspects take on new significance, however, when they are viewed in relation to the problem of man's relation to himself. Some ways in which Christians have spoken of sin receive clarification also from such a view.

It should be remembered that Christians have seen man's sinfulness expressing itself in two basic ways which at first appear to be opposite to each other. Man may rebel against the Creator, break his law, reject his love—thus he sins against God in the first way. He may, however, try to live by his own resources, seek to save himself—then he sins in the second way. Because of this duality in the ways of sinning there is difficulty in keeping clarity about the meaning of certain words. From one point of view Christians have often expressed themselves in agreement with what Greeks and others have held: there is a higher aspect of human nature, related in some way to reason and conscience. This aspect of man is in a peculiar way capable of responsiveness to God. Hence it may be spoken of as the spirit of man. Thus the apostle Paul writes in one place that "The Spirit itself beareth witness with our spirit, that we are the children of God."[18] But Christians have been sensitive to the fact that the very possession of a higher part may give man the illusion that by it he may save himself. Then what ought to be spirit becomes, in the religious sense, flesh; that which could be higher becomes lower. And the most dreadful sins which Christianity names are often those connected with the assertion of man's highest powers. Thence arise the insufferable acts of self-righteousness which render him insensitive to others, the intellectual self-deceptions which make him blind to the evil he does, and the religious pride which hides his own sin from him. With this caution about the terms "higher" and "lower" in our minds, we may turn now to a consideration of sin in its several aspects.

---

[17] Galatians 5:17, K.J.V.
[18] Romans 8:16, K.J.V.

Man's rebellion against his Creator is at the same time a rebellion against himself. It is a betrayal of his true nature, and Christians have generally agreed that he is aware of this fact. Often the manner of speaking of his rebellion has been in terms of the notions of law and conscience. Man as a sinner is man as a lawbreaker, and yet in conscience he is aware that the law he breaks is right and just. Paul wrote, "I delight in the law of God, in my inmost self, but I see in my members another law at war with the law of my mind and making me captive to the law of sin which dwells in my members."[19] About the content of the law to which reference is made in this connection Christians have differed, as well as about the capacity of man to define it. Some have felt that law in the most general sense is that which human reason recognizes as just; that which is given in some specific code, the Ten Commandments, or something else. The point on which they agree, for the most part, is on the matter of man's failure to live up to that which he himself approves as good. This is the law for him, and his awareness of it is a reflection of his basic relation to the God who made him.

His sinful attempt to find inward unity by dealing with it himself often takes the form of defining it in a rather limited way so that he feels that he lives up to it. He may also, of course, constantly choose courses of action which dull his conscience to the point where it no longer condemns him no matter what he does. Thus in the Tempest, when Antonio suggests the murder of Sebastian's brother, the latter interposes:

> But, for your conscience,—

To which Antonio answers:

> Ay, sir; where lies that? if 'twere a kibe,
> 'Twould put me to my slipper: But I feel not
> This deity in my bosom: twenty consciences,
> That stand 'twixt me and Milan, candied be they,
> And melt, ere they molest![20]

One may also try to get conscience on the side of his sinful self by rationalizing his own actions—as some moderns would put the matter: giving the wrong reasons for what he does. He may also discover that the keeping of the law of conscience as he knows it, or living by reason and justice, of abiding by some set of customary religious regulations leaves him with a sense of emptiness or frustration. Here, perhaps, is

---

[19] Romans 7:22f.
[20] William Shakespeare, "The Tempest," Act II, Sc. 1, *Works,* p. 1145.

to be found the explanation for those passages in the writings of the apostle Paul in which he speaks of himself as being, according to the law, blameless.[21] In many ways, Christians have pointed out, man seeks to come to terms with a law which is written deep into his being as a creature of God.

He may, of course, come to the discovery of a deeper law, that which is bound up with the redemptive character of God. This has within it dimensions that are not envisioned by a viewpoint which makes justice and conscience ultimate. A gift has been given in which a demand is recognized. Man is called upon to love both his God and his neighbor in a self-abandoning way. As man becomes aware of this law, deeper levels of self-dividedness are disclosed, for close to love is its opposite hatred. A scholar who has delved deep into the life story of Martin Luther tells us that at one point in his development he was oppressed by a deep sense of his own inability to love as the faith told him he should. As he continued his efforts he came finally to the point where he hated the God who called upon him for love.[22] Paul looked back on the law which he had kept blamelessly and blamed it for leading him to the rejection of Christ and to persecution of his church.[23] The deeper law would never have so betrayed him; that law he knew in Christ, but it had also been known in his Hebrew heritage. It had told men that they must not covet; when that law came Paul died. And yet to it he gave assent. Hence arose that war within himself at its deepest level; here was the root of self-hatred.

The man who rejects the divine gift may seek elsewhere to find the love which his spirit requires. He may try to find the love he needs within himself; then he is betrayed into a self-preoccupation which is often erroneously mistaken for genuine self-love. He may also make inordinate claims on the love and devotion of others, attempting to secure from them the love he denies to himself. He may also reject the demand which accompanies the divine gift. In various ways he seeks to diminish its scope. "After all," he may say when he is confronted with the commandment of Jesus, "I am only human, and God doesn't really expect anything like this of me!" Against Jesus' explicit words is the tendency to apply the commandment of love only to friends and family, to place the unloved and the unlovable outside the circle of concern. He may attempt to sentimentalize or, indeed, even to trivialize the redemptive

---

[21] Philippians 3:6.

[22] Heinrich Boehmer, *Road to Reformation,* John W. Doberstein and Theodore G. Tappert, trans. (Philadelphia: Muhlenberg Press, 1946), p. 98. Used by permission.

[23] Philippians 3:6.

love of God himself: "God will forgive," said Voltaire, "it's his business." [24]

To speak so is, of course, not simply a rejection of redemptive love; it is blasphemy, violation of the holy. As we have seen, sin so conceived is seldom if ever encountered in its purity in Hebrew or Christian thought; it is rather a quality of sin; it is that which is connected with the sense of guilt in the religious sense. The person who is guilty feels that it is he himself who has sinned; hence he must accept responsibility for his action. But he assents to the judgment that his action has been sinful. Thus Paul says that his mind assents to the affirmation that the law is "holy" as well as good.[25] The self-dividedness which response to the presence of the Holy evokes in man is probably nowhere so clearly stated as in the quotation from the book of Job which has already been introduced,

> Now my eye sees thee;
> therefore I despise myself.[26]

The attempt to bring unity to the self while recognizing the reality of the Holy has most often expressed itself within the area we normally call religion. It is that fact which has aroused a constant skepticism about religion on the part of Christian writers. Sometimes in elaborate ritual men seek to manipulate the divine and convince themselves that they are at peace with him. In other instances people who profess to despise liturgies find their own ways of dealing with guilt in manners which are really ritual in character though they do not recognize them as such. There are those who make contributions large or small to religious purposes, who devote hours to the service of the church, who do all sorts of religious deeds in order to try to bring the holy to term with them, and to make it possible for them to live with themselves.

To be at enmity with himself—this is one way of speaking of the perversion of the creature. His unity has been broken; no self-determination in the full sense can be his, for two selves seek to determine him and neither wholly succeeds. His creativity is inhibited, for that which would create is hampered by that which disturbs him, or his potential creativeness turns to destructiveness. Of his sociality the next chapter will speak; here it should be pointed out at least, however, that he who finds it hard to love himself may find it impossible to love anyone else. Man's reason either condemns him as it traces a justice by which he does not live, or it becomes the servant of his lower self trying to find him plausible

---

[24] Quoted by Emil Brunner in *The Mediator*, p. 447.
[25] Romans 7:12.
[26] Job 42:6.

excuses for not doing what he ought. All aspects of his life are affected by his dividedness.

So deep is his plight that his situation becomes one of bondage. As we have seen, he seeks in various ways to come to terms with himself, but each of these simply reveals the impossibility of his attempts. The terms Christian writers have used to speak of that which binds man have been many; they have given variant expressions to a single conviction. We cannot understand what Paul means by the term "flesh," unless we take into account that for him it was an objective power. It had him in its grip; and yet he was responsible for its hold upon him. The word "sin" as Paul uses it also has reference to a veritable power, as do other terms like "death." Sometimes with Paul and in the history of Christianity the forces which work in man against God are grouped together as particular manifestations of a kingdom of evil with a ruler, the Devil or Satan. There are cases of a peculiarly virulent sort in which a servant of Satan, a demon, actually possesses a person. But even when such terms are not used, the hold of sin on the life of man, the vigor

MAN AND HIS ENEMIES Dreadful companions accompany man on his journey through the world. *Knight, Death and the Devil.* Albrecht Dürer (Courtesy of the National Gallery of Art, Washington, D.C. Gift of Russell Allen)

of the self which resists the Spirit, is described in terms of an unbreakable bondage. So does it take possession of a man that he may be said to have "an evil nature" which has been superimposed upon the good nature which is his by reason of his creation by God.

Man's bondage is the worse because it does not seem to rob him of his awareness that he ought to be free. Hence he struggles against himself. And yet, as we have seen, his attempts to set himself free always turn out to be efforts of his lower self; they are compromises which do not take into full account the stature of spirit. He may, of course, give up the struggle. Then he becomes less than a man. Then he is delivered to despair.

3. GOD, MAN, AND SELF

In terms of the attitude we are examining in this chapter we might call despair the experience of radical self-condemnation. The despairing man recognizes that he has sinned and that his own resources for dealing with his sin are inadequate and futile. Christian faith has recognized this; in answer it has echoed a word from the First Epistle of John, "We shall know that we are of the truth, and reassure our hearts before him whenever our hearts condemn us; for God is greater than our hearts." [27] Man, finding it impossible within his own resources to forgive himself, has been able to do so because of the assurance that he is forgiven by God.

The despair is appropriate, however; for self-forgiveness is no easy matter. But Christians have been convinced that forgiveness by God is no easy matter either. As we have seen, they point to the cross of Christ as the evidence that God takes sin even more seriously than man does —or even can. There the forgiveness of God has been made known in its utter self-abandoning fullness.

Christians have been convinced, too, that there are links between God's decisive redemptive act and their own lives. Some have found them peculiarly in the Scriptures. Thus Luther once remarked that when the devil condemned him, he turned to the Bible.[28] In some liturgical services the minister reads "comfortable words" [29] to assure the people

---

[27] I John 3:19f.

[28] Martin Luther, *The Table Talk of Martin Luther,* William Hazlitt, trans. and ed. (London: G. Bell & Sons, Ltd., 1911), p. 268.

[29] *The Book of Common Prayer,* p. 76.

that their plea for pardon has been heard. Some Christians have found a link between Christ and their own lives in the words of ministers or priests, believing that Jesus spoke to the apostles and their successors when he told them that whosoever sins they remitted would be remitted. Still others, or even the same ones under other circumstances, find in the words and actions of friends, parents, or counsellors the objective reality which brings the forgiveness of God to them. Others seem to find an assurance in the depths of their own beings when these are responsive to the promptings of God.

Whatever the specific link may be between God's action and man's situation, Christians have usually agreed that there was some specific work of the Spirit which made the redemptive love of God actual in the life of the believer. But this work had its active human counterpart in a response of man. The puzzle of the divine and the human, which we have noted before, is present here. It may be stated thus, in the words of Paul Tillich: that a man is "accepted in spite of being unacceptable" and accepts his acceptance.[30] The terms we are using in this chapter are these: man forgives himself as God forgives him. The human forgiveness is predicated on the divine; the divine forgiveness is actualized in the human.

4. MAN AT ONE WITH HIMSELF

We come now to a point on which Christians honestly differ. No credal statements nor clear pronouncements of scripture settle the issue. Christians give different answers to the question, "Is it proper for a Christian to love himself?" Some, careful to note the difference between right and wrong self-love, affirm that it is. Thus Bernard traces the development of love in the life of the person from the stage at which he loves himself first and even loves God for his own sake to the point where he loves God first and then himself for God's sake.[31] Others feel that so prone is the person to inordinate self-love that to allow him to feel that a certain amount of it is right will betray him into allowing himself too much. After all, Jesus counselled a man to "hate himself," to "deny himself," and said that he who seeks his own soul must inevitably lose it.[32] Fur-

---

[30] Paul Tillich, *The Courage to Be* (New Haven: Yale University Press, 1952), p. 164. Used by permission.

[31] Saint Bernard, *On Loving God,* William H. van Allen, trans. (South Wales: Caldey Abbey, 1909), pp. 51-67.

[32] Luke 14:26; Mark 8:34; Matthew 10:39.

ther, self-love is so often a pathological compensation for self-hatred, that to encourage it at all seems to be courting trouble.

If the term "self-love" is to be used, clearly it must be employed with great care and clarity; often other terms will bring out the desired meaning better in specific contexts. However, this is certainly obvious: some terms must be used to express the Christian conviction that a work of God goes on in the human life such that man is brought into right relations with himself, and that his self-hatred and self-condemnation are overcome. Here as elsewhere the work of God does not cancel out the self-determination of man; God acts and because he acts man is able to act. Because of God's love in redemption man is able to overcome his self-hatred; he accepts God's love of him. He makes this love his own. Many in our time speak of this action as "self-acceptance." Having confronted God's redemptive love man comes to a new apprehension of God's creative action as also an act of love. Man recognizes himself as a creature, precious to God in his own uniqueness. It should be clear from what has been said, however, that self-affirmation might lead to self-trust, and the redemptive relationship to God would then be lost. Here again a human action—predicated on a divine action—is called for. Man must join in the battle against himself. This is at least part of the meaning of self-denial. We may well conclude that the question of whether to use the term "self-love" or not is really academic. The person who is capable of loving himself aright really does not care.

We have already noted certain aspects of man's unification in the chapter on man's response to redemption. With the expressions which grow out of it the remainder of the book will be largely concerned. It may be helpful here, however, to note its general character and point out the manner in which it contrasts with the dividedness of life which sin brings about.

The love of God frees a man from the self-condemnation which goes with willful defiance of his Creator. He is forgiven for his breach of the divine law. He then is able to live at peace with his reason and conscience, recognizing their limited validity and grateful for the measure of guidance they provide for his actions. The love of God also releases him from the self-hatred that accompanies his recognition of the deeper law which redemptive love discloses to him. That law is by its very character a call for a renewal of spirit; if it is kept in the attitude of slavery, it has been betrayed. If the law of redemptive love requires that a man love in abandonment of his own concerns, taking up his cross and following Christ, then only a keeping of it which is in the spirit is valid. And just this is what the gospel speaks about: a new spirit which gives man the inner drive to live the life of love. But this is no easy thing. Again and again does Paul speak of the need to overcome the resistance of the flesh. The love of God also releases a man from the sense of self-abhorrence which belongs to this awareness of having violated the demands of the Holy Reality. In its place is the divine forgiveness, coming from the awesome One before whom man trembles. With that forgiveness comes a new awareness of the real place of religion in life, that of relating man in truth to that God who dwells "in the high and holy place."[33]

The forgiveness of God also renews the createdness of man, makes of him "a new creature." The various powers of his being are now released for a significant self-expression. The person is valued in his uniqueness as a creature and counselled to express that uniqueness in ways that give glory to God, bring good to his neighbor, and give him a sense of expressing his whole self. Man's body is part of the unity of his being and has a rightful part in all that he does. Man is capable of a self-determination which is itself a gift of the Spirit. His creativity can express itself in the ways that are appropriate to his own capacities and abilities. Of his sociality we shall say more in the following chapter.

And yet the limitations to perfect unity remain. Some of these are bound up with the social context in which he lives and will come before us later. Others are within him, where the temptations to division are always present. The various powers of the personality may become focal points for the flesh which lusts against the spirit. The Christian may have to follow the example of Paul and "pommel" his body.[34] He must beware of self-righteousness, of thinking of himself more highly than he ought to think. The powers that would drag him down to sub-human levels of living or tempt him to defy God by pretensions to super-human abilities are ever at work in his life. Against these he must offer active resistance. At the same time, he must realize that his resistance is not wholly his own doing; it arises from the work of the Spirit. He will fall before temptation from time to time, and he must seek the renewed forgiveness which will make it possible to be at peace with himself. That which he does and that which God does for and in him come together. Neither is complete without the other. Of the strange way in which they supplement each other Paul spoke in his advice to the Philippians: "Work out your own salvation with fear and trembling;

---

[33] Isaiah 57:15.
[34] I Corinthians 9:27.

for God is at work in you, both to will and to work for his good pleasure." [35]

5. MAN IN THE MODERN WORLD

The wholeness of historic Christianity held a tension in man's attitudes toward himself. It reminded him that he was "a little lower than the angels," crowned with "glory and honor." [36] It also told him that he was at war with himself and his God, and yet God had acted on his behalf to restore him to his creatural dignity. Medieval mystics probed the endless varieties of man's self-loves, seeking to discover the depths that they might help him ascend the heights. Luther and Calvin were convinced of his "total depravity," while they recognized at the same time the greatness of his original endowments and his redemptive possibilities. As the vision of faith's wholeness faded, the tension relaxed.

The Renaissance, and with it much of modern culture, emphasized the greatness of man's powers and was reluctant to admit his failures. Into the spirit of affirmation of man's greatness went a Christian contribution; to it were added others from several sources. Sometimes the assertion of man's powers was accompanied by a rejection of Christianity, with its allegedly gloomy outlook.

> Glory to Man in the highest!
> for Man is the master of things.[37]

Sometimes traditional faith was reread and reformed; that which was out of keeping with the modern spirit was set aside. Where emphasis fell on man's intellectual and moral powers, the conception of God was accommodated to man's intelligence. Mystery was driven out, and man was proclaimed capable of thinking God's thoughts after him. Jesus was seen as the great moral teacher; no need was there for him as savior, since man needed not saving but educating. The bondage of the will was discarded as incompatible with the true spirit of Christianity:

> When Duty whispers low, *Thou must.*
> The youth replies, *I can.*[38]

---

[35] Philippians 2:12f.
[36] Psalm 8:5, K.J.V.
[37] Algernon C. Swinburne, "Hymn of Man," *Swinburne's Collected Poetical Works* (New York: Harper & Brothers, 1924), I, 764.
[38] Ralph W. Emerson, "Voluntaries," *Poems by Ralph Waldo Emerson* (Boston: Houghton Mifflin Company, 1897), p. 180.

A future time was envisaged here on this earth when the contradictions of human existence would be overcome, and men could live at peace with their brothers in a realized kingdom of God.

Where emphasis has fallen on religious experience, there has been a greater awareness of the darker side of the picture. A profound awareness of sin and guilt have been seen as implicit in the experience itself. There has been some tendency, however, to define the content of the redeemed life rather narrowly. By withdrawing from the world or defining their relations to it in simply moral terms, men have escaped awareness of the tensions that continue to make themselves felt when the total context of life is taken into account. The saved man is pictured as the man of a rather easily definable moral character, not one who is in daily need of repentance because of his involvement in a problematical world.

A minor current of attitude, however, has also run through recent centuries, emphasizing the weakness and even the perverseness of man. Sometimes this has been unrelieved by any reminder of the grandeur seen by Christian faith. Weariness with life and sickness of the spirit were characteristic of late German romanticism. And men like Leopardi and Schopenhauer gave in to a gloomy pessimism.

There were Christians, too, who remembered the historic heritage in its wholeness. Pascal spoke of both the grandeur and the misery of man.[39] John Wesley went up and down the land of England preaching with incredible energy man's need for grace and God's willingness to supply it. Northampton heard and trembled as Jonathan Edwards described the plight of "sinners in the hands of an angry God." [40] And in nineteenth century Denmark Søren Kierkegaard wrote his anguished outpourings concerning the depth of the gulf between God and man, and yet found comfort in the thought that "as against God we are always in the wrong." [41]

The events of the present century have rendered men sensitive to the voice which speaks of the wholeness of historic Christianity. They listen in sympathy as it speaks of man's depravity, with respect as it speaks of his dignity, and with hope as it speaks of his redemption.

---

[39] Blaise Pascal, *Pensées,* W. F. Trotter, trans. (New York: The Modern Library, 1941), p. 129 (number 409).

[40] Jonathan Edwards, *Representative Selections,* Clarence Faust and Thomas H. Johnson, eds. (New York: American Book Company, 1935), p. 155.

[41] Søren Kierkegaard, *Either/Or,* Walter Lowrie, trans. (Princeton: Princeton University Press, 1949), II, 283ff. Reprinted by permission.

READINGS

From the Bible

1. The problem of man's inner division is set forth in Romans 7 and Galatians 5.

2. The coming of wholeness is recognized in Romans 8.

3. Job struggles with God and himself throughout the book which bears his name; see especially chapters 3 and 42.

From Historic Christianity

1. Augustine, *Confessions,* is the story of a tortured person being drawn toward peace. Special attention might be given to books 1, 7, and 8.

2. Bernard of Clairvaux, *On Loving God,* analyzes the transformations of human love responding to the love of God. Greek and Biblical notions of love are reflected.

3. John Wesley, *Journal,* describes an ardent search for the assurance of God's love and the manner in which it was answered. The one volume edition of Percy Livingstone Parker (Chicago: Moody Press, 1951) is selective. The relevant portions are pp. 31-66.

FOR STUDY AND DISCUSSION

1. In what ways can religion become a technique for dealing with guilt?
2. Is there any proper self-love? If so, how does it differ from wrong self-love?
3. Does Christian faith have anything to say about self-acceptance which differs from the views of a "secular" psychologist?
4. Do evangelists tend to oversimplify the human situation?
5. How can religion which is merely a device by which a man achieves self-acceptance be distinguished from religion in which a person receives acceptance from God?

VIII

MAN AND HIS FELLOWS

Though Christians differ on the matter of the propriety of speaking favorably of man's love for himself, they are agreed that it is entirely proper for man to love his neighbor. Jesus' identification of the second commandment has impressed itself on the entire history of the faith. It has not always been clear, however, that the commandment has important implications for the conception of human nature.

The question "What is man?" is of pressing concern at the present moment of history. In our time we have seen tremendous movements develop within which man becomes simply a member of a mass. In the process he becomes de-humanized; he is swallowed up in a vast collective. No longer does he think, decide, or act for himself. The reaction of many has been a strong assertion of the preciousness of individuality. Our Western heritage has been regarded as a treasure house of significant ideas and institutions which dignify and protect the individual. And this has been natural, for surely one of the leading threads that has been woven into the texture of Western life is that of regard for the individual's rights and privileges.

The Western emphasis on individuality has been linked in a significant way with the Christian faith. And some in our time would contrast Christian individualism with totalitarian collectivism. However, there are others who find in historic Christianity something that is not exactly the same thing as the sort of individualism prized during the past few centuries. Indeed, they feel that an individualistic Christianity is one that is not true to its own deepest rootage. It is one of those simplifications which omit important aspects of the ancestral heritage of faith.

These thinkers tend to feel that a recovery of historic Christianity involves a new sense of the social dimensions of human nature. The Christian vision, they point out, sees man as social in his essential and created being. It views the brokenness of life as in part the estrangement of man from his fellows. And it envisions a redemption which is not simply the reconciliation of individual souls with their maker, but a renewal of fellowship with God which is at the same time a fellowship with his children.

Perhaps the alternatives before us are not those of individualism or collectivism. Others may emerge as we turn to consider man's attitude toward his fellows in the light of the Christian vision.

1. "LOVE THY NEIGHBOR"

The early Christians did not make love of neighbor an item in their creeds. Perhaps it was too obvious to them that it was part of their faith for them to feel the need for stating it; and it did not enter into the controversies which some of the credal statements helped to settle. That they were aware of it as essential is easy to see from their writings. At a very early time it was expressly stated that a man at odds with his brother should be reconciled before he partook of the Lord's Supper. And a statement on church order from early in the third century gives us a vivid description of that which was expected of converts to Christianity.[1] The prospective church member went through a preliminary examination, then a probation period of three years before he could be examined again with a view to being baptized. At the second examination he was expected to indicate that he had performed works in keeping with the spirit of the faith he intended to profess, deeds of love toward those about him. The early church took for granted that love of neighbor was part of the Christian life.

---

[1] Hippolytus, *The Apostolic Tradition of Hippolytus,* Burton S. Easton, ed. and trans. (Cambridge: The University Press, 1934), pp. 41ff. For regulations concerning the Lord's Supper see "The Didache," Cyril C. Richardson, *Early Christian Fathers,* p. 178.

The matter was clear, of course, in the New Testament they chose for their own. The picture of Jesus which the gospels present shows love to be at the very heart of his teaching. The two great commandments he enunciated were those which enjoin love to God with heart, mind, soul, and strength and love to neighbor. In response to the question regarding the identity of the neighbor he told the familiar story of the good Samaritan.[2] Neglect of the deeds of love toward others was tantamount to neglect of the Christ himself. On the other hand, those who had visited the sick and the prisoners and had given food to the hungry and drink to the thirsty had done these things to him.[3] In the sermon on the mount he spoke with particular clarity of the manner in which the children of the kingdom were expected to differ from others. No special virtue lay in doing deeds of kindness to friends and relatives. But those who were Christ's followers were to love their enemies, do good to those who hated them, pray for those who despitefully used them.[4]

In these matters they were to reflect the character of God. And here we come upon another important aspect of the teaching of Jesus. God's redemptive love was to be the measure of man's attitude toward others. Here was the new law, rooted in the nature of God himself. And the early Christians were convinced also that Jesus in his death had showed forth the sacrificial character of God's love in a decisive way. Here his own teaching about God, his own life's total direction, and his teaching about man's relation to his neighbor came together. Men were to love one another as God in Christ had loved them.

When Jesus enunciated the great commandments, he was summarizing the law and the prophets, he was expressing his understanding of the heart of his inherited faith. And when the Christians chose the Old Testament as part of their scriptures, they included many significant and often beautiful exhortations to love of neighbor. The law and the prophets, said Jesus, hang on the two commandments;[5] and, indeed, the ancient writings are full of them. Israel had a deep sense that each must care for the other. And its laws included concern not simply for fellow Israelites but for the stranger in the gates. Particularly were the poor and the weak singled out as objects of special provision.[6] The prophets

---

[2] Luke 10:27, 29-37.

[3] Matthew 25:31-46.

[4] Matthew 5:43-48.

[5] Matthew 22:40, K.J.V.

[6] Cf. Leviticus 19:10. See Norman H. Snaith, *The Distinctive Ideas of the Old Testament* (Philadelphia: The Westminster Press, 1946), pp. 86ff.

ever linked men's relation to their God with their treatment of one another. In scathing words did they denounce those who came with offerings into the courts of the Lord but did injustice to their fellows. It is true that at certain points the teaching of the Old Testament was particularistic; in the name of their God the early Israelites exterminated their enemies and even in late times a prophet called Nahum expressed fierce joy at the fall of Nineveh. But there was another strain in the teaching of the great prophets. If Israel had received special blessings, it was that she might share her knowledge of God with the world and all men might come to know him as they had.[7] Her vision of the future included a time when the knowledge of the Lord would cover the earth "as the waters cover the sea." [8]

Paul followed Jesus in regarding love of the neighbor as a summary and fulfillment of the law.[9] But, as we have seen, he saw a stubbornness in man which makes it impossible for the law to make him good. The commandment that should have brought life brought death instead. It is interesting to note the specific commandment he chose to illustrate his point; it has special reference to love of another. In the seventh chapter of Romans he wrote:

> I should not have known what it is to covet if the law had not said, "You shall not covet." . . . When the commandment came, sin revived and I died.[10]

Law could not produce love. Here the Spirit must act to overcome the rebellion of man, and when the Spirit overcomes the desires of the flesh it can produce its fruits. Of these he spoke in his letter to the Galatians; the first in his list is *love*.[11] Against it and the Spirit's other fruits there is no law. Through the centuries God by his law had prevented the people from living lives of total lovelessness; this was its positive value. And that value was fulfilled, as Paul saw it, with the coming of Christ. He who possessed Christ's spirit would have faith, and hope, and love.

In his First Epistle John summarizes the various themes we have noted in beautiful fashion. He sees the inseparability of the two great commandments: "for he who does not love his brother whom he has seen, cannot love God whom he has not seen." [12] He indicates the dependence

---

[7] See, for example, Isaiah 49:1-7.
[8] Isaiah 11:9.
[9] Romans 13:8.
[10] Romans 7:7, 9.
[11] Galatians 5:22.
[12] I John 4:20.

of our love for others on God's love for us: "We love, because he first loved us." [13] And he puts into three short words the conviction about the nature of God which lies behind the attitude toward his brother that is demanded of man: "God is love." [14]

2. LOVE AND THE NATURE OF MAN

The declaration that God is love refers primarily to his redemptive nature, utterly self-giving and sacrificial, as Christians have seen it made known in the cross of Christ. It also refers to his constant self-giving in the creation of the world and his care for it. "Even the hairs of your head are all numbered," said Jesus.[15] And he told his disciples that God is aware of the fall of a sparrow.[16] Christian thought here as elsewhere moves from redemption to creation. In a similar way the love of man for his neighbor should be, first of all, self-giving and sacrificial. Man must stand ready even to die if the need arises. But his love should also express itself in a constant concern for the good of others, calling forth many acts large and small in all the relationships of life.

If there is similarity between the love of God and that of man, it is because there is a link between God and man. Christians have sometimes referred to this as the image of God in human nature. As God's creative and redemptive acts spring from his very nature—and this is the meaning of the assertion that God is love—so creative and redemptive acts of man spring from his true nature. Of course, we must remember that man's true nature has been obscured by what some Christians have called his second or sinful nature; he does not want to be himself. Hence a commandment comes from God telling him what he must do; and in so doing telling him what he must be. If we agree with the Christian thesis that the commandment to love one's neighbor is derived from the God who created man, we must draw the conclusion that the commandment tells us something of the nature of the person to whom it is directed. And if man redeemed does in fact, though in limited measure, love his neighbor, it is because he is thus expressing his true, created nature. If man is redeemed to life in community, we may infer that he was created for life in community. The true man, God's creature, loves his neighbor; thus he expresses his essential nature.

---

[13] I John 4:19.
[14] I John 4:8.
[15] Matthew 10:30.
[16] Matthew 10:29.

And yet man, though linked to God, is different from him. He is not an originator of love in the absolute sense. "We love, because he first loved us."[17] Now if the relation of the divine and the human which has been noted at many points of the preceding exposition is a true one, then we may say that God's love often comes to man through human agencies. Then to respond to the love of God means not merely that a man must love his neighbor; it means too that he must be open to receive love from his neighbor. It may be important to remember that the love of God is not bound to any given channel; sometimes the love of God may come to a person through the very hatred of others. But one of its normal vehicles is their love—human, self-determining love; and that love is to be received in gratitude as God's gift.

Perhaps some light has now been thrown on the assertion which has been made previously, that historic Christianity sees man as essentially social. Attitudes which have become dominant within our culture over the past few centuries have tended to obscure this aspect of the Christian vision. In part these are due to a neglect of one aspect of the wholeness of the historic faith in favor of another—that which envisions the preciousness of the individual in his uniqueness. The Christian conviction about the individual has been reinforced by the heritage of Greece, in which there was much which pointed to the primacy of the individual human being. It must not be overlooked that the Greeks saw bonds between individuals: Oedipus suffered that he might save his people; Aristotle saw man as "a political animal."[18] And yet when attention was given to the ultimate reaches of the human spirit, the Greeks tended to focus on the solitary. Thus the Epicureans counselled the pursuit of pleasure while the Stoics taught men to live by reason and virtue. The two schools appear to be diametrically opposed. And yet the pleasures which Epicurus proposed were those which none could take from a man: he must so live as to be self-sufficient. And the virtue which the Stoics taught was that of the aristocrat who was able to bear anything because of the divinity within him: the good man must be self-sufficient. And though Oedipus suffered to save his city, he emerged as other Greek heroes, a solitary individual grand in his isolated facing of what fate imposed upon him.

The past few centuries have given preference to the Christian emphasis on the individual and the Greek portrayal of the solitary. They have placed the word *freedom* at the very center of the vocabulary

---

[17] I John 4:19.

[18] Aristotle, "Politics," Benjamin Jowett, trans., Book I, *The Basic Works of Aristotle,* Richard P. McKeon, ed. (New York: Random House, 1941), p. 1129.

which speaks of man. And freedom has often been defined in such a way as to identify it with self-sufficiency.[19] The free man of modern ideals is like the rational man of the Greeks; both are sufficient to themselves. They need no one.

Christianity itself responded to the ideals in the culture around it and emphasized one part of its ancestral heritage at the expense of another. Where attention was focused on religious experience, especially, did the individual come to the fore. Individual religious experience was for many the very center of Christian faith; everything else revolved around it.

Historic Christianity in its wholeness sees man as essentially bound to his neighbor, both by the need of expressing love toward him and by the need of receiving God's love through him. And though during the past few centuries, Christians have often defined their faith in ways which obscured this conviction, theologians of our time are discovering it again. Some relate the Christian assertions to the emphasis in contemporary social psychology on the creative role of the community in the development of the individual. The subtle ways in which the love of the mother for the tiniest infant contributes to his security has been pointed out.[20] The manner in which the play group helps the youngster to define himself has been noted again and again. The child locked in the garret for years and emerging at the last incapable of fully human responses is described on the pages of sociology books.[21] For the Christian he illustrates the manner in which the very love of God can be shut off from its creative effects in the lives of human beings by the stupidity or cruelty of their fellows.

It is important to see here that community and the individual are correlatives of each other. Christian faith insists on the preciousness of the individual creature. Hence, Christians can join with others who are concerned for freedom in the face of the contemporary threat to individuality in the development of a mass society. But they will not set community and individuality in opposition to each other. A collective cannot act creatively to produce individuals; it destroys them. But a true community will; indeed, a true community depends on the recognition of the importance of individuals. Only significant, self-determining

---

[19] See Emil Brunner, *Christianity and Civilisation* (New York: Charles Scribner's Sons, 1948), I, 111f.

[20] Henry Nelson Wieman has related Christian faith and insights from Social Psychology in penetrating ways. The illustration of the mother and baby is one he used in a group discussion when I was present. Used by permission.

[21] William F. Ogburn, Meyer F. Nimkoff, *Sociology* (Boston: Houghton Mifflin Company, 1940), p. 5.

COMMUNITY IN CONTEMPORARY CHURCH ARCHITECTURE Pews surrounding a central altar help participants to be aware of the corporate character of their common worship. The Church of Saint Clement (Episcopal) in Alexandria, Virginia. Joseph H. Saunders, Architect (Charles Baptie, Annandale, Virginia)

individuals can contribute to the life of true community; and only true community can play a creative role in the development of such individuals.

For Christian faith the individual is self-determining but not self-sufficient. His life is essentially bound with the lives of others. This is true because of his own true nature. And his own nature is what it is because of the character of God whose image he bears.

3. SIN AND SOCIAL SOLIDARITY

"Inasmuch as ye have done *it* unto one of the least of these my brethren, ye have done *it* unto me." [22] In these words Christians have traced the inextricable connection between deeds done to man and sins against God. It is impossible to hurt the children without doing damage to their Father. They can be hurt in either of two ways: by active malice or by passive neglect.

If we retrace our analysis of sin, we shall find that at every point it can be seen to have specific reference to man's misdeeds against his brother. That refusing to love his neighbor is a defiance of the Creator's law needs no comment after what has been said. It may be remembered, too, that Paul's list of the works of the flesh includes such items as "strife, jealousy, anger, selfishness." [23] The flesh is not simply the bodily aspect of man; it includes man's self-preoccupation fighting against his obligations to others. And sin against the neighbor is violation of the holy, too, for it involves a disregard of the sacredness inherent in every person's fundamental relatedness to God. Whenever man refuses love to his neighbor, he is sinning against God.

But he can sin also by refusing to receive through his neighbor the love of God for himself. Then, too, he defies the creator who made him to live in partial dependence on others. He asserts his flesh by imagining himself to be self-sufficient. And he refuses to see the relation to God that is the deeper content of his neighbor's deeds toward him.

Whenever he is unable to enter into relations of giving and receiving with those about him, he experiences bondage. He is caught in a trap of self-concern which makes it impossible to express himself freely toward them or accept freely their treatment of him. A false self-love develops within him, out of all true proportion. He demands more of

---

[22] Matthew 25:40, K.J.V.
[23] Galatians 5:20.

others than he should, or he refuses to recognize what they are ready to give. He withholds his own affection from them because he has to give it all to himself. But Christian faith speaks of a grace which can come to such a man, usually at the hands of others, which makes it possible for him to enter into free relations with them as he comes to a true acceptance of himself. Then he can become a self-determining creature, with true sociality and active creativeness. Authentic self-love is not the opposite of right love of others. The two are bound up with each other. Man's relations within himself and his relations to others cannot be separated; what has been said in the preceding chapter about self-hatred and self-love can be understood correctly only if this is recognized.

At still another point Christian thinkers have seen a relationship between man's sin and his sociality. It is suggested in an ancient and in many ways primitive story.[24] When the Israelites stormed the Canaanite city of Jericho, they were commanded to devote all the booty to the Lord. Soon thereafter they were defeated as they sought to storm the city of Ai. Seeking the reason for their defeat, their leader Joshua discovered that it lay in the sin of a certain Achan, who had hidden part of the booty from Jericho in his tent. The curse which had fallen on the whole people as a result of his action was removed by killing him and his entire family. Many centuries later the prophet Ezekiel proclaimed that ancient ideas of corporate guilt must be set aside; "the soul that sinneth, it shall die,"[25] said he. But even his great name could not eradicate from the faith of Israel a conviction that was set forth in cruel fashion in the story of Achan. And this conviction has become part of historic Christianity, too. It is this: that men are bound together in sin. The lives of men are so interwoven with one another that it is never possible to assign the guilt for any wrong action totally to any one person. Others, even relatively righteous people, bear some of the responsibility for it. Our emphasis on individuality during the past few centuries has tended to obscure this for us. But it is appropriate that prayers in the liturgies of the church should read, "We, poor sinners, confess unto thee."[26]

Christian people have often neglected to take seriously the importance of sins against their neighbors. Sometimes their very preoccupation with their relation to God has led them to take lightly their relations to others.

---

[24] Joshua 7.
[25] Ezekiel 18:4, K.J.V.
[26] *Service Book and Hymnal*, p. 1.

At other times they have been simply neglectful. They have not taken seriously the commandments of the gospels. They have allowed rather commonplace moral maxims to be guides for conduct rather than the hard words of Jesus. To make the self-giving character of God the rule for human life is no easy thing.

It is important to note on the other hand, however, that at times love of the neighbor has been interpreted as the entirety of the gospel; the second commandment has been taken seriously and the first disregarded. When this has happened, a concern for created beings has replaced devotion to the Creator. The sin of neglecting the neighbor is replaced by that of neglecting God. In the end the result is that a false love of the neighbor replaces the true. For he who truly loves his neighbor takes into account that in his life which relates him to God.

4. LOVE AND REDEMPTION

If man's relation to himself and his relation to his fellows are as closely bound up with one another as they seem to be in sin, they must be just as close in redemption. Historic Christianity has asserted that this is the case. The redemptive love of God reaches man through his fellows; and he who receives it is commissioned to transmit it to others.

The connections between God's love, man's faith, and man's love for his fellows have received repeated attention through the centuries. There are differences of opinion among theologians on these matters. And yet, there is a general unity of opinion that the specific sort of love of which Christianity speaks—self-abandoning, redemptive love—arises only as there is a trust on the part of man which is in itself a response to God's love of him. A rather simple story may bring to focus some of the matters of which Christian thinkers have written.

The motion picture, *The Best Years of Our Lives,* traced, in part, the inward story of a sailor returning to his home town after having lost both of his hands during the war. Where fingers had been there were now mechanical hooks, which he was able to manipulate with considerably dexterity. But the man was deeply disturbed by reactions to him; the stares of children evoked his anger, and the treatment accorded him by others always seemed unnatural. His difficulties were deepest in the sphere of his relations with the girl he had left behind—to whom he now returned. He had loved her, and she had returned his love; their expectation had been that on his return they would be married. Now he found that he could not be sure of her love, and he could not give her the love that he wanted to. After a conversation in which she had tried to assure him of the genuineness of her continuing love for him, he burst out, "I've got to work this out for myself." Perhaps he thought she was simply being noble and that he would have to live with her nobility throughout his life. Possibly he thought she was being upright, sticking to her man through thick and thin. Perhaps he felt that she was condescending to his condition and he would have to live with her pity. In any event, he rejected the offer of love. Later in the story came a scene in which she saw him without the hooks on his arms, saw him in his full helplessness. And somehow it became clear to him at that moment that she was neither noble, nor righteous, nor condescending. Her love for him was genuine. Then he could love her in return—and their marriage came soon.

The whole could be fearfully sentimentalized. And yet in its straight simplicity the story can be taken as a parable of some central assertions of Christian faith. A man may have difficulty in trusting the divine love; and when he has such difficulty, he is unable to open his own love. But when it becomes possible for him to trust, then he can love. The person who is intent on saving himself simply does not have the capacity for loving others. He may act morally toward them, he may do good deeds on their behalf, he may seek the way of religious devotion to the limit. It is only when he entrusts himself to the love of God with which he is loved that his life is opened so that he can love others for their own sakes, not for the sake of his own salvation. But when he does so trust the love of God, that love is reflected in his own life. He is bound to others by God's love for him.

5. PERSON AND COMMUNITY

The Christianity of the past few centuries and of the present has not always been aware of the implications of the law of love for the nature of man and for the nature of religion. It is a commonplace nowadays to say that "Religion is a personal affair." And yet it is questionable if the faith of the church through the centuries could be taken as supporting such a statement without serious qualifications.

The emergence of the emphasis on individual religion is certainly understandable. Reaction against dogmatic uniformity in the churches and against governmental supervision of thought was inevitable. Man must find his own faith if it is to be truly his own. The modern world has undergone a development that is parallel to that of ancient man. From earliest times religion was a group matter; the stoning of Achan's family is a survival of such a conception. But after that came a time when the individual stood out against the group, when he asserted his own primeval relationship to the divine. So it was in Greece when Socrates defended his own course of action before the Athenians. So it was in India when the Buddha received his enlightenment under the Bo tree. And so it was in Israel when men like Jeremiah found a relationship with God even in their utter loneliness. This is the stage of religion which Alfred North Whitehead found of crucial significance; he defined religion, therefore, as "what the individual does with his own solitariness."[27]

However, a further development appears to be necessary, one in which it is seen that the same God who is related to the individual at the veriest depths of his being is related also to the group. This development it seen at various places. In Christianity it receives expression in the notion that the Spirit who acts in the deepest places of the individual soul is also the creator of the church. It also receives expression in the conviction that love is the only adequate word to describe the profoundest relations between God, man, and men. Love is that relationship in which the difference of the other is taken into account, and yet the bond between the other and oneself is not broken. Christianity has also spoken of its vision of the end in terms of a kingdom of God. Here the reality of history and of social relationships is not denied. Men's relations with each other are fulfilled and made whole.

The present emphasis on the individual is, as we have seen, in part a reaction against a threatening collectivism. And yet simply to assert the individual may not be enough. Isolation and alienation may become intolerable, and then the forfeiture of the self to some collective may ensue. Historic Christianity offers a faith which affirms the individual without surrendering his relation to others; which affirms relationships without denying the individual. Whitehead's definition points to a necessary part of the process of religious development. Another necessary part is recognized by him too. "The topic of religion," he says, "is individuality in community."[28]

---

[27] Alfred N. Whitehead, *Religion in the Making* (New York: The Macmillan Company, 1927), p. 16. Reprinted by permission.

[28] *Ibid.*, p. 88.

READINGS

From the Bible

1. The laws of ancient Israel recognized man's concern for others, as in Deuteronomy 14:29f., Leviticus 19.

2. The prophets were shocked at men's treatment of others. Amos 2, Isaiah 1, Jeremiah 22.

3. Jesus emphasized love for others in various teachings: Matthew 5-7, Luke 10:25-37.

4. Paul and John made love of others a central aspect of true faith: Romans 12, Galatians 6, I John 4.

From Historic Christianity

1. Calvin, *Institutes,* II, viii, gives "An exposition of the moral law," interpreting the ten commandments with the notion of love to the neighbor as a central principle.

2. Dante, *The Divine Comedy,* "Inferno," canto 11, uses the notion of a bond of love between men as a key to the classification of sins.

3. Martin Luther, *Christian Liberty,* could be used here too, because of its relating of love of neighbor to faith in God's Word.

FOR STUDY AND DISCUSSION

1. James A. Pike, *Doing the Truth* (Garden City: Doubleday and Company, 1955), p. 65, describes the complexities that may be involved in a situation involving infidelity. Here is material for thought and discussion on the solidarity of sin.
2. The notion that the man of our time is a "mass man" has been set forth many times. To what extent is it justified? What relevance does Christian faith have for the problem? What, concretely, can Christians do about it?

3. The loneliness of the individual in contemporary society has been pointed out by many. To what extent is the problem a real one? What relevance does Christian faith have for the problem, and what can Christians do about it?
4. In what important respects is faith an individual matter: in what respects is it social?
5. A study of some contemporary novels or plays would be appropriate here, for example, Franz Kafka, *The Castle*.

IX

AREAS OF RELATEDNESS: PERSONS

Two dimensions of Christian faith are now in view. The Christian vision has been traced out, and the several aspects of man's relatedness have been delineated. While man's fundamental attitude, that toward God, has received no separate and extended treatment, reference to it has been made again and again. Its character is implicit in the Christian vision, and it has come to light at those points in the preceding analysis at which the dimension of vision and that of attitude have been seen to intersect.

The Christian vision sees God as the loving Creator who has made man and his world good; as the holy Reality to whom man is responsible and against whom he has rebelled; as the forgiving Redeemer who restores man to wholeness and to fellowship with himself and his neighbors. Man's attitude toward nature, himself, and others is determined by the conviction that any relationship of life can be used by God in a creative way; any relationship may tempt man to deify the creature or neglect the Creator; any relationship may be used by God redemptively, and all are included in his redemptive purposes.

We shall be turning now to more specific matters than those which have engaged our attention to this point. In this chapter we shall examine some areas of man's relations to himself and his neighbors; in the following chapter we shall be looking at some of the groups in which man's life is involved. We shall have to expect less help from credal statements and from particular statements in the Bible. Only on the most general matters can we expect widespread agreement among Christians living under diverse conditions in many centuries. Circumstances of life change with time and place. But as we go along, we may be surprised at the amount of guidance we can receive from the historic faith even on rather specific matters.

As we turn to them, we shall note the manner in which the several areas of man's relationships are interrelated, and the way in which the dimensions of vision and attitude intersect again and again.

1. WHAT SHALL I DO?

A man's choice of vocation is one of the major decisions of his life. What sort of person he is going to be depends in no small measure upon the sort of thing he is going to do. On a matter of so great concern as this, Christian faith ought to have something to say; and theologians of our time are convinced that it does. The very word *vocation,* as everyone who has had even the slightest brush with Latin knows, betrays its religious derivation. It is connected with *vocare,* to call; and a vocation was at one time, at least, regarded as a response to a calling from God. That for many in our time it has lost its religious reference is fairly obvious, and reasons for this fact are not hard to find. The secularization of life has progressed to such an extent that many find no reference to the Eternal in anything they do; to think of vocation as a calling from God would be very strange to them. The spiritualization of Christianity in many churches has also tended toward a loss of the sense of vocation for many. The religious "calling" has come to be so identified with the ministry or missionary endeavor that the religious dimension of other occupations often goes unnoticed. Theologians of our time sometimes look to historic Christianity to discover a meaning in vocation which many of our contemporaries do not see. We shall follow their example. It is not our concern, however, to set forth any full-fledged doctrine; we shall simply draw some of the more obvious implications of the Christian vision and attitude for an understanding of vocation.

That a man's attitude toward God must be central and that it determines all the others is a point on which Christians would agree. Hence to regard one's vocation as a calling from God would seem to be natural, and, indeed, primary. All else follows from this, and without this there can be no properly Christian thinking about vocation at all. This is not to say that the call will come as an audible voice heard by the human ear; rather the calling may emerge in the concrete situations in life in which the presence of God is regarded as the primary factor in decisions which must be made. Thus a person may "hear" God calling him as he studies the results of an aptitude test which shows him something of himself that he could not know without it.

It is important here to note that no unification of life encompasses all of it. Vocation is rightly a dedication to God, but commitment must be all-inclusive. Hence a man's vocation cannot be the whole of his life. A person is committed to God in his work and in his play, in his eating and his sleeping, in all of his life. If this is not the case, a vocation may easily become a false God, claiming all of a man's devotion. More than one person has measured his total life by his success in his occupation; his work drives him like a cruel taskmaster. It is like the law of which Paul spoke, calling on him for more than he can deliver. It is possible, too, of course, for a man's vocation to play too small a part in his life. Against this Christian moralists have had much to say. Even with sincere people who work hard, their vocations sometimes are not seen within a religious context of meaning. Often people who feel a genuine sense of dedication about their efforts in Sunday School or Youth Work in the church, find no special significance in their day to day work. They know it is important to be honest, to do a good day's work; but they do not regard their labor as response to a call from God. It would seem, however, that a proper attitude toward vocation in line with the primacy of God in life, is one which sees it as a major facet of one's total dedication.

That a man's attitude toward his neighbor is one characterized by love, by willingness to be bound to him in giving and receiving—this has important implications for vocation, too. He must recognize in his vocation his dependence on others, past and present, and be willing to acknowledge his debt to them. He must also seek to serve them through that which he does. In Ephesians there is a passage in which the thief is told to stop his thieving and take up an honest means of making a living. The motive suggested for the change is particularly interesting. He is not exhorted to be honest so that he can be a good citizen; he is told to work so that he will have something to give to others.[1] This

---

[1] Ephesians 4:28.

would be true conversion—from living from others to living for them. So often has vocation—as service to others—been stressed that it probably needs no further word. There is one aspect of it, however, so troublesome in view of the present state of society that a word or two should be said about it. It would seem that man must accept responsibility for the effects of his actions on others. In the modern world this is very difficult. Often it seems that people who are genuinely devoted to others in terms of personal service do not take responsibility for the broader social effects of the work in which they are engaged. The question has become particularly acute in the matter of atomic scientists: to what extent are they responsible for what others do with what they have discovered? In present day complex society it is exceedingly difficult to say unequivocally that any vocation is a service to others.

A man's attitude toward the nature around and within him will also have important implications for his vocation. Whenever spirit and body are set over against each other, important effects on views of vocation appear, and during the past few centuries the outlook of men on nature has had its effect upon their attitude toward work. Emphasis on the spiritual to the detriment of the physical has led to a prizing of those occupations which require nothing of the hands; for example, the gentleman is one who uses only his mind. And the view that nature is simply something to be exploited for financial profit has robbed men of a sense of communion with her in their work. Occasionally we are reminded of the possibilities inherent in work which brings man close to things physical. Thus a recent short story tells of a man and his wife who through many years have worked together as fishermen in their own little boat. On one voyage which has taken them far from the ordinary seaways the old man suddenly collapses and dies. The story is primarily concerned with the actions and thoughts of the woman as she tries to keep things under control while she waits for needed help. Throughout the story one feels the strong sense of her attachment to her husband, their work, and the ocean. These are summarized in the passage:

> . . . even now she was one with him and was no longer capable of thinking of herself as a separate entity, even while staring full face into his deadness. . . . They had always taken from the sea. Yet they had taken with a reverence which, while unspoken, was a real and a true thing, she knew.[2]

---

[2] Tom Filer, "The Last Voyage," *Prize Stories 1959: The O. Henry Awards,* Paul Engle, ed. (Garden City: Doubleday and Company, Inc., 1959), p. 271. Reprinted by permission.

It is, of course, possible for matter to be distinguished from mind in such a way that the spiritual is underestimated too. And often it seems, at least to college professors, that many people think the only people who work are those who do something with their hands. For Christian faith man's work properly relates him to the earth and to his own body which is drawn from it; and yet it is such that his own prior relation to God is kept clear.

Treatment of man's relation to himself has been deferred to the last, though it is central in the matter of vocation. Here, as elsewhere, Christian faith insists that he who seeks his life will lose it and only he who loses it will find it. The man who looks only within himself for guidance in the matter of vocation is likely to find little. But when he relates himself to God, his fellows, and his world, he may find much. And he should. With appreciation he can acknowledge those capacities and abilities which he has received from God and determine to develop and express them in ways that are creative. In trust he will, however, be able to look at himself objectively, recognizing his limitations. Because he is able to accept himself, he is able to accept what others can tell him about himself, in counselling, in testing procedures, in any of the ways that are available to him. He will not be surprised if deciding on a vocation proves difficult, for he is a free, self-determining human being, helping to create himself as he makes decisions. No vocation, perhaps, gives full scope to the possibilities within him. And yet he will try to find some definition for his life lest it be over before he has done anything with it. As he discovers the ways of expression which are appropriate to the gifts within him, he will surely enjoy himself, and enjoy his own expressions. But he will be delivered from a devouring self-preoccupation as he constantly turns to the world around him, the people beyond him, and the God to whom he is committed.

The Christian vision tells him that God is his Creator. Therefore, in gratitude he will use his own gifts creatively. It tells of the rebellion of men against their maker. Therefore, he will recognize the ambiguities of his situation and will be saved from disillusionment as he recognizes the sin that ever clings to his world and to himself. It tells also that God is redeemer, and bids him use his gifts in ways that serve redemptive purposes.

2. "WHO IS MY NEIGHBOR?"

If the question "What should I do?" focuses attention on the person in his concrete particularity within a web of relationships, the question

"Who is my neighbor?" [3] focuses attention on the other—also in his concrete particularity and within a web of relationships. The question as it appears in the gospels was asked in order to get clarification concerning the meaning of the love commandment. And the answer was given by the telling of a story. Thus even the mode of answer called attention to the fact that the concrete, the particular, the specific person in the specific situation is the neighbor, the one who is to be loved. He is to be loved simply because he is there.

The second commandment presupposes the first, and it is not to be confused with it. God is the primary object of love, and he is loved because of his own love for the person. He who has known that love in its indifference to merit is to reproduce the same kind of loving in his own life. Love of man for man is to reflect God's way of loving. "Be merciful," said Jesus, "even as your Father is merciful." [4] He makes the rain fall on the just and the unjust, and the children of the kingdom are to love without discriminating among the objects of their love. They are to love them that hate them, pray for those who despitefully use them. Without asking whether the neighbor is deserving or undeserving, the Christian is commanded to love him.

Such love presupposes God's love for the person who gives it. And it presupposes also a continuing action of God in human life, creating, judging, redeeming. The Christian simply acts in the situation and leaves his action to God for what God can do with it. His act is done in trust.

And yet the Christian does seek to do the loving action in the concrete situation as best he knows how. This does not mean that his action is one of love in some of the more common uses of the term. The action may be very painful to the other. The Christian may not particularly like the other. The action of love is simply the one which is for the good of the other insofar as it is possible for the Christian to define it in the given situation.

Because men and situations are to some extent alike, some definitions are possible; hence, some principles for action can be set forth, and these can be very helpful. However, it is important to see that no set of principles can fully define the person or the situation. The devotion of the Christian can never be diverted from God's demand that he do the deed of love for the specific person; the Christian is not devoted to principles as such. Here Christian thought diverges from emphases which sometimes appear under the influence of Greek thought: Plato calls for

[3] Luke 10:25-37.
[4] Luke 6:36.

love of the ideal of justice. And it is different, too, from the strand in Jewish thinking which emphasizes devotion to the law as the guide for action toward individuals. The need of the person at the time must be the primary consideration. Indeed, Christian faith, with its keen sense of the ubiquity of sin, has noted that devotion to law or principle can be a means of avoiding the demand of love in its fullness. Jesus pointed out again and again the manner in which people who were devoted to fulfilling the law used their very devotion as a tool for the oppression of others. A man might excuse himself from caring for his parents by devoting his money to God; [5] he might use his concern for keeping the Sabbath to blind him to human need around him. There is scarcely any subject on which he expressed himself with more bitterness than on this. Cruelty to others has been cloaked by devotion to principles again and again. There is hardly a person more heartless toward others than the one who is always right.

And yet principles and laws may have their limited value. This is because, as we have noted, people and situations do bear some similarity to each other. The early teachers of the church soon found it necessary to set forth certain general statements about how Christians should act toward other people, and their successors have been at work ever since. Theologians differ on the extent to which principles should be guides for Christian action. Some insist so strongly on the uniqueness of persons and situations and the dangers of self-righteousness that they are inclined to deny their value almost entirely. Others feel them to be extremely helpful and of the greatest importance for Christian action in the world. They agree, however, in insisting that the second commandment must be taken to mean love for the person in a specific situation.

3. FAITH AND FRIENDSHIP

If the Christian is commanded to do the deeds of love toward his neighbor and the latter is defined as the person who is at hand, in need of his ministrations, there would seem to be no place for the preferential love which is indispensable for friendship. And, indeed, certain sayings of Jesus would point to such a conclusion. One of the major differences between the children of the kingdom and others is that they treat all men as those others treat friends: "If you salute only your brethren, what more are you doing than others?" [6] In another passage he urges

[5] Mark 7:11.
[6] Matthew 5:47.

people giving a feast to invite the poor and the afflicted rather than simply their own friends.[7] The teachings of Jesus on this point are of a piece with his viewpoint on various human relationships. None of them can stand in the way of an absolute devotion to the will of God, and that will includes love for the neighbor, whoever he happens to be.

Once the divine priority is established, however, there seems to be no reason to quarrel with the natural fact that certain people are drawn into bonds of special friendship. Jesus himself chose a group to be his special companions, and the gospels speak of others who appear to have been especially close to him. The gospel of John in particular presents a very sensitive interpretation of Jesus' relation to the disciples in terms of friendship. His last hours mark a turning point in his relationship to them. Henceforth, he says, they will be no longer servants but friends.[8] Early Christians also recognized as a legitimate and treasured part of their own heritage a classic story of friendship, that of David and Jonathan. David's lament belongs to the world's great literature:

> Jonathan lies slain upon thy high places.
> I am distressed for you, my brother Jonathan;
> very pleasant have you been to me;
> your love to me was wonderful,
> passing the love of women.[9]

Friendship, then, would seem to be an aspect of the created order, growing out of the concrete particularities of individual creatures. And yet, like other aspects of creation, it can stand in the way of that devotion to the Divine which must be placed first in human life.

The experience of friendship illustrates in an especially vivid way the relations of love and trust. The friend is the one to whom one can entrust himself and his thoughts without fear of betrayal. One knows that what he says will be met with understanding and sympathy. The other will reply in honesty, "speaking the truth in love"[10] even when that truth is hard to face. There will be occasions when the other is hurt within the friendship, and the hurt is particularly deep and distressing by reason of the friendship itself. But the hurt will be taken into the other, felt as his own, and there will be forgiveness and restoration.

Because of the interrelatedness of the divine and the human, however, the experience of friendship may involve levels of reality which transcend

---

[7] Luke 14:13.
[8] John 15:15.
[9] II Samuel 1:25f.
[10] Ephesians 4:15.

personal relationships. The trust of a friend may help to engender that self-trust which has trust in God as its other pole. Indeed, unless the friendship points beyond itself and yields such trust, there is grave danger of its becoming pathological. The person who depends solely on his friend is in a very dangerous situation so far as his own life is concerned. He will develop fixations or obsessions with regard to the other. But if friendship opens out into a larger trust, it can be of the greatest significance; and as it so opens it will be enhanced. The person who trusts God ultimately can form friendships in which he does not simply use others for his own ends. Such use may be rather obvious and distasteful, but it may also be exceedingly subtle. The person who seeks only persons who agree with him or minister to his own ego, who is fearful lest others threaten his own securities, is not free in his friendships. He who trusts God can love his friends; and friendship can be a means by which such trust comes into being.

A moving passage in Augustine's *Confessions* reveals the author brooding over the death of a friend. The passing of the other reveals the pathos of friendship; for if he was treasured, his going is a loss. Augustine summarizes his own resolution of his difficulty in a sentence which seems an appropriate conclusion to this section and an introduction to that which follows: "Blessed is the man that loves Thee, O God, and his friend in Thee, and his enemy for Thee." [11]

4. FORGIVENESS

That the neighbor is simply the person who happens to be at hand, standing in need, and that he is to be treated with the spirit that is natural in friendship—these matters create difficulties. For the neighbor, even if he is actually a friend, will sometimes do that which arouses our resentment. Here the love commandment encounters its greatest resistance. And yet the New Testament is clear on this point, that forgiveness must be given and received. Jesus teaches his followers to pray:

> forgive us our debts,
> As we also have forgiven our debtors.[12]

He tells a story of two men who are servants of the same master. One is forgiven a staggering debt by his lord only to turn around and demand full payment of a trivial debt owed by his fellow servant. The story

[11] *Confessions of Saint Augustine,* p. 58. (IV, ix).
[12] Matthew 6:12.

ends with the unforgiving servant thrown into prison.[13] The implication is that the forgiveness of God is itself withdrawn from the unforgiving. In another place Jesus speaks of a man on his way to the temple with a gift to present to God. He remembers that his brother has something against him. Jesus tells him to go, be reconciled to his brother, before he presents his gift.[14]

To give and receive forgiveness is, rather obviously, no easy thing; and Christian faith underlines its difficulty. The emphasis on the self-determining character of man implies that that which is to be forgiven is, to some significant extent, a voluntary act; it comes from the person's own self. Hence to forgive someone else means that we take into account that he has done something as a self-determined act. He does not need to be forgiven for actions for which he cannot rightly be held responsible, even though they may arouse resentment in us. With them our problem is simply rational; they are explainable and we have to bring ourselves to understand them. But with self-determined acts the situation is different. We have to admit the malice and our own reaction to it. Likewise in seeking forgiveness, we have to admit to ourselves and to someone else that what has been done was a self-determined action. We must willingly accept responsibility for it. Further, the act of forgiving as well as that of seeking forgiveness must be self-determining. It is we who must forgive, and it is we who must sue for forgiveness.

There are strong reasons to suggest that from the point of view of Christian faith both the offering and the seeking of forgiveness are, as purely human actions, impossibilities. Here the law which says we must forgive encounters the bondage which keeps us from keeping it. But the understanding of the law as bondage comes with release from it; Christian faith speaks of forgiveness by God. In analogy with human forgiveness, it sees in the cross of Christ God taking the hurt of human sin upon himself and transforming its effect into free forgiveness. And the act of the cross is re-enacted in human life by the Spirit. Thus there is a human action, a self-determined act, which is made possible by a divine action which is beyond human contriving. Every human act of forgiveness is at the same time a divine action, without which it would be impossible. "Let all bitterness and wrath and anger and clamor and slander be put away from you, with all malice, and be kind to one another, tenderhearted, forgiving one another, as God in Christ forgave you." [15]

---

[13] Matthew 18:23-35.
[14] Matthew 5:23f.
[15] Ephesians 4:31f.

5. THE FAMILY

In the family the human experience of forgiveness occurs in its greatest fullness. Here the hurt of evil done is deepest, and here the resource of forgiving love is greatest. Hence it is natural that some of the richest analogies for divine forgiveness are drawn from family life. The classic story of all time is that of the prodigal son. Back of it is the great verse from the Psalms:

> Like as a father pitieth his children,
> So the Lord pitieth them that fear him.[16]

Paul spoke of the new life which he experienced when he ceased to think of God as lawgiver as a veritable adoption into sonship.[17]

Not all that is said of the family in the New Testament, however, is favorable. On occasion Jesus spoke words which seemed to indicate that he had slight regard for it. When his mother and brothers came to take him home because they thought he was beside himself, he asked coldly, "Who are my mother and my brothers?" and answered his own question, "Whoever does the will of God is my brother, and sister, and mother." [18] Similarly, Paul spoke of the primacy of devotion to God. Since a Christian's first duty is to serve Christ, the interest of simplicity itself seemed to him to dictate that he not choose a wife who would expect him to try to please her.[19] These negative words of Jesus and Paul reflect, of course, their keen sense of the primacy of God in human life. The family in particular is a dangerous rival by reason of the very love and affection it engenders. Hence, it can easily become a false god, claiming the devotion that is owed to the high and holy Lord. The several members of the family, too, by reason of the affection in which they are held, may claim the divine prerogatives. Thus Jesus says flatly, "If any one comes to me and does not hate his own father and mother and wife and children and brothers and sisters, yes, and even his own life, he cannot be my disciple." [20] Illustrations of the tendency of family members to become false deities are common in literature. Thus the father in *The Barretts of Wimpole Street* [21] in his very self-righteousness demands a

---

[16] Psalm 103:13, K.J.V.
[17] Galatians 4:5f.
[18] Mark 3:33, 35.
[19] I Corinthians 7:33.
[20] Luke 14:26.
[21] Rudolf Besier, *The Barretts of Wimpole Street* (Boston: Little, Brown and Company, 1931).

loyalty that cannot be rightly accorded any human. The mother in *The House of Bernarda Alba*[22] ruins her children in the attempt to guide their lives totally. And the child in *My Son, My Son*[23] brings his father to destruction by becoming the false center of the family's life.

The family and its members can be saved from false deification by a realization of the divine love. And that realization can come, in part, through the agency of the family itself. In it is a treasury of human love which can be traced to God. And when it is so traced, the family can be seen in its proper creative role in human life, God's creation being used for his creative purposes. While Jesus and Paul both insisted on the primacy of devotion to God, they did not deny the traditional viewpoint of their people that family life is good.

For both the conviction of the goodness of the created world seems to have involved the goodness of the physical aspects of the family. Negatively, neither seems to be touched by tendencies sometimes present in Greek thought which regard sex as in itself evil. Jesus certainly recognized that there might be circumstances in which devotion to God might preclude other relationships,[24] and he himself, of course, did not marry. Paul frankly said that he felt that it was better to be single, but he connected his statement with the notion that the present age was nearing its conclusion.[25] On the other hand, Jesus spoke of childbirth as bringing great joy to the mother.[26] And for Paul the analogy of husband and wife was used to suggest the profound relationship of Christ and the church.[27] Christian faith has inherited with its view of creation the Hebrew attitude toward life and its beginnings. The physical is no evil thing intruding upon the unsullied goodness of the spiritual. Sex is part of God's good creation. Hence the purity that is demanded with reference to it. Paul recoils from the thought of the Christian being joined to a prostitute, not because he has done something physical, but because he has shared that which belongs to Christ—his body—with someone who cannot properly share it.[28] Sin of this kind has a peculiar seriousness because the body is so intimately a part of the personality.

---

[22] Federico Garcia Lorca, "The House of Bernarda Alba," *Three Tragedies of Federico Garcia Lorca,* Richard L. O'Connell and James Graham, trans. (New York: New Directions, 1947).

[23] Howard Spring, *My Son, My Son* (New York: The Viking Press, Inc., 1938).

[24] Matthew 19:12.

[25] I Corinthians 7, especially verses 1, 7, 29.

[26] John 16:21.

[27] Ephesians 5:32.

[28] I Corinthians 6:15ff.

Hence that which is good should be used for God—"Glorify God in your body." [29]

The importance of the unity of the family, and its significance for the enjoyment of life and for the developing of people has been a constant theme in Christian history. Jesus saw the establishment of the family relationship in the light of the Genesis story, a man and woman are to become one flesh. Paul speaks often of family relationships as he writes to his friends. From the Christian vision and attitudes it is not difficult to draw implications for the nature of the family, and these have had significant influence in the forming of Western culture.

The problem of the family might be stated in this way: it is that of being a community within which persons come into being. There must be mutual love and understanding, there must be give and take, there must be respect for the integrity of the various members. The family is a matrix of special importance within which the creative work of God goes on, developing minds and characters. But the family must ever look beyond itself. It is set within a wider network of relationships of which it must ever be aware. And it must recognize its own ultimate loyalty to a Reality which is beyond it and yet works within it.

READINGS

From the Bible

1. Often noted as a man with a sense of vocation is Nehemiah. See chapters 1-6, especially 6:3.

2. The friendship of David and Jonathan is described in I Samuel 20ff. The lament of David for his friend and King Saul is a classic: II Samuel 1:19-27.

3. The relation of Jesus and his disciples is described in terms of friendship in John 13-17.

4. The first pair is described in Genesis 2 and 3.

5. Paul's views on marriage are given in I Corinthians 7 and 11.

---

[29] I Corinthians 6:20.

From Historic Christianity

1. John Calvin, *The Institutes*, III, x, 6, is a brief statement of the Reformer's views on vocation.

2. Augustine, *Confessions*, Book 4, is a meditation occasioned by the death of a friend.

3. Martin Luther, *Table Talk*, "Of Marriage and Celibacy" is a collection of comments on a variety of themes.

FOR STUDY AND DISCUSSION

1. Arthur Miller's *Death of a Salesman* points up many of the problems of this chapter as they confront a contemporary: self-identity, vocation, family, forgiveness.
2. In what senses, if any, are church vocations different from others?
3. Does God expect me to forgive people if they are not willing to admit they are wrong? Can I love people I do not like? Can there be love without understanding?
4. Is the church partly to blame if people today have perverted attitudes toward sex?
5. Study the marriage service in several Service Books.

X

AREAS OF RELATEDNESS: GROUPS

By the very title of a book Reinhold Niebuhr arrested the attention of the Christian world to the consideration of a problem. He called his volume *Moral Man and Immoral Society*.[1] In it and other writings he has insisted that there is a great difference between man's involvement in close, interpersonal relationships and his involvements in large groups. He has further insisted that Christian faith has something important to say about both. Neglect of the differences has led to confusion in thinking and has sometimes had disastrous consequences in action. Christians who have sought to apply in a simple way the ethical precepts of their faith which have relevance to intimate relationships to the larger spheres of life have been utterly ineffective; they have even made it easier for unscrupulous people to exploit them and others. On the other hand Christians who are concerned about love in the intimate relations of life but deny its significance for the larger areas have been irresponsible with reference to society; they, too, have made it easy for the un-

[1] Reinhold Niebuhr, *Moral Man and Immoral Society* (New York: Charles Scribner's Sons, 1936).

scrupulous to exploit them and others. What is needed is an understanding of Christian faith which will discern the differences between the various areas of life and point up the relevance of the gospel to all of them.

We are not concerned here, of course, with setting forth Mr. Niebuhr's views. Nor do we essay the delineation of a Christian doctrine of economics or politics. We shall, however, seek to come to some understanding of man's attitude toward the groups of which he is a part in the light of the Christian vision.

1. THE CHARACTER OF GROUPS

It is not surprising that Christians have found difficulty in defining the attitudes they should adopt in their relations to groups. The problem is no easy one. Further, for a number of reasons the New Testament largely disregards it. The early church stood in expectation of the imminent coming of the kingdom of God by an act of divine intervention in human history. There was no thought of any transformation of society by their efforts; it would soon be transformed by an act of the Almighty. Connected with this is a second reason for apparent disregard of group relations in the New Testament. While there was much concern for the transformation of individuals and small groups of people, these were considered, for the most part, in limited contexts. Paul suggested the freeing of a runaway slave to his owner,[2] but made no effort to deal with the institution of slavery itself. In view of the cataclysmic end of history soon to come, why should there be an attempt to change things in any radical way? Much of the moral guidance of the New Testament writers has to do with the behavior of people in a fairly simple society and has to do with relations of a rather elementary kind.

It is small wonder, then, that many Christians have drawn the conclusion that the Christian faith is concerned with man's individual conduct and his close personal relationships. Some through the centuries have looked for the coming of God's kingdom in their lifetime and have turned away from the present world and sought to prepare themselves for participation in the next. Others have simply felt a genuine responsibility to deal justly and lovingly with their more immediate neighbors and have sought to extend the influence of the gospel in the world as a spiritual force, but have not given themselves to efforts to

[2] Philemon 15-19.

change society in its larger aspects. Still others have tried to apply the ethic which is appropriate to the individual and his interpersonal relationships to the larger groupings of society.

A closer look at the New Testament itself might yield the judgment that none of these courses of action is true to its spirit. While little is said directly of the larger groupings of life, there are a few very important passages which have a bearing upon man's attitudes toward them. Further, there is a great deal implicit in the outlook of its writers to which attention must be given. It is important to see, too, that for the most part they reflect viewpoints which are stated with greater fullness and clarity in the Old Testament. The law and the prophets have much to say about man's relations to the groups about him.

If we focus attention on the Christian vision, we can rather easily see some important implications for man's involvement in groups. These have appeared already in the examination of the family. We have seen that a group is a sort of entity in itself, and that this fact has to be taken into account in any treatment of it. By creation of God, man is the kind of being who forms groups and who finds in them assistance in fulfilling the creative potentialities of his world and of his life. He can enjoy, realize, do with others what he cannot achieve by himself. The Christian must take into account the givenness of man's group life in its concrete character. This is part of the way God made the world. However, man's rebellion is reflected in all that he does, and it infects his group life in ways that have a certain character. Man sins as a member of a group in ways that he does not sin as an individual. It is easy to see that men of some moral sensitivity would never do to each other as individuals what they do to each other through the groups to which they belong. However, God has acted to redeem man in all of his life; he seeks to extend his Lordship over the entire range of man's living. Hence the life of groups cannot be set outside the range of God's redemptive concern and activity. And yet, within the present world order, redemption is realized only in part. Man's group life, like his individual life and his interpersonal relations, is redeemed only in part.

2. ECONOMIC LIFE

The involvement of groups in economic life is dramatically set forth in a scene from *The Grapes of Wrath.* A dust bowl farmer discovers a tractor coursing over land he has always used. In anger he confronts the driver, threatening to "pot" him "like a rabbit" if he comes too close to the house he considers his own. The driver of the tractor replies that he is not to blame for what is going on. Behind him is a bank, and back of the bank a group in New York who say, "'Make the land show profit or we'll close you up.'" The farmer's desperation is reflected in the words, "'But where does it stop? Who can we shoot?'" [3] The men in New York have nothing against the farmer; they are responsible to stockholders for whom they are trying to make money. But the farmer is bereft of his livelihood.

Christian faith, however, cannot be indifferent to his welfare. And its concern is not simply to see that his soul is saved. For deep within it is the conviction that a man's body is good, that it is God's creation and must be treated with respect. That a man have enough to eat, that he have the means of putting clothes on his back, that he have a measure of security—these are matters for which Christians are properly concerned. "Distribute to the poor," [4] was part of the answer Jesus gave to a man who came seeking to find out how to inherit eternal life. The story of his feeding of the multitudes is told by every one of the gospel writers. And back of Jesus is the heritage of attitude in the faith of the Hebrew people. Their laws made provision for man's physical needs, and their prophets would not allow Israel to forget the destitute and afflicted. That man's economic life is within God's creative concern is deeply woven into the whole fabric of Christian faith. There is an economic factor in all that is creative in human life, not simply in the more obvious needs of men for food and clothing. That which contributes to the growth of his mind, to the enriching of his sensitivities, to the joy of his everyday living rests on an economic base. Schools, museums, roads, governments, churches—all of these cost money.

And the creative possibilities in economic processes are increased by the development of group activities. As soon as man emerges from the most primitive situation, he allies himself with others in ways which secure and protect his means of livelihood. Schools, governments, and churches not only cost money, they require the organized effort of groups of people.

And yet there is within the Christian heritage a strong suspicion of money. "You cannot serve God and mammon," [5] said Jesus; and part of the answer to the question about eternal life was "Sell all that you

---

[3] John Steinbeck, *The Grapes of Wrath* (New York: The Viking Press, Inc., 1939), pp. 51ff. Used by permission.

[4] Luke 18:22.

[5] Matthew 6:24.

have."[6] And if the apostle did not say what is often attributed to him—"money is the root of all evil"—he came close to it: "The love of money is a root of all kinds of evil."[7] Here, of course, is applied to money that suspicion of all created things which is characteristic of Christian faith. Money is an object of special concern simply because of what it can buy. Perhaps there is no way in which world-mindedness can be expressed more directly than in the love of money. The real trouble lies in the temptation to make of the economic the final security of life, to put one's trust in it. The temptation comes to everyone, since economic anxiety is universal, and it is easy to think that overcoming it will secure one's peace. And yet to seek to overcome that anxiety by money alone is to give in to it, to send life into the frustration of unfulfilled and unfulfillable desires. Dante gave vivid pictures of those who made the amassing of money the goal of their lives; in hell they pushed weights around a circle and then pushed them back again to the point from which they had started.[8]

But the poor man too may be driven to economic anxiety; getting rid of money does not mean that one is delivered from its hold. Indeed, poverty and wealth alike tend to debilitate man. The concern of the Bible for the poor is, perhaps, more than simply a concern that they be fed and housed. Few, indeed, are the saints who like Francis can wed lady Poverty and find a happy marriage.

As the creative possibilities of economic factors are compounded by their involvement in group activities, so are the evils. People simply do to each other in groups things that they would not do as individuals. The corporation executives in New York do not intend personal injury to the dust bowl farmer, but they are simply caught in an economic situation. Or are they? Here is a real problem for Christian faith. If they are truly caught, there seem to be inescapable economic factors which are fully determinative of life. And this is just what the Marxists have said: economic forces determine man's life and destiny. The view is not to be set aside lightly. A plausible case can surely be made for a large measure of determination of life by socio-economic forces. And Christian faith will be sensitive to the role of the economic in life, to the fact that sin is deeply woven into the texture of life. Paul Tillich

---

[6] Luke 18:22.

[7] I Timothy 6:10. American Revised Version (New York: Thomas Nelson & Sons, 1901).

[8] Dante, *The Divine Comedy*, "Inferno," VII.

has pointed out that forces were created by the industrial revolution which hang like a fate over modern man's living.[9]

The Christian reply to the Marxist claim does not seem to be a denial of the significance of the economic factor in human life. Rather, it seems to be a proclamation of what in first century terminology was called the victory of Christ over all the evil powers that held man's life in bondage. Christian faith speaks of a power that can rescue man from the illusion that economic anxiety is the ultimate anxiety. It frees him at the center of his being, from the anxiety which is sin.

It does not free him from economic anxiety directly, nor from responsibility in the economic order. Indeed, it seems to say to him that, being freed from the final hold of his economic fears, he may deal with them redemptively. Because he is not ultimately anxious, he may deal with his less than ultimate difficulties. He will seek a measure of security for himself and his family which will make it possible for him to live in some sort of decency. At the same time, he will work for those arrangements in economic life which will secure for all the maximum opportunity for freedom, creativeness, and community. And yet he will not be utopian. He will recognize the continuing fact of sin in human life. He will freely confess his own guilt and the guilt that is involved in his membership in groups which exploit other groups. Such confession, however, will not bring an easing of responsibility. Because of his confrontation with the forgiving love of God, he will seek to use for redemptive ends the resources which his economic involvements make available to him.

3. THE POLITICAL ORDER

In the political realm the deification of the finite sometimes takes literal form: divine prerogatives are claimed by the state, often by its central figure the king or emperor. This fact faced the Christians in earliest times and brought on the most dramatic of the persecutions. The Roman emperor was regarded as a god, and his people were to recognize him as such. If they refused, they were traitors to the government and blasphemers against religion. When the Christians refused, they were forced to take the consequences. This is the situation which is reflected in the Book of the Revelation with its strange stories and pictures. It is a book intended to give courage to those under persecu-

[9] Paul Tillich, "The World Situation," *The Christian Answer*, Henry P. Van Dusen, ed. (New York: Charles Scribner's Sons, 1945), p. 5.

tion, and it describes in sometimes fantastic imagery the struggle between the Roman empire and the kingdom of Christ. An image of a beast is set up and men are forced to worship that image or be slain. The author thinks of the empire as completely evil. It brings dreadful woe upon the Christians who will not recognize its pretentions to divine authority, but in the end it will be destroyed and God and his saints will reign forever and ever.[10]

Sensitivity to the dangers inherent in political power has been characteristic of Hebrew and Christian attitudes toward government throughout history. One strand of tradition that is preserved in the stories about the choice of Saul as king of Israel reflects it clearly. The people come to Samuel, clamoring for a king. All the surrounding peoples have one; why should they not? The reaction of the prophet is that the people are rejecting the rule of God over them. A king will enslave them and bring all sorts of calamities on them. He finally yields to their wishes, however, and Saul is selected.[11] It has been pointed out that the devising of a system of checks and balances which restrained any branch of government in this country from too great an exercise of power was due in part to the influence of men who held Christian convictions.[12] They were so fearful of the temptation to sin that would lie before any person or group given too great a measure of authority that they devised a scheme by which it would be effectively restricted. The issue on which some German Christians repudiated the Nazi regime was on its claim to control the totality of men's lives. This they took to be the modern counterpart of the demand for emperor worship. Indeed, Paul Tillich remarked on one occasion that one could not understand the hold of Adolf Hitler upon the German people unless one saw that for them he was a "Christ figure." Some Christians, at least, renounced him and experienced the wrath of "the beast." [13]

It must be recognized, however, that the very possibility of demonic pretentions on the part of governments is bound up with something which in itself is positive and good. All devils were angels at first. This insight lies behind an attitude toward government on the part of Christians which seems to be the very opposite of the preceding. The Book of the Revelation sees Rome simply as the beast; other New Testa-

---

[10] Revelation. See ch. 13.

[11] I Samuel 8. See Fleming James, *Personalities of the Old Testament,* pp. 77ff., on sources for the stories of Samuel and Saul.

[12] Richard Hofstadter, *The American Political Tradition and the Men Who Made It* (New York: Alfred A. Knopf, Inc., 1948), ch. 1.

[13] Revelation 13.

ment writers see matters very differently. Thus Paul wrote to the Roman Christians, "Let every person be subject to the governing authorities. For there is no authority except from God, and those that exist have been instituted by God." The ruler, he goes on, "is God's servant for your good." [14] And in I Peter appears a similar word. "Be subject for the Lord's sake to every human institution, whether it be to the emperor as supreme, or to governors." The exhortation concludes with brief imperatives: "Honor all men. Love the brotherhood. Fear God. Honor the emperor." [15]

Sensitivity to the positive significance of political power has been as characteristic as suspicion of it in the determination of Christian attitudes toward government. Along with the strand of tradition which we have already seen to be present in the stories about the choice of Saul is another which is also reflected in the biblical accounts. According to the view reflected in it, the decision to select a king for Israel is the expression of a perfectly natural development on the part of the people. The days when God ruled them through judges is now at a close, and the time when he will exercise his authority through kingship has arrived. Saul is the first choice, and his selection and crowning are glorious events.[16] His failure to live up to the expectations he has aroused lead to his eventual rejection and the choice of David in his stead. But even during the time when David is a fugitive from Saul, he steadfastly refuses to lift up his hand against "the Lord's anointed." [17] The king has been chosen by God, his anointing is a ritual act of the greatest significance. To kill the king would be a sacrilegious as well as a traitorous act. Some scholars hold that some of the Psalms reflect enthronement rituals in ancient Israel; in them the king is given an honor which is of the highest sort. He is even spoken of in terms of divine sonship: "You are my son," says the Deity, "today I have begotten you." [18] It is this attitude of highest reverence for the ruler as a servant of God, ruling in order to secure the will of the divine over the people, that is reflected in the writings of Paul and Peter in the New Testament. It lies behind the viewpoint that has been common in historic Christianity of seeing the ruler as God's vicegerent. When the ruler himself or the ruling group in a democratically oriented society is Chris-

---

[14] Romans 13:1, 4.

[15] I Peter 2:13, 14, 17.

[16] I Samuel 9:1-10:16. See Fleming James, *Personalities of the Old Testament*, pp. 77ff.

[17] See, for example, I Samuel 24:10.

[18] Psalms 2:7.

tian, conscious of responsibilities to God, the ideal government is realized, according to a strong tradition in the Christian church. From the time of Constantine to the present there have been innumerable attempts to set forth the character of "the Christian prince" and "the Christian commonwealth." And even where specific religious influences on government are repudiated on principle, as in the case of the United States, Christian thinkers have urged their people to recognize the positive significance of government. In a recent television program a distinguished jurist led his audience on an imaginary tour of a courthouse, remarking that for him it was a sort of temple.[19]

The perennial problem of Christians has been that of deciding the point at which a government ceases to serve the purposes of God and begins to usurp the divine prerogatives. The agony of the earliest believers is reflected in a remark by the author of the Book of the Revelation: the beast "deceives those who dwell on the earth."[20] And in our time many German Christians, trained to think of loyalty to the state as their God-enjoined duty, faced a fearful battle with their consciences before they turned against the Hitler regime. The question of the duty owed by Christians to communist governments is a debated problem of the present day. Like other decisions involved in Christian faith, it is one which always has to be made in the concrete situations, fraught with the anxieties involved in finite existence.

In a general way the basic attitude of the Christian toward the state may be delineated in terms of the focal points of the Christian vision. His primary duty is to love God with the whole of his being and seek his lordship over all of life. Insofar as the political order can be a means by which God can exercise his lordship, the Christian must support and revere it; when it seeks to usurp that lordship, he must resist it. His second duty is to love his neighbor; and insofar as the state provides opportunities for the exercise of that love, he must avail himself of them; to the extent that it prevents that love, he must seek to change it or even actively resist it.

Because he sees God as the creator of all things, and specifically of men made in his own image, the Christian sees the state as existing for the good of men. It provides the setting within which the potentialities of men are, in part, realized. Man must be to a significant extent self-determining, and no state can be permitted to take his freedom from him. He has a mind which is capable of training and is the servant

---

[19] The late Joseph Nye Welch.
[20] Revelation 13:14.

of his self-determination; it is appropriate that the state educate him. He is made for community life, and the state affords means by which men's relations with one another can be regulated in ways that benefit all. The Christian recognizes that he fulfills his responsibilities as a citizen because of his allegiance to God. As Paul sees it, he will do out of conscience what some do because of legal regulation.[21] It is significant that Paul speaks of love as the fulfillment of the law of the state as well as the law contained in the Old Testament. He passes immediately from a discussion of paying taxes, obeying magistrates, and giving honor to legal authorities to a listing of the duties toward neighbor as they are given in the ten commandments. Love fulfills civil as well as moral law.

Because men in their rebellion against God act in ways that are hurtful to others, it is appropriate that restraints be imposed upon them. The man who refrains from harming his neighbor because he fears the punishment which will ensue does not fulfill the law of God which is seeking full and willing lordship over his life. But he fulfills that part of God's will to lordship which expresses itself in concern for the welfare of the other: God does not want his children to be hurt! Further, the Christian expresses his love for his neighbor by seeking to protect him from harm in all the ways he can; the enactment and enforcement of law are among the ways in which he may do so. He will even favor laws which make it impossible for him to encroach upon his neighbor's freedom and dignity. However, the Christian recognizes that the sinfulness of man may express itself in the deification of the state itself; against this he must ever be wary.

The state appears also to offer possibilities for the exercise of the redemptive dimension of God's lordship over life. As Paul saw the Jewish law to be a "custodian until Christ came," [22] the Christian may see the civil law as pointing toward redemptive fulfillment. An account was given recently of an enactment in a certain locality which forced men into new patterns of relatedness. They were somewhat amazed to discover new avenues of appreciation and understanding which came as a result of a law. Christians rightly see the rehabilitation of criminals and juvenile delinquents as an objective of criminological practice.

The redemptive actions possible through political means are fairly limited, however. The sort of love that is the theme of the New Testament can only with difficulty characterize the actions of a political en-

---

[21] Romans 13:5.
[22] Galatians 3:24.

tity. This is true also with reference to the state as a theater for the creative work of God and for the deeds of love of the Christian. Here we come to a crucial problem involving the fact that the large group appears to call for an expression of attitudes which are different from those appropriate to the small. It is fine to turn the other cheek to the individual who strikes you on one, but it is no easy matter to make forgiveness a basis of international relations. It seems that the best that can be sought in the group contexts of human living is justice rather than love. And it seems, further, that the state has to be in a position to enforce its commands. Even Paul was aware of this: the ruler "does not bear the sword in vain." [23] How can this be squared with the Christian ideals of peace and gentleness and meekness? The problem has been perennial for Christians. There seems to be a dilemma in the very involvement in political life. If the Christian does support the government and seek for the doing of justice with the use or threat of force, he seems to be betraying his own dedication to love as the final law of life. But if he does not seek for justice and give support to the institutions of government, he withdraws his neighbor's protections and his own and invites anarchy. Throughout the centuries the dilemma has faced Christians repeatedly; it is before them today in poignant fashion.

The problem of the Christian is that he seeks to be a citizen of God's kingdom and of man's. The human political order will lose its meaning if it is understood as serving earthly ends without recognizing ultimate responsibilities. And yet the ultimate responsibilities must be freely recognized, not coerced. To Caesar must be rendered the things that are Caesar's; to God the things that are God's.[24] But Caesar is God's servant, whether he knows it or not.

4. RACIAL GROUPS

Both the problems and the possibilities of group activity in the economic and political spheres are enhanced by the fact of race, for race groupings often become economic and political in character. In Germany the myth of the master race was connected with a totalitarian political structure, and economic motivations were involved in the treatment of the Jews. Thus racial and economic forces worked together with political in the compounding of a veritable citadel of sin. What

[23] Romans 13:4.
[24] Matthew 22:15-22.

has been said about economic and political groupings may, therefore, be taken for granted as we turn to a consideration of Christian attitudes toward racial groupings. We should, however, give attention to some matters which are primarily connected with race.

In no area, perhaps, has the difference between the individual, person-to-person relationships and that between groups been so significant. In America the white man generally feels that he has been personally kind, even generous to individuals of other races. In turn, those of other races have had relations of genuine friendship across race lines. At the same time, however, the white will enter into group arrangements which deny to other races access to natural resources, to economic and educational opportunities, and even to the protection of law. And those of other races will enter into actions as a group which they would not undertake against individual whites. Both groups easily fall into self-righteousness in defense of their actions. The white points to what he believes to be the moral superiority of his race over others. The races which have suffered discrimination easily allow the relative justice of their claims to betray them into a sense of absolute rightness which cannot be questioned. And so long as sins are cloaked in self-righteousness, there can be no penitence pointing toward redemption. Instead, the sense of guilt increases; and there can be no doubt that the violence and intransigence which marks much of the current relationships among racial groups grows, in part, out of feelings of guilt.

Christian faith speaks soberly of the requirements of redemption and hopefully of its resources. In the cross of Christ it sees a price paid, so to speak, by God in his identification of himself with men. And it sees the need for such identification to be repeated by his followers. A group of students at a recent meeting were deeply moved as they sought for a time to assume the role of people of some race other than their own, trying to understand how they felt in the various situations of life. They came away with a profound sense of the difficulties involved in changing inherited patterns and at the same time of the urgent need to see these patterns changed.[25] And it would seem, at least, that where honest efforts have been made to find what is right in a given situation, unexpected redemptive resources have appeared. Christians must act in expectation—while they will recognize the depth of resistance.

As a penitent standing before the divine judgment and forgiveness, the Christian may see something of the implication of his convictions

[25] The National Student Assembly, Y.M.C.A., Y.W.C.A., at the University of Illinois.

about creation for the relations among racial groups. He can recognize the preciousness of uniqueness and look with gratitude at the differences among men which make it possible for them to act creatively in a diversity of ways that contribute to the good of all. And yet he will not look upon differences as reasons for asserting the superiority of certain groups to others. Self-determination is a sacred right of the creature, and no group can exercise the sole right of determining the rights of others. When it undertakes to do so, it deifies itself. When, on the other hand, it relinquishes its efforts to do so, it opens itself to creative and redemptive possibilities working through the very groupings which do exist.

5. THE CHURCH

The Christian is involved in one group by reason of the redemptive act of God, for one phase of that act was the creation of the church by the Spirit. The early Christians did not think of themselves as solitary individuals who had responded to the same Lord; they were members one of another, members of the family of God. As the ancient Israelites had been constituted into a people by entering into covenant with their God at Mount Sinai, so had the church been constituted by a new covenant in Christ. They were his very body, having many members; each had his own duties to perform. Christ loved the church as a man loves his bride who is his very self. The members of the church are so related that "if one member suffers, all suffer together; if one member is honored, all rejoice together." [26] And yet the church is human, and throughout the New Testament runs that duality of attitude toward it which characterizes the attitude toward other groups. In the very letter in which Paul described the church as the body of Christ, he warned its people by recalling the experience of Israel: baptized in the Red Sea and fed with manna in the wilderness, they were rejected because of their disobedience. He implies that Christians who have been baptized and have received the supper of the Lord must not become presumptuous concerning their spiritual welfare; they, too, may be rejected. The Book of the Revelation contains seven letters to churches which illustrate both aspects of the duality: each contains threat and promise. Thus the church at Laodicea is addressed:

> I know your works; you are neither cold nor hot. Would that you were cold or hot! So, because you are lukewarm, and neither cold

[26] I Corinthians 12:26.

> nor hot, I will spew you out of my mouth. For you say, I am rich, I have prospered, and I need nothing; not knowing that you are wretched, pitiable, poor, blind, and naked. . . . Those whom I love, I reprove and chasten; so be zealous and repent. Behold, I stand at the door and knock; if any one hears my voice and opens the door, I will come in to him and eat with him, and he with me.[27]

The positive valuation of the church is based on the conviction that it exists by the redemptive act of the Spirit. When God's love was poured out on men, it aroused a trust which opened the doors of their love for each other. And it was natural that those who responded should be drawn together with special bonds. The law of their relationship with one another was that they were to love one another as Christ had loved them. They were to live in constant acknowledgment of his redemptive power. They would even exemplify the love of God, and in so doing they would be a means by which it could reach others. They were to love all men, not simply each other. And they were to be a redeeming fellowship because of their own humble awareness of the redemptive resources by which they lived.

As men responding individually to the redemptive love of God became new creatures and thus realized their authentic creaturehood, so men responding socially could become a new humanity. They could realize in the church the social dimension of their creatureliness. It is as natural for men to be bound to one another in their religious life as in their politics, their economics, their family life. Hence life in the church is natural; it reflects the true sociality: one which recognizes its reference to God. Because men are members of a body with a single head, they are members of one another. Thus they realize their true freedom; for a church must be based on the decision of man. But it is not a matter of casual choice, which might or might not be made. Like other choices of the Christian, the decision to be part of the church is a result of the action of the Spirit at work in his life—an action which is, in part, carried on through the church itself. The church which is true to itself will be one in which the creaturely possibilities of man are brought forth in a community of interest and concern. Men nourished within it will be creative men, using their minds with full freedom, because they belong to a community in which they encounter trust and love.

The very importance of the church, however, invites it to self-deification. In the interests of seeking to bring men under the sway of God's

---

[27] Revelation 3:15-20.

will, it may inhibit freedom, control thought, discourage courageous action. The church may close itself up within itself, refusing to share its love with others, particularly the sinful and the needy. It may turn into a group which thinks of itself as the good people, those who have chosen God rather than having been chosen by him. It may ally itself with forces which preserve the evils of some given social order. Indeed, the sins it may commit have been pointed out so frequently in Christian history and in the present, that reference to them need not be multiplied here.

Because it constantly falls into sin, the church must ever seek renewal by the Spirit. Realizing that it does not exist in and by itself, it knows that its very existence is by the constant creative act of God. It does not live for itself either. It points to the redemptive act by which it came into being and toward the whole family of mankind which it seeks to serve. And it points to the kingdom of God which stands before it as judgment and fulfillment.

One of the recurrent problems of the Christian life is that of adjudicating the claims of the several groups of which a person is a member. Still more difficult is the problem of decision with reference to the relations of the groups themselves. Economic groups are perennially at odds with the government. Often the church is at odds with both. Historically the problems involved in the relations of groups have been treated many times; but the circumstances under which men have written have affected their writing to a great extent. On these matters there is wide difference of opinion even on the part of dedicated and intelligent Christians.

Particularly in the matter of the relations of church and state has there been diversity of viewpoint. To some it seems crystal clear that the church should be the ruler of the state and seek to bring it under the sway of the rule of God. To others it is just as clear that the church should be a department of the state, charged with responsibility for the religious welfare of its people. To still others it seems obvious that church and state must be separated and even that they are concerned with totally different things.

If, then, we are seeking to set forth attitudes consonant with historic Christianity on these matters, it seems possible to report simply diversity of opinion. However, it should be possible to say a word or two that can be derived by implication from the vision and attitudes of faith.

The multiplicity of groups itself has certain values. If each is as prone as it seems to be to arrogate to itself prerogatives which are pretentious, then it may well be checked by others. More than once the church has

THE STATE PATRONIZING THE CHURCH An empress presenting a chalice becomes the subject of a work of art which adorns the wall of a church. Panel showing Empress Theodora and members of her court. Copy of original mosaic in the Church of San Vitale, Ravenna (536-547 A.D.). (Courtesy of the Metropolitan Museum of Art, Fletcher Fund, 1925)

been kept from overstepping itself by the fact that the government prevented it from doing so. Likewise the state has been saved from totalitarianisms by reason of the restraining influence of the church. Further, the creative potentialities of each can contribute to the other. The church is interested that the minds of men be developed; hence it sustains educational programs. But it does not assume the burden of educating the entire citizenry of the country.

What distinguishes the church is that it explicitly points to a Reality which gives meaning to the life of the other groups and determines their responsibilities. It includes within itself the interests of all. Hence it is, in one sense, the inclusive group. And yet it seems to be consistent with its character that it be free, that its effect on other groupings should be by persuasion rather than coercion. However, its freedom cannot be taken to mean a relinquishment of responsibility toward the other groupings. How that responsibility shall be exercised is a matter for perpetual study and renewed decision.

Beyond all groups stands the everlasting kingdom. In its life they find their final meaning. Through it runs a river with the water of life. And along its banks grow the trees whose leaves are for the healing of the nations.[28]

READINGS

From the Bible

1. Economic injustice was a major target for the preaching of the prophet Amos.

2. A positive attitude toward the state is reflected in Romans 13, I Peter 2:17, and I Samuel 9:1-10:16.

3. A skeptical or antagonistic attitude toward the state is reflected in Revelation 1, 3, 12, 13 and in I Samuel 7:3-8:22, 10:17-27, 12.

4. The Israelites had entered into a covenant with their God whereby they were constituted into a people of his choosing. See Exodus 19, Joshua 24. The Christians thought of themselves as the people of the new covenant: Hebrews 10, I Peter, Jeremiah 31.

From Historic Christianity

1. Clement of Alexandria, *The Rich Man's Salvation.* A second century Christian confronts the problem of money.

2. Martin Luther, *Secular Authority: To What Extent Should It Be Obeyed?* The reformer here analyzes the obligations of the Christian to the political orders.

3. John Woolman, *Journal,* is the account of a nineteenth century Quaker incensed about slavery.

4. Part II of Walter Rauschenbusch's *Christianizing the Social Order* (New York: The Macmillan Company, 1909) gives a Liberal's conception of a major task of the church.

---

[28] Revelation 22:2.

FOR STUDY AND DISCUSSION

1. To what extent (if any) is the following criticism justified? The Christian church is so identified with privileged classes in our society that little leadership in economic reforms can be expected by the church.
2. Is a Christian in a communist country bound to obey the orders of his government?
3. Whites have justified their resistance to the Supreme Court decision regarding school segregation on grounds of conscience; some negroes have defended their participation in lunch counter demonstrations on grounds of conscience. What is the relation of conscience to political authority?
4. Should religion be taught in the public schools? If so, what kind?

THE EXPRESSIONS

XI

INDIVIDUAL WORSHIP

If you drop a stone into the clear waters of a New England pond on a cloudless day, ripples will radiate from a center. If you drop another stone at another point in the pond, ripples will radiate from a second center. And yet the wavelets spreading from different centers will be much alike by reason of the clean, clearness of the water, by reason of the blue of reflected sky.

The expressions of Christian faith are like ripples radiating from many centers on a broad surface. Here appears a pattern of worship, there a cathedral, somewhere else a cup of cold water given in the name of Christ. Among them all is a similarity. And, if our analysis to this point has been correct, this is true by reason of a common vision and common attitudes.

We turn now to a consideration of the expressions of Christian faith. The broad surface may be divided into a few large areas: worship, literature, and art; action, association, and thought. These again may be divided and even subdivided. The area of worship comes before us first. Of the various ways in which it could be subdivided, only one concerns us. Because man is an individual, a self-determining being, he will sometimes worship alone; because he is social, he will sometimes worship with others. Individual worship is the subject of this chapter.

1. THE CALL OF A PROPHET

The sixth chapter of Isaiah has long been regarded by Christians as a classic instance of individual worship as they understand it. In it is reflected almost every one of the elements of vision and attitude which have been described in the preceding pages. Since it is brief, it can easily be given here in full:

> In the year that King Uzziah died I saw the Lord sitting upon a throne, high and lifted up; and his train filled the temple. Above him stood the seraphim; each had six wings: with two he covered his face, and with two he covered his feet, and with two he flew. And one called to another and said:
>
> "Holy, holy, holy is the Lord of hosts;
> the whole earth is full of his glory."
>
> And the foundations of the thresholds shook at the voice of him who called, and the house was filled with smoke. And I said: "Woe is me! For I am lost; for I am a man of unclean lips, and I dwell in the midst of a people of unclean lips; for my eyes have seen the King, the Lord of hosts!"
>
> Then flew one of the seraphim to me, having in his hand a burning coal which he had taken with tongs from the altar. And he touched my mouth, and said: "Behold, this has touched your lips; your guilt is taken away, and your sin forgiven." And I heard the voice of the Lord saying, "Whom shall I send, and who will go for us?" Then I said, "Here I am! Send me." And he said, "Go, and say to this people:
>
> " 'Hear and hear, but do not understand;
> see and see, but do not perceive.'
> Make the heart of this people fat,
> and their ears heavy,
> and shut their eyes;
> lest they see with their eyes,
> and hear with their ears,
> and understand with their hearts,
> and turn and be healed."
>
> Then I said, "How long, O lord?" And he said:
>
> "Until cities lie waste
> without inhabitant,

and houses without men,
  and the land is utterly desolate,
and the Lord removes men far away,
  and the forsaken places are many
  in the midst of the land.
And though a tenth remain in it,
  it will be burned again,
like a terebinth or an oak,
  whose stump remains standing
  when it is felled."
The holy seed is its stump.

The experience begins with the Holy Lord, not with the worshipper's self-analysis. The shaking of the house, the billowing of smoke, the cries of angelic beings proclaim the awesomeness of the scene. The Lord is seen, but not described; his train simply fills the temple. The Holy one is also the Creator, and his glory is reflected in heaven and earth, in the nature which has come from his hands.

The response of the prophet is immediate: "Woe is me!" The sense of sin is upon him, and it includes the feeling of violation of the holy as well as some sort of moral guilt: "I am a man of unclean lips." The prophet's sinfulness does not isolate him, however; even in the depth of his own experience, he remembers his oneness with his people. Like him, they are people of unclean lips.

The Holy Creator is also the Redeemer. An angelic being takes coal from the altar, touches it to the prophet's lips, and declares his forgiveness. He is reconciled to God, and by an action initiated by the divine.

The Redeemer is also active in human life, and he engages the prophet in his activity. He calls Isaiah to the assumption of a vocation. Previously his holiness had overwhelmed the prophet with a sense of sin, but God does not now overwhelm him to the destruction of his humanity. He seeks and gets a free, self-determining response—"Here am I, send me."

Within the experience is also the impulse to action by the prophet toward others. God sends him to them. And he must act for their true good, for the good as God defines it for them, in spite of the fact that they will not like it. They will reject the prophet, but he must still do his work on their behalf. He will become poet and political figure, he will express that which is in him; but his main concern is not the expression. His central concern is to do the will of God which he understands to be for the true welfare of God's people.

The experience of Isaiah was particularly rich and full. Other experiences which deserve to be defined as worship are far more simple; some are very different in other ways. Before we look at them it may be helpful to try to come to some understanding of just what individual worship is.

2. THE CHARACTER OF CHRISTIAN WORSHIP

The analogy between the friendship of human beings and the relations of men with God has already come before us. Because of it, worship may be compared with certain phases of relationships involved in friendship. Let us imagine a specific situation. Two friends have been having difficulties with each other. They come together to talk things over. As they explore the meaning of their friendship, they come to a point where they declare themselves to one another as friends. Perhaps they shake hands. Then they speak of things they are going to do which are bound up with the fact of their friendship. Perhaps they go right from conversation to some common activity. Now let us imagine still another situation. This comes out of personal recollection. Many years ago, before we were divided by distance, a certain friend and I were almost inseparable. We were constantly together, sharing ideas, moods, actions. We walked and talked, we played and worked, we shared problems and joys. One summer day we had taken a long drive and spent some time at a lake. In the evening we returned. I suppose that the drive took about an hour. Afterward I realized that we had spoken scarcely a word the whole time. And yet I felt that somehow our friendship had expressed itself in a very deep and real way in the sharing of our silence.

Every human experience is complex. While it has a center, it also has peripheral aspects; and at its edges, so to speak, it merges, sometimes almost imperceptibly, into other experiences. The experience of worship is no exception, and we shall misunderstand it if we seek to regard it as more simple than it actually is. And yet it has a certain character which the illustrations from friendship may help us to describe. In the first, the actual declaration of friendship was at the center; all else moved toward this or emanated from it. Around it were circles of experience which related directly to it. The friendship relation itself was the subject of conversation; it was also directly involved in plans that were made. Just these plans, not others, were made because two people were friends. The conversation itself emerged out of many experiences in the past and eventuated in actions beyond itself. At its center were certain words, and these were important. And yet the very saying of the words was significant only within an atmosphere of personal sincerity and mutual trust. The experience of shared silence also emerged out of a wide background of experiences; without them it could not have occurred. While no words were spoken, it was exceedingly meaningful. That it issued in specific actions is doubtful; that it affected the character of many is certain.

Moments of realization of friendship, spoken or unspoken, are not the whole of the relationship. If two people are friends, that fact will affect a great deal of what they do, even when they are absent from one another. Within the total relationship, however, the moments of realization are of great significance. The analogy with worship can now be drawn. Faith is a total relationship with God, affecting the conduct of all of life. And yet it is important that there be times of realization of that relationship. In themselves these may be rather complex, but at their center will be some moment at which the relationship itself is declared, by speech or silence.

The inadequacy of the analogy of friendship is as important as its relevance. One member of the two, God and man, is the high and holy One who inhabits eternity. And this fact qualifies the entire relationship between them. It must be taken into account in every theology. It is a determinant in man's response to the world and in his treatment of his fellows. In worship it becomes central; it is felt. Hence there emerges within the worship experience the sense of awe. Some writers have spoken of it as the feeling of creatureliness.[1] It is of the essence of worship.

But it is not all. And one way of speaking of certain convictions central to Christian faith is this: the high and holy One, without diminishing his holiness in any way, enters into a relationship with his creatures which is like that of human friendship. He overcomes the separation between them which qualifies all that they think and do and say. It is important for that relationship that at times it should come to specific realization, that it be declared. Herein lies the significance of worship.

Its character, as Christians interpret it, will be determined by the nature of God and man and the character of the relationship between them.

> Because God is holy, there will be awe;
> because God is good, there will be thanksgiving;

---

[1] Rudolf Otto, *The Idea of the Holy*, p. 8.

because God is righteous, there will be confession;
because God is loving, there will be release from guilt;
because God is concerned for the person, there will be petition;
because God is concerned for all his children, there will be intercession;
because God is active, there will be resolution.

3. CREATOR AND CREATURE

To be an individual is no easy thing. It involves a willingness to take risks, to make decisions without full knowledge of circumstances, to accept the anxieties that are bound up with finitude. It is especially difficult in our time when pressures toward security and conformity are imperious and when the trends of life are in the direction of mass-mindedness. Even historic Christianity becomes a way by which men escape the path toward difficult selfhood. Its words about church and creed and Bible seem to afford comfort and stability.

And yet historic Christianity is not fully recovered if its emphasis on the individual is lost. It enshrines the stories of men who were summoned by God to the hard task of being themselves. It is aware of difficulties involved. But it points also to resources. It points out that true individuality is the correlative of community, and it asserts that the depth of individual life is its relation to God.

At this point, individual worship is of paramount importance. Central in it is the moment in which the individual says "Thou" to God; and this happens in response to the conviction that the person is addressed by God; God has said "thou" to him. Here is the moment of confrontation when men no longer think about God, or act a certain way because of his demand on their lives, or celebrate his goodness in a song. Because Christian faith makes this moment central in worship, its view differs from others which appear from time to time in the religious literature of the world. There is no merging of man into the divine; he is not lost like a droplet in the ocean of God's being. Reinhold Niebuhr quotes with approval the saying of a Christian thinker, James Denney, "I would rather be saved in Christ than lost in God." [2]

We have looked at Isaiah's account of his call. Experiences like it are described by Jeremiah and Ezekiel; like Isaiah, these prophets are profoundly convinced that at the very beginning of their work God summoned them to a task. He is the same Lord for all three, the judging

---

[2] Reinhold Niebuhr, *The Nature and Destiny of Man,* II, 113.

and redeeming God active in human history and engaging them in his work. But the experiences themselves are very different. Jeremiah's is simple conversation; the prophet does not answer the summons with alacrity. He pleads his youth and weakness. But God promises to make him like a wall and gives him a commission

> to pluck up and to break down,
> to destroy and to overthrow,
> to build and to plant.[3]

Ezekiel's call comes at the climax of an exceedingly complicated vision, the "wheels within wheels" of the familiar spiritual.[4] In no case was the individuality of the prophet dismissed, though in the case of Jeremiah it was to be changed. And in each case the character of the call was markedly different from the others. God's method of calling the prophet was suited to the prophet's character; his individuality was respected and utilized.

All three speak of their call as a turning point in their lives. After it they were different persons from those they had been before. Though they did not use the terms, we seem justified in saying that the call was a creative act of God. And their response to it was their participation in their own creation. The divine and the human are interrelated. The worship experience was the central point of a self-definition with respect to their lives and their work. In the case of Jeremiah, at least, it was at the same time a redefinition. Here we have come to a central significance of private worship as we look at it against the background of Christian vision and attitude. It is a focal point for an act in which God creates and man participates in his own creation. If man is to become an individual, he must define himself; and worship is the point at which self-definition occurs in confrontation with God.

This does not mean that man seeks through a worship experience to evade the hard duty of serious thought and earnest searching. Worship is no substitute for aptitude tests, the help of counsellors and friends. It makes it possible for these to be more, rather than less, helpful. For in worship man confronts that Reality before whom there can be no pretenses, by whom he is loved no matter what his weaknesses may be. If he can enter fully into its spirit, he will be delivered from self-delusions, willing to accept himself and do that which is within him to do.

---

[3] Jeremiah 1:10.
[4] Ezekiel 1 and 2.

Self-definition does not take place within a vacuum, however. A man is what he is in relation to things around him. And here again worship as seen from the perspective of Christian faith will appear differently from worship viewed in some other ways. For the Christian, worship is not the experience of the reality of God in contrast to the unreality of the world. The world itself is real, and it is good. But here is a problem, for the world does not appear good sometimes. And yet, as in the case of the person, it is possible that within worship a redefinition occurs. That in the world which seemed bad can be overcome. Paul tells us of a thorn in the flesh which was sent to buffet him. Three times, he says, he prayed that it might be removed. The answer came, "My grace is sufficient for thee: for my strength is made perfect in weakness." [5] Thus that which had seemed inimical was turned to Paul's benefit. A world may be redefined in worship so that it becomes—for us—what it was not before, God's creation.

Self-definition involves man's relation to people as well as things. The prophet was aware of a sinfulness which he shared with his people, and he was called to serve them. Here again a Christian view of worship is at odds with some others. No "flight of the alone to the Alone" [6] is sufficient. Right relations with one's fellows is, indeed, a prerequisite to proper worship. "If you are offering your gift at the altar," said Jesus, "and there remember that your brother has something against you, leave your gift there before the altar and go; first be reconciled to your brother, and then come and offer your gift." [7] The counsel was applied to participation in communion services in the early church. Prayer on behalf of others has also historically formed a part of private worship. The modern may well find himself in difficulties with some views of the efficacy of such prayer; but he will scarcely quarrel with the notion that intercessory prayer means, at the very least, the honest expression of concern for others before God. And it cannot be restricted to prayer for friends and family either. It must include even those who despitefully use one. When prayed for, they cease to be enemies; they are redefined as God's creatures, standing in need of his redemptive concern.

Worship, then, can be God's creative act in which men participate by defining and redefining themselves, their fellows, and their world. In it they will probably redefine God too.

---

[5] II Corinthians 12:9, K.J.V.

[6] Plotinus, "Enneads," VI, 10, *The Essence of Plotinus,* based on the translation by Stephen McKenna, compiled by Grace H. Turnbull (New York: Oxford University Press, Inc., 1934), p. 222.

[7] Matthew 5:23f.

4. TYPES OF WORSHIP EXPERIENCE

Experiences of worship differ with individuals. They also differ with the same individual at different times. We do not step into the same river twice, as the ancient philosopher pointed out, because it is not the same river.[8] Nor are we the same person. Christian faith has always assumed that private devotion was part of the continuing life. From earliest times we have indications that Christians were expected to pray every day. Jesus assumed personal prayer as a part of life, and he spoke the memorable words: "When you pray, go into your room and shut the door and pray to your Father who is in secret; and your Father who sees in secret will reward you." [9] Indeed, private prayer and meditation seem well-nigh universal in religion.

The experience of the call, which we have examined in the writings of the prophets, is simply a rather crucial experience of self-examination involving a major life decision. That it should take the form of worship at a central point is natural. Other major decisions may take on much of the same quality, for they, too, involve definition of ourselves, our fellows, and our world. The gospels, especially that of Luke, speak often of the importance of prayer in the life of Jesus. It is noteworthy that he spent much time in prayer at times of special decisiveness in his career. Thus, before the choice of those who were to be his special companions—the twelve—he is described as spending an entire night in prayer.[10] In a similar manner, the decision about a job, marriage, an important move may well be accompanied by an act of worship.

There may also be worship experiences of rather more than ordinary significance in the life of the person from time to time because of the development of his own life. He and his world are different when he is a youth of seventeen, a young husband and father at thirty-seven, and a man approaching retirement at fifty-seven. The meaning of faith will also be different.

Moods of worship will also accompany experiences of unusual sorts. The grandeur of a scene in nature may move a person to wonder and praise. Thus in the twenty-ninth Psalm we have the reflections of a man who has seen in the passing of a storm a witness to the greatness and power of God. Some act of undeserved kindness at the hands of others

---

[8] Heraclitus, "Fragments," Milton C. Nahm, ed., *Selections from Early Greek Philosophers* (New York: F. S. Crofts & Co., 1940), p. 93.

[9] Matthew 6:6.

[10] Luke 6:12-16.

may move him to thanksgiving. On the other hand, some deep disappointment may drive him to serious consideration of the question about the meaning of his own life, to the question about the locus of his ultimate trust; here, too, some expression of worship may be evoked. In and with his God he seeks to come to some resolution of his problem.

A particularly vivid experience of confrontation with God is likely to be the focal point—so far as awareness is concerned—of a radical life transformation. One may have a sense of being under the judgment of God, unable to secure his own release from actions rooted in the kind of person he is. This will be followed by an assurance of God's favor, coming in one way or another, and the release which accompanies response to it. The literature of Christianity is full of instances of such conversions. Afterward everything seems changed. The apostle Paul wrote of his own experience as one in which God revealed his Son in him; what things he had regarded as gain became refuse.[11] Life had a new focal center.

But the greatest number of worship experiences are less spectacular than these. Christian life involves a discipline, and acts of personal devotion have an important part in it. There is need for constant renewal of one's trust in God and of the life that belongs to it. Every day is different from the preceding, even though no revolutionary changes have been made. The flesh has to be conquered again and again; the Spirit of God must find ever renewed response in the spirit of man.

Sometimes individual worship is a moment interrupting an experience of another kind. A friend of mine who is a scientist told me of a moment of ecstasy which came near the completion of a long and complicated experiment. In the most humdrum circumstance of life there may emerge a reason for simple expression of gratitude to God. In a church service, when people are bound to one another in common worship, there may come a moment when the individual retires into his solitariness.

Children are intrigued by the fact that no two leaves are alike. People are even more different from each other than leaves, and if their personal worship is to be sincerely reflexive of their individualities, it will vary from one to another in an infinite number of ways.

5. REDEEMER AND REDEEMED

In some of the experiences that have been noted emphasis falls on the relation of the Creator to the creature. In others, it falls in another

[11] Galatians 1:6, following the Greek; Philippians 3:8.

place, upon the relation of the Redeemer to the redeemed. The two are not separated in human experience. In the call of Isaiah which made him a prophet he describes his own profound awareness of sin and the act by which God declared his forgiveness. And yet there are some experiences of worship in which the one or the other becomes central.

The early Christians were convinced that in disclosing his redeeming love God had made it possible for them to enter into a newer and richer life of private devotion than they had previously known. Thus, Paul speaks of the opening of a way by which the Christian can use, in his address of God, the intimate word, "Abba"—my Father.[12] This is possible because of God's action. Thus the establishing of the relation of Redeemer to redeemed is parallel to the action by which the Creator-creature relation is brought about. There is a divine action in which the human being participates. Individual worship, which is a realization of God as redeemer and man as redeemed, is a divine action in which a human action participates.

This action is no easy thing. Early Christians believed that the cross showed the length to which God would go in his love to reconcile man to himself—and the extreme was necessary because of the obstacles which stood in his way. Making his love effective in the lives of men, however, meant overcoming further obstacles. The New Testament writers were convinced that there was an action of God in the lives of men which continued his act in the cross. Sometimes they spoke of it as the Divine Spirit working in the human spirit. In the passage which has been noted in the writing of Paul he says, "When we cry, 'Abba! Father!' it is the Spirit himself bearing witness with our spirit that we are children of God."[13] The difficulty encountered by the Spirit is recognized in the same context: "We do not know how to pray as we ought, but the Spirit himself intercedes for us with sighs too deep for words."[14] If it is difficult to be an individual, to realize in worship the relationship of creature to Creator; it is also difficult to realize the relationship of redeemed to Redeemer.

The significance of worship in the realization is that, in it, the human being says "Thou" to God the redeemer. And he recognizes that he can do so only because of God's action toward him. In some of the Psalms we are permitted to overhear the penitent addressing his forgiving Lord. The thirty-second and the fifty-first are of special interest, and ought

---

[12] Romans 8:15, Galatians 4:6.

[13] Romans 8:15f.

[14] Romans 8:26. The concluding words in the K.J.V. read: "with groanings which cannot be uttered."

to be read in their entirety. A few verses from the latter, however, give us a clue to their content.

> Have mercy on me, O God,
> according to thy steadfast love;
> according to thy abundant mercy
> blot out my transgressions.
>
> Against thee, thee only, have I sinned,
> and done that which is evil in thy sight.
>
> Purge me with hyssop, and I shall be clean;
> wash me, and I shall be whiter than snow.[15]

In the very presence of God the Psalmist defines himself as a sinner and is redefined as a forgiven man.

Sensitivity to the seriousness of sin has meant that the notion of God as forgiving Father has a central place in the religious consciousness of Christians. They are apt to be dissatisfied with "worship, for the most part silent, at the altar of the Unknown." [16] Even a Power "not ourselves which makes for righteousness" [17] is not adequate for their devotion. It is certainly proper that a walk in the woods amid the glories of springtime should arouse the spirit to grateful wonder, but to find in this the summit of worship is to lose sight of the reaches of religious experience. A God who is not personally encountered is not a God against whom one sins or by whom one is forgiven. In Christ, Christians are convinced, they have met God as their forgiving Lord; hence, they frequently offer their prayers in his name or for his sake. Indeed, sometimes they address their prayers directly to him or to the Spirit. They also may introduce into their worship patterns reminders of God's forgiving love. Some symbol, like the cross, may help them to focus attention on it, or the reading of passages from the Bible may bring it to their remembrance.

Acknowledgment of sin is obviously appropriate in acts of private worship. It follows upon, it does not precede, awareness of God's love. As we have noted, it is only the assurance of the absoluteness of God's

---

[15] Psalms 51:1, 4, 7.

[16] Thomas H. Huxley, "On the Advisableness of Improving Natural Knowledge," Alburey Castell, ed., *Selections from the Essays of Thomas Henry Huxley* (New York: Appleton-Century-Crofts, Inc., 1948), p. 13.

[17] Matthew Arnold, *Literature and Dogma* (New York: A. L. Burt Company, n.d.), p. 75. In this phrase Arnold, the nineteenth century Christian liberal, reflects the focusing of attention on morality which we have noted as typical of his time: see chapter I.

mercy that makes it possible for man to endure the realization of his own guilt. "Forgive us our debts" and "lead us not into temptation"[18] have their place in every Christian's prayer. It is proper that he should think of specific sins and give thought to ways in which he can avoid their repetition. At the same time, it is important that dwelling on sin should not become morbid. Such a spirit expresses a lack of trust in God's forgiveness and may be an evidence of misplaced pride.[19] It is even possible for a worship act to become a sort of technique by which the self seeks to overcome its own guilt. In the end, it is self-defeating, however, for we are able to forgive ourselves truly only when we are forgiven by God. Worship begins and ends with his love.

Repudiation of the notion that prayer may be a means by which a person deals with his own guilt is only one part of a conviction that is connected with Christians' awareness of the seriousness of sin: worship itself may be perverted.

One of the commonest perversions is that which regards worship as a technique by which man manipulates the Divine. Prayer then becomes a means by which man secures from God that which his own heart desires. He wants rain to fall, sickness to be healed, football games to be won; so he prays. Now it is important to remember that Christian faith never sanctions the denial of the creature's individuality. That he should have desires is natural. Indeed, again and again Jesus bids his disciples to pray. And yet at the same time he speaks of the need for their desires to be transformed. He also reminds them: "Your Father knows what you need before you ask him."[20] And the gospels describe him in the garden of Gethsemane, praying that a cup of suffering might be taken from him, and yet willing to accept the will of the Father as his own.[21] Honest expressions of one's deep desires is important to prayer, but it must be accompanied by willingness to have one's desires changed. Here, as always, it is important to remember that prayer is a divine-human action in which there is a dual participation.

Worship can become sinful also when it is confrontation with false gods instead of the true One. Christians are repeatedly reminded that the deities of family and race and nation did not lose their power when the ancient baals were destroyed. Much that is called prayer is purely partisan. Indeed, the gospels tell us that the temptation to bow before

---

[18] Matthew 6:12f.

[19] See the perceptive treatment in Donald M. Baillie, *God Was in Christ* (New York: Charles Scribner's Sons, 1948), pp. 160-171.

[20] Matthew 6:8.

[21] Matthew 26:39.

the prince of evil was real for the Christ.[22] Our childhood pictures have obscured for us part of what is intended by the temptation story. They depict a devil with recognizable horns and a scarcely concealed tail. But such a figure would not have offered true temptation. Jesus was confronted by one who quoted to him the sacred scripture of his people. It was only after struggle that he put the false god out of the way so that he could receive the comfort of the true One.

Worship becomes sinful, too, when a man uses it to evade his total responsibility to God. He tries, by saying the words, to convince himself that he is doing the deeds. Against such false worship the entire prophetic movement in ancient Israel was set, and Jesus quoted with approval one of its greatest exemplars: "Well did Isaiah prophesy . . . 'This people honors me with their lips, but their heart is far from me.'"[23] And lest men think too highly of prayer as such, they may be reminded that of no one did the Christ speak in words of more withering scorn than of him who went up into the temple to pray and began with the words, "God, I thank thee that I am not like other men."[24]

The tendency for worship to usurp the place of total commitment to God is not difficult to understand. And many of those in our time who are concerned for a recovery of historic Christianity are convinced that it has been a marked characteristic of the past few centuries. There has been a tremendous emphasis on individual religious experience among Christians. Those of a conservative orientation have emphasized the need for a conversion experience of a rather dramatic sort, and sometimes of other subsequent experiences, second blessings. Preaching has been such as to evoke emotional response; indeed, the entire service of worship has had a strongly emotive tone. Groups for informal prayer and Bible reading have been drawn together. On the other hand, some Christians of a more liberal orientation have also stressed religious experience. For them, religion is "morality touched by emotion."[25] Worship is so conducted as to produce aesthetic response.

Against the emphasis on experience there has been a pronounced reaction among contemporary theologians who have been concerned to recover historic Christianity. Many have stressed the objective elements in Christian tradition. They feel that the emphasis on religious experience permitted a neglect of theological thought which could give significant

---

[22] Matthew 4:1-11.

[23] Matthew 15:7f.

[24] Luke 18:11.

[25] Matthew Arnold, *Literature and Dogma,* p. 48. Here Arnold, the great phrasemaker, joins two concerns typical of liberal faith.

guidance for Christian thinking in a time like our own. It also diverted attention from issues which called for ethical and social response on the part of Christians. And the emphasis on the individual led people to a disregard of the supporting matrix of the church about his life.

Perhaps, at times, the pendulum of reaction has swung too far. Historic Christianity has found an important place for individual religious experience. But it has viewed it within the context of a total faith. And it has seen that if it is rightly viewed, there are important lines running from it to all the expressions of Christian faith.

READINGS

From the Bible

1. Conversations between God and man in which each maintains his individuality are described in Genesis 18 and Jeremiah 14.

2. Many Psalms reveal a succession of moods in converse with God.

3. The book of Jeremiah reveals a lonely and sensitive person, who freely pours out his soul to God, but who never forgets his relation to his people. For example, chapters 4, 5, 9.

4. The temptations of Jesus reveal much about the nature of private worship: Matthew 4, Luke 4:1-13.

5. References to prayer are frequent in the teachings of Jesus; see Luke 11:1-13; 18:1-14.

From Historic Christianity

1. Thomas a Kempis, *The Imitation of Christ,* is one of the most universally loved among the many classics of Christian devotion. Many others could be mentioned.

2. Saint John of the Cross, *The Dark Night of the Soul,* describes the mystic's journey into the Divine Light.

3. Friedrich D. E. Schleiermacher, *On Religion, Speeches to its Cultured Despisers,* is an effort to derive all of religion from its central

feeling or intuition. Speech two is on the nature of religion, and speech five is on the specific religions.

4. John Calvin, *Institutes,* III, xx, is a treatment of prayer from the viewpoint of its author's biblicism.

FOR STUDY AND DISCUSSION

1. How can some order be brought into the devotional life without turning it into an effort to manipulate the Divine?
2. What use can be made of the Bible in private devotion?
3. What use can be made of poetry in the life of devotion? By what criteria do you choose appropriate poetry? What contemporary poetry might be used?
4. Is music a help or a hindrance to private devotion?
5. Study some pictures, traditional and contemporary, with a view to judging their possible help or hindrance to private devotion.

XII

CHURCH WORSHIP

If two Christians meet on Sunday morning and one says to the other, "I am going to church," the other may answer, "So am I." Each assumes that the other is on his way to a service of worship. This is not because worship is the one focal point from which all that happens in the church radiates. It is rather because it is the focal point that is characteristic of the church. Other groups have business meetings and educational programs. But the church alone—or its equivalent in some other faith—is the group which makes its relation to the divine explicit at all times; and in its worship it expresses that relationship purposely and directly. As it is natural, from a Christian point of view, that man as an individual should worship, it is also natural that he should join with others in a church and that his church should have common worship.

The two men may be going to very different churches. One may be on his way to a service with set and stately ritual, the other to a service conducted with utmost freedom. It is no easy thing in our time to say of any form of worship, this is the Christian way. And when we seek to do some justice to the variety that has characterized Christian worship through the centuries, we are faced with formidable difficulties. It may be possible, however, to see that some of the patterns of worship which have persisted within the church have been such as to give appropriate expression to the Christian vision and attitudes.

1. THE CHURCH WORSHIPS

No classic description of the church at worship can be taken from the Bible and set beside the solitary experience of Isaiah. And yet, many Christians have experienced in corporate worship those moods which are reflected in the experience of the prophet. They have become aware of a holy Reality to whom they have responded first in adoration and praise, then in contrition and confession of sin. They have heard a word from the Eternal declaring them cleansed and so have come anew to wholeness. Ready for a second word calling them to dedication and action, they have heard it, too, and have gone out from the service with new resolution and courage.

Even the consciousness of oneness with others which is essential to the worship of the church is present in the experience of Isaiah. His is no solitary flight of the soul to God. When he becomes aware of his sin in the presence of the divine holiness, he cries out, "I am a man of unclean lips, and I dwell in the midst of a people of unclean lips." [1] And when he receives a call from God, it is to go and speak the word of the Lord to them. Often Christians of our time, sitting in the midst of a congregation, fail to feel their oneness with their fellows as the prophet did when he was all by himself. The emphasis on the individual which has been an important aspect of the past few centuries has reflected itself in significant ways in Christian worship. Many have come to expect experiences of a highly individualistic sort from corporate worship; and when these have not been forthcoming, they have been disappointed. Such experiences may take place; there may be in the midst of a service of corporate worship a moment in which the person is drawn into solitary communion with his Lord. But unless the person has come to feel his corporateness with the fellowship of believers in the act of worship, he has missed something essential. Sometimes there will come moments when the communion of the worshippers with one another will be a felt reality, almost tangible in its character. Then will come that point in the worship of the group which is analogous to the confrontation of the individual with God: the worshippers will say "Thou" to God, and "we" of themselves. The people will become a church.

This comes about by no human action or engineering. It may be

[1] Isaiah 6:5.

earnestly sought, but it cannot be secured. Like the worship of the individual, that of the church is a divine-human action in which men can act because God acts. The church is no thing which simply exists. It is ever being created by the Spirit. And it participates in its own creation through its worship.

The very order in which the several moods follow one another in the experience of the prophet is natural; and it has reflected itself often in the worship patterns of the church. Adoration has been followed by confession and then by the effort to seek some guidance and incentive for significant living. And yet the pattern has not always been such; indeed, it is important to note that there have persisted throughout Christian history two currents of attitude toward the patterning of worship. Both are already present in the New Testament itself. There are scathing words about the manner in which people who follow all the correct forms depart from the spirit of devotion and the doing of God's will. "This people honors me with their lips, but their heart is far from me." [2] On the other hand are the strong strictures of Paul against the babel and confusion of worship as it was being carried on in Corinth. If an outsider were to come to the church, the apostle remarks, he could think he was in a madhouse. "Let all things," he advises, "be done decently and in order." [3] The two currents of attitude have their parallels in all of Christian life and thought. On the one hand, it must be acknowledged that God is the free and sovereign Lord and he is bound by no forms or patterns. He can communicate with man under any conditions; his word is "not bound." [4] On the other hand, it should be seen that there are places where we might more likely expect him to speak than in others. There are disciplines which the church like the individual accepts because "God is not a God of confusion but of peace." [5] From New Testament times certain types of services have persisted up until the present. The order in which the various elements have appeared has, of course, varied from time to time and from group to group, and still does. And yet there are some basic similarities of practice even where the externals at first seem to differ to a very marked degree.

One type of service which has had a constant history throughout the life of the church is that which includes preaching. We hear of it in the New Testament and in the earliest Christian literature. Even in the second century it included the main elements which are common today.

---

[2] Matthew 15:8.
[3] I Corinthians 14:40, K.J.V.
[4] II Timothy 2:9, K.J.V.
[5] I Corinthians 14:33.

It has generally comprised acts of praise, such as hymns or psalms; readings from the Scriptures; prayers voicing adoration, confession, intercession, and petition; and preaching.

Common, too, among Christians have been services which include all or most of these elements but omit preaching. The richest sources of such acts of worship in the church have been the monasteries, with their disciplines of devotion for the various hours of the day. Even outside of them, however, there have usually been churches where certain periods of the day are signalized by appropriate acts of worship. No visitor to Cambridge in England should fail to go to Evensong at King's College Chapel. There in the midst of architectural beauty he will hear the soaring voices of men and boys joining in the responses, and he will listen also to lessons from the Old and New Testaments read according to an order which relates each service to those before and after it. Churches which on principle reject the use of prescribed prayers also have their acts of worship in which hymns are sung, the scriptures are read, and the people join in prayer.

Almost universal among Christians is the observance of the Lord's supper. It goes back, of course, to the very times of beginnings, the very time of the Christ. Early in its history a pattern developed which formed the nucleus of that which is used in many churches to this day. It came to include acts of praise and contrition, readings from the Scriptures, the saying of a creed, the offering of the elements, and prayers of petition and intercession. It reached its climax in a great prayer which included the words of Jesus and called for the Spirit to come upon the elements that they might feed the spirits of the worshipers; then came the actual receiving of the bread and wine by the ministers and congregation. Some churches have explicitly broken with this tradition and have sought to come to a more literal repetition of the actual supper itself as it is described in the New Testament. The New Testament account is simply read; the church may read its covenant as a reminder of the obligations it has promised to keep; prayers—often extemporaneous—are offered over the bread and the wine which are then given to the people. As Christians have not celebrated the supper alike, they have not understood it alike. It has been a center of controversy among them. In some ways this has been very unfortunate; and yet it points to the fact that the celebration has been so meaningful that people have been thrown into conflict by their very attachment to it. So it is that people have differed in their interpretations of what their remembrance meant, but they have recalled with deep feeling that in the night in which he was betrayed their Lord took bread and broke it.

EARLY CHRISTIAN WORSHIP A second century Christian depicts the Lord's Supper on the wall of a catacomb. *The Eucharist.* Catacomb of Priscilla, Rome (Alinari-Anderson Photo)

On still another act of worship that has persisted through the centuries Christians have been divided, sometimes fiercely. From earliest times baptism has been associated with entrance into the church. But whether those baptized should be adults or infants, whether they should be immersed, have water poured on them, or be sprinkled—these and their significance have been matters over which Christians have quarreled. For all that, they have remembered the simple pictures presented in the gospels: Jesus receiving baptism at the hands of John, the risen Christ commanding his disciples to go and teach all nations, "baptizing them in the name of the Father and of the Son and of the Holy Spirit." [6]

Along with these services have gone certain others which have persisted because of the continuities of human experience, of the need to solemnize the special moments of life. Thus, throughout Christendom there have been wedding ceremonies, services of ordination, funeral rites. And there have also been services which have been especially treasured by certain Christian groups.

Gradually there developed within the early church a pattern connecting worship observances which recurred annually. Many groups

[6] Matthew 28:19.

continue to find meaning in it, while others who reject it in principle actually observe much of it in practice. The Christian year—as it has come to be known—begins with Advent, a period of preparation looking toward the coming of the Christ. Then comes the great celebration of that coming, the Christmas season. This ends at Epiphany, after the familiar twelve days, commemorating the coming of the wise men to Bethlehem and signifying the manifestation of the Christ to the nations—the missionary outreach of the church. Ash Wednesday introduces a season of penitence and self-discipline, Lent, which is preparation for the solemn events at the close of Jesus' life. The remembrance of his last week begins with the pageantry of Palm Sunday and moves toward the gloom of Maundy Thursday, when he last broke bread with his disciples, and Good Friday, when he was put to death. Then comes the great Easter Festival, the center from which the whole year developed. Fifty days after Easter marks the coming of the Spirit, the birthday of the Christian Church. This is followed by Trinity Season, signifying the full disclosure of "God in three Persons," which lasts until, with Advent, the year begins again.

Throughout the centuries the greatest variety of worship has been found in the Christian churches; this is due, in part, to convictions of the Christian people regarding the freedom of God. Both the variety and the uniformities are rooted in the Christian vision and attitudes. To them and their specific expression in worship we now turn.

2. CELEBRATION

It has become a rather bitter joke among ministers that they see many of their parishioners at the Easter service and only then. There is, of course, sound reason for choosing this as the day to go to church if one does miss all other services; for Easter is the celebration of the central point in the drama of redemption. As we have seen, the Christian year developed, backward and forward, from Easter. And yet Easter itself was not observed as an annual celebration in the earliest churches; it grew out of the Sunday service. For the earliest Christians every Sunday was Easter, the "first day of the week" on which the Christ arose victorious over sin, death, and the devil. It was their analog to the Jewish Sabbath, the seventh day of the week which had long been set aside for rest and worship.

It is appropriate that on the first day of the week Christians should celebrate the central redemptive act of God, and in a sense all worship radiates from this center. The full range of Christian worship may be viewed as the celebration of all the acts of God in redemption and in creation. Here it has something in common with worship as part of the general religious life of mankind. Whatever else worship is, in all cultures, it seems to include celebration. This is a point at which corporate worship is needed to complement private devotion. Even a bit of good news will send a man scurrying to his friends with the word, "This calls for a celebration." There is something about joy of any kind that calls us to company with others and to some sort of overt expression of response to it.

In a sense the church celebrates its own existence, as the creature of God's redemptive action. Indeed, the New Testament reflects the consciousness of the early Christians that they were a colony of heaven, the people of a new era in human history; and this consciousness called for joyous expression. The pictures of heavenly adoration in the Book of the Revelation may well be taken as reflecting worship acts of the early Christians who thought of earthly praise as the anticipation of heavenly. Living creatures, elders, and thousands upon thousands sing praises to the Lamb and the Ancient of Days:

> Worthy art thou, our Lord and God,
> to receive glory and honor and power,
> for thou didst create all things,
> and by thy will they existed and were created.[7]

The fact that worship can be conceived as the celebration of the existence of the church, however, constitutes a temptation: the church may glorify its own acts rather than those of God. As the individual can sin in worship, so can the church. In ways that are often very subtle, worship may serve to encourage in the church a false sense of its own righteousness, of the finality of its doctrines, of the perfection of its ritual observances. The very emotional coloration which is given to all things through the celebration that occurs may serve to obscure the truth that the finite can never pretend to be infinite. Only when the church looks to the Spirit which ever creates it can its worship be true to itself and its Maker.

The celebration of God's acts of creation and redemption is an element in almost all of the worship services of Christian churches. It finds

[7] Revelation 4:11ff.

particularly congenial expression in congregational and choral singing. Here the primitive church entered into a rich heritage from Judaism. In the book of Psalms was already at hand a collection of poems which invited men to "come and see what God has done." [8] There were recounted his mighty acts in the making of the world and in the life of Israel. To these the Christians eventually added poems of their own, the hymns of the Christian people. Spoken words have also been uttered in the spirit of celebration. It is not strange that from the very early centuries of the Christian church until the time in which we live, ministers and congregations have said to one another:

> Lift up your hearts!
> *We lift them up unto the Lord!* [9]

and

> Praise ye the Lord!
> *The Lord's Name be praised.*[10]

3. CONTRITION

The mood of celebration is not the only one which is appropriate to the disclosure of God's redemptive love. For that love is known also as holy, and before it man is aware of his own creatureliness and rebelliousness. And as the prophet cries out, "Woe is me! for my eyes have seen the King, the Lord of hosts!" so do his fellows cry, "We are a people of unclean lips." [11]

The divine disclosure comes first, and the patterns of Christian worship have most generally sought to provide the opportunity for it to occur. Services often begin with declarations of the call of God to men to worship him and with hymns that set forth the majesty of the high and holy One. These are followed in many patterns of worship by specific acts of confession and contrition. In their fullness these acts begin with the declaration of the divine mercy, offered freely to the person who is penitent. Only when man knows that God has turned toward him will he turn from sin. Thus the longer form of invitation to confession in *The Book of Common Prayer* [12] is full of assurances of the divine

[8] Psalms 66:5.
[9] *The Book of Common Prayer,* p. 76.
[10] *Ibid.,* p. 25.
[11] See Isaiah 6:5.
[12] *The Book of Common Prayer,* p. 5.

grace which comes to meet the person who is called to repent. Then follows the act of confession itself. It is important to note that this uses the pronoun *We*. This is no confession of private sins; it is the public confession of the gathered congregation. After it is a second assurance of grace, a word from God in which the people hear their own forgiveness declared. The basis on which this word is spoken may differ in different groups by reason of variant interpretations of the locus of the authority to forgive sins. Thus those Christians who make the Scriptures central will be helped by "comfortable words" [13] from them, while others who give special powers to the clergy have an assurance by reason of the declaration itself made by the minister. The whole act begins and ends with God's forgiving love. The reading of the Scripture and the preaching of the gospel are also to be seen as ways by which the divine word of forgiveness and reconciliation is offered to sinful man.

The service of baptism, which is almost universally connected with entrance into the church, also emphasizes the mighty act of God overcoming man's utter incapacity to fight successfully against sin and death. Those who baptize adults by immersion emphasize this in their very symbolism. For them the words of Paul have special significance:

> We were buried therefore with him by baptism into death, so that as Christ was raised from the dead by the glory of the Father, we too might walk in newness of life.[14]

Those who baptize infants tend to compare and contrast the ceremony with physical birth. It effects, or at least symbolizes, that the child is born into the household of faith which is the creation of the Spirit of God.

The observance of the Lord's supper also calls attention to men's humble response to God's redemptive acts. The simple service of non-liturgical churches is an occasion of solemnity and deep seriousness. With the reading of the words of Jesus the people are reminded of the body and blood which were given, of the fact that when they eat the bread and drink the wine, they show forth the Lord's death till he come. In services which reflect a tradition which arose soon after New Testament times there is a complex of moods which follow upon one another. There are alternations of joy at the wonder of God's love and sorrow at the thought of the sufferings and death of the Christ. The spirit of the people is movingly expressed in the prayer which in some orders precedes their partaking of the elements:

---

[13] *Ibid.*, p. 76.
[14] Romans 6:4.

> We do not presume to come to this thy Table, O merciful Lord, trusting in our own righteousness, but in thy manifold and great mercies. We are not worthy so much as to gather up the crumbs under thy Table. But thou art the same Lord, whose property is always to have mercy.[15]

In every service of worship which is taken seriously by those who participate in it, there is a sense of need for an act of God by which he will create his church anew. This alternates with a happy response to the greatness and goodness of God revealed in his works in nature and history. The two moods are both present in the progression of the Christian year. The joy of Christmas is preceded by Advent, the joy of Easter by the seriousness of Lent and Good Friday. God's disclosure of himself brings praise and contrition; neither is complete without the other.

4. CLARIFICATION

The church which says "Thou" to God should have some sense of what it means when it says "we" of itself. And this sense is part of what it seeks in its worship. It is natural that it should try to find it after it has been assured of the forgiveness of sins. The prophet was prepared for his own self-definition by the searing of his lips. And the church may be prepared to recognize what it is created to be after it has become aware of the depth of redemptive love. Hence there is a certain reasonableness in an ordering of worship which places acts of self-definition by the church after acts of adoration and contrition.

Definition, of course, is an intellectual process, and there has been an intellectual element present in Christian worship throughout the centuries. This is not to deny moods of awe in the presence of impenetrable mysteries, nor is it to minimize the place of emotion in the experience of worship. It is rather to say that along with awe must go mental awareness, and along with mystery must go meaning. Already in New Testament times there were those who were so entranced by emotional moods that they tended to disregard rationality altogether. For them the speaking with tongues was the highest form of spiritual expression. Paul speaks very plainly to them. He remarks that even flutes or harps must give off sounds that are distinct, and that a trumpet call must be clear if it is to summon men to battle.

---

[15] *The Book of Common Prayer*, p. 82.

> What am I to do? [he asks] I will pray with the spirit and I will pray with the mind also; I will sing with the spirit, and I will sing with the mind also.[16]

Intellectual elements permeate services of worship. A sensitive reading of the liturgies of almost any church will reveal a great deal that is loaded with theological significance. The words of hymns also are capable of carrying important meanings. There are, however, certain elements in many services of worship in which the intellectual element comes to the fore. Some churches include the saying of a creed in all or most of their services, and others read a church covenant from time to time. In this way they define themselves in terms of what they believe. The reading of the scriptures speaks to the mind as well as being a proclamation of the forgiving love of God. And, of course, preaching is intended to address the reason as well as the feelings, and will. Indeed, preaching might be interpreted as the attempt to define for the church what it is at the present moment in the light of the Christian revelation.

Even in services where preaching is not included definition is important. One of the most insistent emphases of the reformers was that the Lord's supper should be accompanied by words which made clear what was taking place; indeed, they made the service available to the people in the vernacular because they believed that word and sacrament were not to be separated. And while the Roman Catholic church has largely continued to use the Latin language in the service of the Mass, it has been zealous in educating its people concerning the meaning of the action which takes place.

The intellectual element brings to a focus one of the most difficult problems related to Christian worship. If a service is a divine-human action, how does the Divine address the mind of the worshipper? Christian faith speaks of a word of God, but there is no audible voice from the other side. The scriptures which are read were written by men, and the sermon which is preached is delivered by a man. How, then, can God be said to speak? The problem is no easy one, and every preacher who takes seriously what he is seeking to do is disturbed by it. Here again, however, we have an instance of a work of God which accompanies a self-determining act of man. Christians have believed that in, through, and sometimes in spite of, the words read and preached, the holy God who is the free Lord of all things can make his own voice heard. "My word . . . shall not return unto me void, but it shall accomplish that which I please." [17]

---

[16] I Corinthians 14:15 and see whole passage.
[17] Isaiah 55:11, K.J.V.

The word which was voiced by the prophets, which became flesh in Jesus Christ, can be heard in the worship of the church.

5. RESPONSE

Throughout the experience of Isaiah runs a series of responses: "I am a man of unclean lips"—"Here am I; send me." [18] Likewise throughout the experience of worship in the church come occasions for response. The people join in the singing of hymns, they read portions of scripture, they read prayers, they say *amens.* Even when they simply listen, they are called upon to respond. Indeed, preaching is never simply the delivery of ideas whose truth does not really matter to the congregation. It evokes decision. The congregation participates in the service from beginning to end; else it is not truly a divine-human action.

It is important to see, however, that the people are called upon to respond; the initiative comes from the side of the Divine. Worship conceived as a manipulation of God, by which he is forced to accede to the will of the worshippers, is out of character with the Christian faith. And their response is social. Made into a company by the Spirit, they say common prayers and sing common hymns.

Some elements in worship are primarily responsive in character. Thus the prayers that are spoken—or unspoken, for that matter—are human responses to a divine invitation. Because God loves man, he calls men to open themselves to his love by prayer; thus can he give them that which he knows they need even before they ask him. Because God loves the whole family of mankind, he calls upon men to pray for others, to make intercessions for all men,[19] thus opening their own spirits to the extensiveness of his redemptive concerns. Prayers of petition and intercession are natural parts of public worship. Usually periods of prayer are so placed in services that their responsive character is clear. Frequently they follow readings from the scriptures in which God's word to the worshippers is spoken. Some groups place the prayer of the church after the sermon itself, thus emphasizing its character of response to the word which has been both read and preached.

There are other ways also in which people express themselves responsively in services of worship. From earliest times it has been customary among Christians to give money or other gifts for the support of the church and the extension of its ministry as well as for the relief of the

---

[18] Isaiah 6:5, 8, K.J.V.

[19] See I Timothy 2:1.

poor. People are baptized, they eat bread and drink wine, they kneel or they stand in reverence. They participate in acts of dedication or make public declaration of their faith.

Part of the response must be carried outside the house of worship, or the service is empty. Beside the sin of private worship, which becomes an evasion of total responsibility to God, is the similar sin of public worship: "This people honors me with their lips," says the Lord, "but their heart is far from me. In vain do they worship me." [20] The temptation to make loving words substitute for loving acts has haunted the Christian church. It is true, too, that some of the love of God to which men respond must be sought outside worship; it must be discovered in the fellowship of the church, in the place of private prayer, in the totality of the common life. Worship alone will not sustain the people of God. Man must enter into a giving and receiving that is pervasive in life. What worship may do for him is to make him aware of that which he ought to receive and that which he might expect to give.

READINGS

From the Bible

1. The ritual for the Day of Atonement or the celebration of the Passover reveals many facets of congregational worship. Leviticus 16, Exodus 12.

2. A variety of problems encountered in a young Christian congregation made up of recent converts is discussed in I Corinthians.

3. Psalm 24 exhibits the pattern of call and response.

From Historic Christianity

1. Hippolytus, *The Apostolic Tradition,* includes descriptions of various services in the church of the third century.

---

[20] Matthew 15:8f.

2. Service Books of various denominations contain services with specific historic backgrounds. *Venite Adoremus,* published by the World Student Christian Federation, Geneva, 1951, contains services from a number of communions.

3. A *Missal* should be consulted for the Roman Catholic Mass.

FOR STUDY AND DISCUSSION

1. In *The Word of God and the Word of Man,* Douglas Horton, trans. (New York, Harper & Brothers, 1957), Karl Barth describes the expectancy that accompanies a church service and raises the question about the fulfillment of that expectancy, pp. 104 ff. What do you think should happen in a church service? Does it happen often? Ever?
2. Do you prefer services with or without a sermon? Why?
3. Study the ritual for the Day of Atonement or the Passover as it is described in the Old Testament and as it is observed in a synagogue today. Could the Christian church learn anything from these in its conduct of worship?
4. All the prayers in a church service should be silent–read together by the congregation–spoken by an individual.
5. The offering ought to be eliminated from the service of worship; all the money matters of the church should be taken care of in other ways than in worship.

XIII

WORSHIP AND THE RELATIONSHIPS OF LIFE

The eighteenth chapter of First Kings tells in dramatic fashion the story of a contest between Elijah, prophet of Israel's Lord, and four hundred and fifty prophets of Baal. Two altars are erected side by side and sacrifices are placed on them; the deities are to be tested in terms of their ability to respond with fire to the cries of their protagonists. In vain do the Baal prophets call on their god, crying long and loud, cutting themselves with knives, while Elijah taunts them with the suggestion that perhaps their god is sleeping or has taken a walk. When time comes for Elijah to call on Israel's Lord, fire comes and consumes the sacrifice. Immediately afterward rain comes upon a land which has been desolated by drought for three years.

The point of the story is that Israel's Lord, the God who has acted redemptively in the history of his people, who demands rightness of action and truth in the inward parts, is also the God of nature. As he conquered Baal, so did he vanquish other gods who sought to claim the people's devotion. But he did not disregard the concerns which were connected with the other gods; he included them—as he included nature, the sphere of the Baals' operation. It was because he included the concerns of all the lesser gods that he could rightly claim the total devotion of his people. They must have no other gods before him—or even alongside of him.

Literal polytheism ceased to tempt the Jews at the time of the exile; it was no problem thereafter. But religious polytheism tempted them as it tempts all people at all times. There are worthy concerns, and these may claim total devotion. There are things which must be trusted to some degree; these may be trusted too much. Here again is the tension of the created and the Creator. We have seen it in the several relationships of life, the tensions which create difficulties for the Christian as he seeks to achieve and preserve attitudes which are in keeping with his attitude toward God. Worship may help him toward the proper attitudes. And yet worship itself may become perverted and add to his temptations. While literal polytheism seldom reflects itself in the language of Christian worship, religious polytheism presents a continuing temptation. Prayers are often, in fact, addressed to the gods of partial concerns, not to the Lord of inclusive concern, the high and holy One.

This chapter is about the battle between God and the gods in the area of worship. It will serve to relate worship to the attitudes which were the subject of the preceding section of the book and to the several expressions of faith which are the subject of the remainder of this section. It will treat of several gods in their rivalry with the one Lord. The alternatives are these:

The god who is *nature* or the God who created nature,
the god who is *oneself* or the God to whom he is precious as a creature,
the gods who are *friends* and *family* or the God who created men for fellowship with one another in him,
the gods who are *groups* or the God who bound men together in "the bundle of life,"
the god who seeks only worship or the God who claims all of life.

1. MAN AND NATURE

If the baals are recognized for the idols they are—that is, if subhuman forces are not made objects of devotion, nature can find its proper place in the worship of the Creator. Because he made it, he can use it for his purposes; it can participate in that divine-human action which is the reality of worship. Its beauty and tenderness, its grandeur and awesomeness, elicit responses of wonder and praise. Its fruitfulness has been the occasion of acts of thanksgiving which have become integral parts of the liturgies of Christian churches. Nature within man, too—his body—can contribute to the fullness of worship. That which he hears and sees, even that which he smells and feels, may affect him profoundly, and often in ways that are too subtle to come to his conscious awareness. Even bodily movement may be expressive of moods. The appropriateness of standing or sitting or kneeling for various parts of worship reflects itself in individual devotions as well as in formalized public services. And yet Christians have been aware of the peril of concentrating too much attention on nature. Those who find their only experiences of worship amidst woods and streams are sometimes disappointed when they seek in them a sort of help from God that comes through people and ideas. Christian faith also reminds the worshipper that God is not bound by the nature he has created, that he can speak to the human spirit where the world excites no sense of awe or obvious occasion for gratitude, and where the bodily situation is not such as to arouse the expectation that a word from the divine would be easily heard. Kneeling or standing may be an aid to prayer, but neither is a prerequisite.

That wedding ceremonies should form part of the rituals of all Christian churches speaks of the continuing conviction of the goodness of the body which is enshrined in attitudes toward marriage and the family. Some of the most telling of Jesus' parables recognized the natural joyfulness that surrounds weddings: he spoke of bridegrooms and their friends, of wise and foolish bridesmaids. It is right that weddings be joyous; it is also right that they be solemn, that those who come to be married know that their relationship is "not by any to be entered into unadvisedly or lightly; but reverently, discreetly, advisedly, soberly, and in the fear of God." [1] Marriage is a high moment in life, a time of celebration; and it is appropriate that its religious dimension be made explicit through an act of worship.

From the conviction that nature is God's creation comes the corrolary that it is available to him for his redemptive purposes; here again the belief of Christians is reflected in their worship patterns. Certain parts of nature, so to speak, have been drawn into specific connection with redemption; they have served as links between the redemptive acts of God in the past and his continuing action in the life of his people in the present. Thus, for example, the waters of baptism have connected

[1] *The Book of Common Prayer,* p. 300.

Christians through the centuries with the death and resurrection of the Christ and even with his own baptism at the hands of John. There has been the greatest variety of interpretation about the relation of water and the Spirit, and yet most Christians have held that baptism in water is a matter of importance, even though baptism in the Spirit is of greater significance. The touch of hands, in confirmation or ordination, has connected Christians across the years. Again, the interpretations have been diverse; and yet Christians remember that the New Testament connects the Spirit in some way with the laying on of hands.

Bread and wine have formed a focal point in one of the most important services of the historic church. Early Christians were vividly aware of the relation of the meaning of the sacrament to their conviction that the world—and specifically the material—is God's creation. With this was connected another conviction which they also regarded as essentially related to the meaningfulness of the service, namely, that Jesus had a real body—indeed, was in all respects a genuine human being. If matter was evil, and if the body of the Christ was a phantom, they said, the sacrament was devoid of significance. Interpretations of the supper have divided Christians, sometimes violently; and yet there has been a common conviction that God's redemptive act in history is linked with the present in some important way through the material elements.

As attitudes toward nature have affected practices of Christian worship, so have acts of worship had their effects on men's attitude toward their world. After a profound religious experience George Fox found that the very earth had a new smell.[2] A character in John Masefield's "Everlasting Mercy" says that after his conversion,

> The waters rushing from the rain
> Were singing, Christ has risen again.[3]

A college student once remarked that he had never noticed the beauty of clouds until his own life had found a center of devotion. He who eats bread from the Lord's table in gratitude may find that he is more thankful than before when he sits at his own table with his family.

The church has fluctuated throughout its history in its attitude toward the physical concomitants of worship; and the fluctuation has reflected, in no small measure, attitudes held at any given time toward

---

[2] George Fox, *The Journal of George Fox* (London: Friends Tract Association, 1901), I, 28. "All things were new; and all the creation gave another smell unto me than before, beyond what words can utter."

[3] John Masefield, *Poems* (New York: The Macmillan Company, 1925), p. 88. Reprinted by permission.

nature itself. Some have been so concerned for the spiritual, intellectual, and moral aspects of faith that they have given scant attention to man's relation to the earth. Others have so fastened their attention on the physical that they have appeared almost indifferent to the moral, intellectual, and spiritual. In the centuries just past there has been a tendency to disregard man's relation to nature; with it has gone a tendency to disregard the physical setting of worship and to lose a sense of the significance of the sacraments. Theologians of our time are hopeful that there will be a reappropriation of the historic attitude of faith toward nature and of worship which will justly reflect that attitude. Here, as elsewhere, worship and the whole life of faith are interconnected. Worship may help to shape an attitude; and that attitude will find its reflection in worship.

2. MAN AND HIMSELF

Christian faith sees man as being, in his individuality and wholeness, a creation of the love of God; as being rebellious against that love in a way which results in his alienation from himself; as being redeemed by the love of God in such a way that his true creaturehood is, within limitations, realized. The worship of the church has reflected these convictions. Their special relevance for private worship has already been traced in some detail; their relevance to the worship of the church has also been noted. In general, it might be said that acts of devotion, solitary and social, seem to be peculiarly appropriate tools through which the Spirit can bring man to wholeness. His individuality is never surrendered to the group or even to God himself. And his finiteness remains; even his most exalted moments are not deifications. In worship his entire person is engaged, his reason and his conscience, his emotions and his will—indeed, his very body. These may be transformed, but they are not destroyed nor disregarded. Selfhood in its totality is precious.

There are some acts of worship in which a man's individuality comes to focal expression. As we have seen, it is natural that certain crucial decisions in the life of a person may evoke expression in private prayer. They may also be recognized within the life of the church. Thus those churches who practice the baptism of adults see in the ceremony a declaration on the part of the one baptized; he is witnessing to all who are present his own faith in Christ and his resolution to live in newness of life. Some churches whose normal practice is the baptism of infants think of confirmation as an occasion when the individual affirms his own faith and pledges his intention to lead a Christian life.[4] It is appropriate, too, that in some cases decisions concerning vocations be publicly declared. This is sometimes done with reference to callings of all sorts; people affirm their intention to do the will of God in whatever work they undertake. Vocations within the church have generally been signalized by ceremonies of ordination in which the person is dedicated to God for the work he is to do.

One aspect of man's inner life is of such importance for worship and its relations to other expressions of faith that it requires special attention. Man is a being who is able to convey and respond to meanings. He can speak and he can listen, he can be reminded of things absent by things which are present. He can use words and he can also use things as signs of other things or even of ideas. The Bible does not analyze him as being responsive to meanings, but throughout it speaks in terms of a God who speaks, of prophets to whom the word comes, of men who should be responsive to what God says. Indeed, the New Testament speaks of Christ as the Word which was in the beginning with God and then became flesh to dwell among men. The message of God's love, proclaimed in preaching, is also called a word from the Lord even though it is announced by men.

It has often been pointed out that there are two important ways in which men respond to words or other signs: rationally or emotionally. Because this is true, signs have at least two significant dimensions of meaning. One, often called the denotative, refers to the meaning which signs have for our reason; the other, often called connotative, refers to the meaning they have for our emotions. How the two relate to each other is a very delicate and difficult problem. Indeed the whole field of the philosophy of meaning has been one in which much work has been done in recent years. Though its complications need not concern us here, a few considerations of a rather elementary character may prove helpful.

We can say, rather simply, in view of convictions which have been common among Christians, that both the denotative and the connotative significance of words and other signs are important for worship; this is asserted because the whole person of man is involved in it. Further, the two cannot be separated, though they may be distinguished.

---

[4] See Orders for Confirmation in various Service Books. Franklin H. Littell, *The Anabaptist View of the Church* (Boston: Beacon Press, 1958), p. 36, points out that churches which practiced infant baptism emphasized confirmation more strongly than they had previously when the Anabaptists began to stress believers' baptism.

It will be remembered that Paul wrote to the Corinthians indicating his own awareness of the importance of spirit for worship; and yet he insisted that the mind was important too.

Later we shall have occasion to look at the significance of words and other signs for the relation of worship to other expressions of faith. Here it may be enough to refer to the rather obvious fact that they have played a tremendously important part in Christian worship throughout the centuries. Words such as *God, Christ, forgive, go, I, we* have appeared again and again. They have had a meaning for the mind—denotative—and a significance for the feelings—connotative. Things like crosses, bread, wine, altars, books have stood for ideas apprehended by the mind and felt by the emotions.

An illustration of the way in which meanings may be built up within an experience can be drawn from the Old Testament: it comes from the stories about the warfare of the Israelites with the Philistines:

> And David said longingly, "O that someone would give me water to drink from the well of Bethlehem which is by the gate!" Then the three mighty men broke through the camp of the Philistines, and drew water out of the well of Bethlehem which was by the gate, and took and brought it to David. But he would not drink of it; he poured it out to the Lord, and said, "Far be it from me, O Lord, that I should do this. Shall I drink the blood of the men who went at the risk of their lives?" [5]

Here the water means more than water usually does; it is a sign of a number of ideas. It means, at the very least, refreshment for the body. It possibly means also remembrance of home and family, since it comes from Bethlehem, the city of David. But after the feat of the mighty men, it means their devotion to David, their very lives. And because of this, it finally means for David something sacred, something he must pour out to the Lord. At the last there comes an act of worship, and into it are incorporated all of the meanings leading up to it. The act reflects the sense that the divine is immeasurably higher than all things human. And yet it seems to deny something, too. Christians and Jews who have responded to other elements in their heritage may well feel that a dedication of the water to God, followed by the grateful drinking of it, might have been a more fitting climax to the story than that which actually took place. The Divine is higher than the human; it denies the finalization of any finite meaning; but, if creation and redemption are affirmed, it also supports and, indeed, fulfills the finite mean-

[5] II Samuel 23:15-17.

ings. Christians have dared to raise to their lips bread and wine that mean far more to them than the blood of David's devoted followers.

The problem for the individual is that of being rightly concerned for his selfhood without being betrayed into selfishness. In terms that have been used here—he must not make himself the center of meaning for his life. If he does so, the pronouns *I* and *me* become the focal points around which his entire vocabulary revolves. That these words are prominent in the hymns and gospel songs of the past few centuries, that they have occurred frequently in utterances from the pulpit, that they have become central in prayers—these are signs that the worship of Christian churches has reflected currents of attitude abroad in a world which treasures individuality. They are indications of a yielding to the temptation—sometimes a very subtle one—to make the individual and his thoughts and experiences the primary concern for worship. Theologians of our time often express the hope that a recovery of the sense that has informed much of the historic worship of the church may help men to acknowledge and celebrate something other than their own ideas and emotions—the mighty acts of God.

3. PERSONAL RELATIONS

The words of the Christ, "Where two or three are gathered in my name, there am I in the midst of them," [6] have been treasured by Christians. They suggest that it is natural for small groups to join in acts of devotion, and that the Spirit may be present in some peculiar way to such acts. There are ranges of experience that are not normally accessible, perhaps not accessible at all, to man as he worships alone or with the full congregation of the church. These come to him when he joins with one or two others. There are, of course, dangers in the worship of the few; they may address their prayers to a deity of their own, whose only concern is their welfare. Like other baals, he must be overthrown if worship is to come to its fullness. The high God looks on the group with tender regard but at the same time is the Father of all men. He loves them more than each loves himself or his fellows, and yet he loves all other men too.

One conviction reflecting itself in the worship of the small group is, of course, the belief that men are essentially social. Friends share interests and concerns; they are congenial with one another; it is natural that they should make the religious dimension of their relationship ex-

[6] Matthew 18:20.

plicit in praying with and for one another. And yet such acts can minister to the development of a wrong as well as a right attitude toward friendship. Jesus pointed out that men must not confuse their natural expressions of affection toward friends with the fulfillment of the divine commandment of love toward all. "If you love those who love you, what reward have you?"[7] It is significant that in this connection he spoke explicitly of the importance of prayers which went beyond the circle of friendship: "Pray for those who persecute you."[8] Intensive prayer might be a force tending toward making a friendship obsessive; it could also help to establish it in its proper place among all the relationships of life because it related friendship itself to its ultimate Foundation.

Families, as well as friends, will naturally worship together from time to time. Recognizing this, Christian churches generally have offered them assistance in formulating their acts of devotion. At the very least, they will "say grace" at the table. If their prayers are restricted, as in the familiar story, to "us four, and no more," they are offered to a tribal god; like all prayers, those of the family must be offered to "the Father, from whom every family in heaven and on earth is named."[9]

A second conviction has had a part in shaping the character of the worship of two or three. This is the idea that the grace of God often comes to a person through the mediation of other human beings. A trusted friend may bring such an assurance of grace that a person can be released from a sense of guilt. Often a minister, a man chosen by the church who has the word of scripture in mind and heart, may be of essential help when a penitent is in need of voicing a confession of sin. Indeed, some Christian groups have held that ministers have special prerogatives from the Christ himself to announce the forgiveness of sins to the penitent. It has been a common experience among Christians to find that certain words of prayer could be addressed to God only in the presence of some fellow human being who brought to them a realization of forgiving and redeeming love.

4. MAN IN THE GROUP

Christian worship of the solitary individual or when two or three are gathered together will rightly include reference to the larger groupings in which man lives. And these, in turn, will express themselves in wor-

---

[7] Matthew 5:46.
[8] Matthew 5:44.
[9] Ephesians 3:14f.

ship, sometimes almost unconsciously. As natural outgrowths of man's created nature, they will rightly make explicit from time to time the religious reference which belongs to their reality. The ambiguities which haunt their existence will be reflected in their worship; economic groups will bow before the idols of the market place and political groups before the idols of the tribe. And it is no easy thing to deliver them from such worship to obeisance before the high God who has no favorites.

Medieval guilds had their patron saints, and they donated windows to cathedrals. In our time farmers meet to make clear the spiritual dimensions of their vocation and express in worship their understanding of their tasks. Labor unions and industries sometimes have chaplains. The lack of clarity concerning the relation of religion to economic life over several centuries has rendered patterns of meaningful worship difficult, however. Parts of the labor movement have had strong anticlerical tendencies, and management has often felt that it is no simple thing to see spiritual dimensions in economic life. Nevertheless there have been "labor priests," and clergymen have sometimes assumed an important role in bringing mutual understandings. Traditional prayer books usually contain intercessions on behalf of workers, farmers, and others; and in recent years there have been additions to the liturgical resources of the church which have revealed a keen awareness of the need of the Spirit to lead men into ways of living which will accord with the dignity of human beings and the recognition of their economic needs.

The religious dimension of the life of political groups has received expression in worship from earliest times. The anointing of a king was a solemn act as it is described in the Old Testament. It may well be that many of the Psalms grew out of ceremonies connected with kingship. The crowning of Charlemagne on Christmas day of 800 is a well-remembered historic event. And the coronation of Elizabeth as Queen of England brought vividly before the peoples of the world a long tradition of Christianity within which a very complex ceremony has evolved. The ceremony was essentially a religious service: it was held in a church, the crowning was by an archbishop, the vows were spoken to God. Even in a land like the United States, where the separation of church and state is a fundamental principle of government, the inauguration of the President is in part a religious act. Prayers are said, and an oath is administered.

However, the worship of the political group presents formidable difficulties. It is a simple fact that it is almost impossible for a group to admit that it has been wrong, and corporate confession is essential to Christian worship. Whoever has listened to one of the mass rallies which attended Adolf Hitler's rise to power can scarcely avoid the judgment that there was a powerful religious element present in them. In outbursts of veritably frenzy people burst into expressions which were actually deeds of devotion addressed to the gods of blood and soil. And these acts contributed to the sense of utter rightness which attended fanatic totalitarians in their policies and programs. It is no wonder that some churchmen refused obedience. As Christians of the second century recognized that their allegiance to Christ forbade them to burn incense before the altar of the emperor, some German Christians remembered that it was written,

> You shall worship the Lord your God
> and him only shall you serve.[10]

The church rightly includes the concerns of all, the one, the two or three, the economic and political groups; and it is appropriate that its worship should reflect these concerns. Its scripture preserves an apostolic admonition:

> I urge that supplications, prayers, intercessions, and thanksgivings be made for all men, for kings and all who are in high positions, that we may lead a quiet and peaceable life, godly and respectful in every way.[11]

The church may, of course, focus its attentions exclusively on itself; its prayers will be for its own people, its own programs, its own interests. But then it ceases to be true to itself, for the church must always point beyond itself to a city which has no temple, "for its temple is the Lord God the Almighty and the Lamb."[12]

5. WORSHIP AND THE WHOLE OF FAITH

One of the most persistent baals in the history of religion is the one who is satisfied with the worship of the lips. Altars have been raised to him by individuals and groups, by nations and churches. Because of him religion has been called "the opiate of the people."[13] Elijahs have repeatedly torn down his altars so that shrines to the true God might be built. He is the Lord who claims the whole of life; of that whole, worship is a part. There are lines running from it to all the expressions of faith

---

[10] Matthew 4:10.
[11] I Timothy 2:1-2.
[12] Revelation 21:22.
[13] Karl Marx, see note 16, ch. VIII.

because Christians share a common vision and common attitudes. In the fullness of Christian worship every other expression is represented; and every other expression can become, during a moment of its execution, an act of worship.

Because of the Christian attitude toward nature, the material can participate in the life of worship. Hence it is not strange that artists and musicians have contributed means by which acts of worship could be enhanced. Churches, altars, hymns, and anthems have shared in "the beauty of holiness." [14] On the other hand the history of art contains numerous instances of men for whom the painting of a picture was, in itself, an act of devotion to God.

Because of the Christian attitude toward the mind of man, thought has a legitimate place in worship. Creeds are spoken, meaningful hymns are sung, and scriptures are read. The sermon seeks to set forth the meaning of the gospel for the congregation in its immediate situation. On the other hand Christian thinkers have expressed in the midst of their theological work the consciousness of standing in the Divine presence. Anselm seeks the help of God as he essays to prove his very existence: "Speak now, O my whole heart, speak now to God: 'I seek thy face; thy face, Lord, do I desire.' And do thou, O Lord my God, teach my heart where and how to seek thee, where and how to find thee." [15]

However, worshippers have seldom been satisfied to express theological thoughts entirely in prosaic language. Even the extempore prayer in a rude church commonly has some literary grace; and the language of devotion that is mirrored in the liturgical books of the various churches constantly verges on poetry. Few sermons lack some passages that are, at least slightly, purple. Also, it is true that from earliest times the gift of poetry has been connected with divine inspiration. Christian poets have sometimes borrowed from their pagan predecessors the forms in which they had sought the assistance of the muses. Milton sometimes invoked both pagan and Christian deities. It was natural that he should pray in a poem:

> . . . What in me is dark
> Illumin, what is low, raise and support.[16]

Early Christian communion services often terminated in the taking of food to the needy, and today most acts of worship by the church include

---

[14] Psalm 96:10, K.J.V.

[15] Anselm, "An Address (Proslogion)," ch. 1, Eugene R. Fairweather, ed. and trans., *A Scholastic Miscellany,* p. 70. Reprinted by permission.

[16] John Milton, *The Complete Poetry and Selected Prose of John Milton* (New York: Random House, n.d.), p. 92.

the receiving of money, part of which goes to the relief of human distress. Thus what begins as Christian worship receives expression in action. On the other hand, even dreary action is sometimes rendered sacred by the remembrance of the words: "As you did it unto one of the least of these my brethren, you did it to me." [17]

Finally, through worship the church comes to a realization of itself, and in worship it gives expression to that realization. A church which does not worship is inconceivable; so is a church which only worships. It is no accident that all the activities of the church—its decisions, its programs, its most menial tasks—commonly call for prayer, and that these become, for those who do them, acts of dedicated service.

Thus it is that worship becomes a focal point from which radiate influences which affect all the expressions of faith. It is not the only center; any expression may become one. Worship influences the other expressions and it is influenced by them. Because we have examined worship as a center in some detail, we shall find it possible to deal with the others more briefly.

READINGS

From the Bible

1. A service of reading, explanation, and response is described in Nehemiah 8.

2. The New Testament gives several accounts of the institution of the Lord's supper: Matthew 25:26-29, Mark 14:22-25, Luke 21:14-23, I Corinthians 12:23-26.

3. Some have seen the character of early Christian worship reflected in the description of heavenly worship in Revelation 4 and 5.

4. Celebration of the marriage of a king's son to a princess from Tyre may be the theme of Psalm 45.

[17] Matthew 25:40.

From Historic Christianity

1. Service books of various denominations should be helpful here.

2. The sacraments can be studied in Thomas Aquinas, *Summa Contra Gentiles,* bk. 4, ch. 56-78; Martin Luther, *A Prelude on the Babylonian Captivity of the Church;* John Calvin, *Institutes,* IV, xiv; and Huldreich Zwingli, *On the Sacraments.*

FOR STUDY AND DISCUSSION

1. How is the Lord's supper celebrated in your church? Could ministers of denominations other than your own lead the service? Why or why not? Are members of churches of denominations other than your own permitted to participate in the service? Is any preparation required or suggested for participation in it?
2. Why is it impossible for all members of the World Council of Churches to participate in a single communion service? Should steps be taken toward broader bases of intercommunion? Why or why not?
3. What is the meaning of baptism in your denomination? Do members of churches other than your own have to be rebaptized in order to join yours? Is some other ceremony required?
4. Compare the regular order of worship in a number of service books.
5. What expressions of faith are neglected in the worship of your church (if any)? What could be done to give them more significance?

XIV

ART

The recovery of Christian faith in our time is more than a reappropriation of theological understandings, ethical insights, and worship patterns of other days. It has effected the appreciation of a rich heritage of art and music, as well as a stimulation to new efforts of artistic creation. As theological analysis has brought an awareness of meanings imbedded in historic Christianity, even when these were set forth in the language of the past, it has made men sensitive to the expression of those meanings in art. And as the meanings of the faith come to take on significance for contemporary artists, they have received new, and sometimes rather striking expression.

Awareness of the massiveness of Christian faith is due in part to recognition of art as one of its significant aspects. The recent past has seen a deepening interest in the creation, the appreciation, and the interpretation of Christian art.

1. THE EMERGENCE OF CHRISTIAN ART

The Christian movement grew out of a Hebrew heritage which was profoundly suspicious of much that constitutes art. The words, "You shall not make for yourself a graven image, or any likeness of anything that is in heaven above, or that is on the earth beneath, or that is in the water under the earth,"[1] were written deep into the consciousness of prophets and people as well as lawmakers. The repudiation of any attempt to make a representation of a divine being occurs again and again on the pages of the Old Testament. Aaron made a golden calf for his people, but his sin and theirs called down the wrath of the Almighty. Jeroboam's act of making shrines at Dan and Bethel was noted by the Hebrew historians as an act of flagrant disobedience; "he made Israel to sin."[2]

Nevertheless, there is indication within the Old Testament of genuine appreciation of certain arts. David's wife disapproved of his dancing before the Lord, but he seemed to feel that he had given a perfectly natural expression to his religious devotion.[3] There seemed to be no hesitation about making the Lord's house and its appointments things of beauty. The attitude of certain Jews toward the temple is reflected in the description given in the book of Exodus of the plans for the tabernacle in the wilderness. The author describes Moses as saying, "See, the Lord has called by name Bezalel the son of Uri, son of Hur, of the tribe of Judah; and he has filled him with the Spirit of God, with ability, with intelligence, with knowledge, and with all craftsmanship, to devise artistic designs, to work in gold and silver and bronze, in cutting stones for setting, and in carving wood, for work in every skilled craft . . . and Moses called Bezelel and Oholiab and every able man in whose mind the Lord had put ability, every one whose heart stirred him up to come to do the work."[4] Here the artist is God's own man, called, inspired, and equipped by him. Though the temple remained ever devoid of anything resembling an image of the Lord, things cunningly carved and woven, things of wood, precious stone, brass, and gold might minister to his praise. Strength and beauty were appropriate in his sanctuary; it was also filled with the sound of music.

> Praise him with trumpet sound;
> praise him with lute and harp!
> Praise him with timbrel and dance;
> praise him with strings and pipe!
> Praise him with sounding cymbals;
> praise him with loud clashing cymbals![5]

---

[1] Deuteronomy 5:8.
[2] I Kings 14:16.
[3] II Samuel 6:16-23.
[4] Exodus 35:30ff., 36:2.
[5] Psalms 150:3-5.

Representational painting is not mentioned in the Old Testament; perhaps the prohibition of images was taken to include it.[6] There is evidence, however, that early in the Christian era the Jews had begun to paint; the ruins of the walls of a synagogue discovered in Dura are adorned with pictures.[7]

Most of the early Christians' attitudes toward art were inherited from their Jewish forbears as a result of the similarity of their convictions. For them too, depiction of the Deity was taboo; anything that smacked of the worship of idols was out of the question. Moreover, any appreciation that might have been connected with the lingering loyalty of a Jewish Christian to the temple and its priesthood was soon dissipated by historic fact as well as theological declaration. The temple was destroyed in 70 A.D., but the Christian writer reminded his fellows that this was no calamity; for "the hour is coming when neither on this mountain nor in Jerusalem will you worship the Father . . . God is spirit, and those who worship him must worship in spirit and truth."[8] Another declared that the temple cultus was forever superseded when Christ, the perfect priest, made the perfect offering in the sanctuary of heaven itself.[9]

The assertion that God is spirit voiced those convictions which had acted in the history of Israel as deterrents of artistic expression. And yet the connected conviction that he had acted redemptively in human history and culminated his work by sending Christ reflected itself very early in pictorial fashion.[10] One can easily imagine that reminders of God's redemptive acts in the past would bring comfort to those in present distress. From the second century come the earliest Christian paintings that have been preserved.[11] On the walls of those miles of tunnels in and about Rome where the Christians buried their dead, they depicted

---

[6] Jeremiah 22:14 speaks of painting a house. There are a few references to cosmetic painting.

[7] M. Rostovtzeff, *Dura-Europos and its Art* (Oxford: The Clarendon Press, 1938), pp. 100-135.

[8] John 4:21, 24.

[9] Hebrews 7-9.

[10] See Walter Lowrie, *Art in the Early Church* (New York: Pantheon Books, 1947), p. 80.

[11] These have been described and reproduced in various places. See Walter Lowrie, *Art in the Early Church.* A set of Kodachrome slides has been selected and described by Roland H. Bainton, *The Panorama of the Christian Church* (Boston: The Pilgrim Press, 1944). A Leader's Guide accompanies the slides; page numbers will refer to it. Arthur L. Frothingham, *The Monuments of Christian Rome* (New York: The Macmillan Company, 1908), is profusely illustrated. The University Prints, Cambridge, has prints of religious art works.

scenes from what was for them sacred history. There was Daniel safe among the lions; there was Jonah emerging from the open mouth of the great fish; there was Susanna being vindicated in spite of the accusations of the elders. These were mighty acts of God. The redemptive concern of God for the Christians themselves reflected itself in one of the most familiar figures of catacomb painting, the *Orans,* or "Praying one." A female figure, probably representing the soul of the departed, was depicted with upraised arms. Redemption pointed to creation, too; for the early Christian artists did not hesitate to picture trees, grass, and flowers. They even introduced what seem to be rather trivial decorative motives; their faith did not inhibit the sheer joy of simple expression for its own sake.

However, early Christian art was a reflection of something other than convictions alone; it was profoundly influenced by styles of art current at the time. Experts have worked diligently to identify these, and their

REDEMPTION IN THE OLD TESTAMENT Remembrance of a mighty act of God in times past encourages early Christians in the face of death and disaster. *The Sacrifice of Abraham.* Catacomb of San Callisto in Rome (third century) (Alinari Photo)

study is a fascinating one.[12] Though it does not concern us here, the manner in which Christian artists responded to influences is of importance for us. It appears to parallel exactly the manner in which Christian theologians responded to thought currents abroad at the time. To these we have already given attention. At some points there was simple assimilation into Christian art of contemporary features. Some aspects of a Christian painting are indistinguishable from those of a pagan one. At other points there was outright rejection; some things were simply not appropriate for depiction by people whose convictions were those of the Christians. Clement of Alexandria, a Christian teacher who lived about 200 A.D., instructed artists of his faith to avoid the picturing of certain symbols which were connected with pagan worship.[13] At other points there was transformation or adaptation of current art forms in order to make them conform to Christian outlooks. And at times the transformation was so significant that it resulted in a new creative thrust within the life of art.

These responses can be illustrated by the development that took place in the portrayal of Jesus. One of our earliest pictures of him is in the figure of the good shepherd carrying lambs on his shoulder while wolves look at them hungrily.[14] Here, of course, is a reflection of the conviction that in Christ God acted redemptively and protected his own from whatever threatened them. The face of Jesus is beardless; to the student of the history of art he looks almost exactly like Hermes. There was simple assimilation of a current theme and style of art. Apparently, however, the Christians were soon disturbed by the resemblance of their Savior to a pagan god, and pictures of Jesus began to look different. There was rejection of a pagan style, even one which Christians themselves had imitated. Soon the Christ began to have a beard—to have those features and that cast of countenance which has become familiar in Christian art. Now this Christ was no absolute novelty. And yet the manner in which he was depicted in about the fourth century became determinative for the entire subsequent history of painting. That portrayal has become creative in art history, a focal point around which many things revolve. In our own time the question has been seriously

---

[12] Charles R. Morey, *Early Christian Art* (Princeton: Princeton University Press, 1942), traces a number of influences.

[13] Hans Lietzmann, *The Founding of the Church Universal*, Bertram L. Woolf, trans. (New York: Charles Scribner's Sons, 1950), pp. 182f.

[14] Roland Bainton, *The Panorama of the Christian Church*, p. 20. Used by permission.

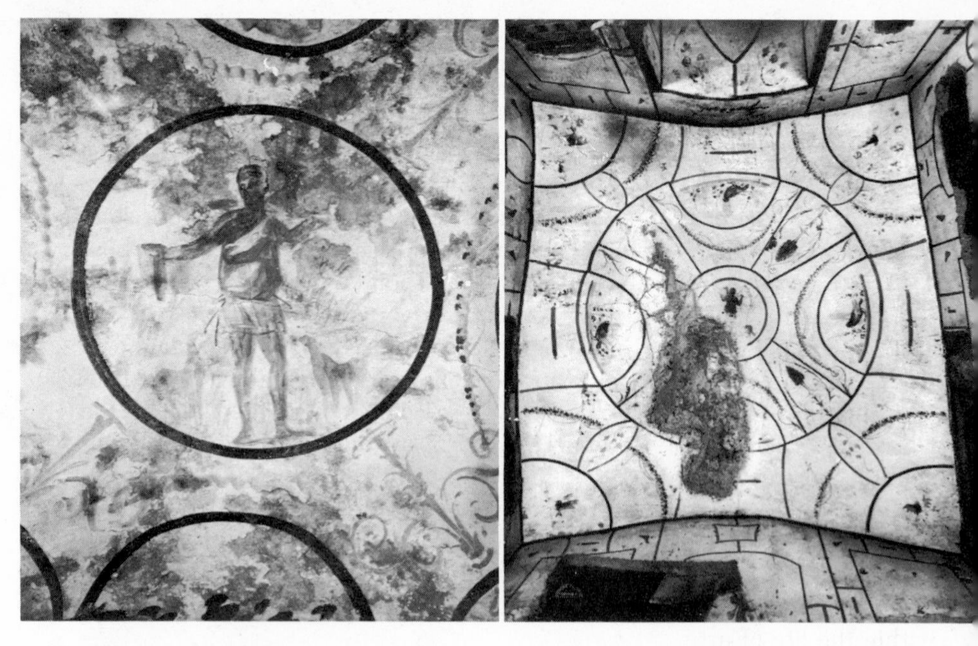

Christ as a beardless youth carries his sheep, secure from the threatening wolves. Catacomb of Domitilla (second century) (Alinari Photo)

The Shepherd, the sheep, and the wolves are surrounded by decorative motifs. Catacomb of Domitilla (second century) (Alinari Photo)

Some centuries later the Shepherd is still a beardless youth, but he and his surroundings are richly adorned. Mausoleum of Galla Placidia, Ravenna (fifth century) (Courtesy of the Italian State Tourist Office)

THE GOOD SHEPHERD IN EARLY CHRISTIAN ART

raised about the adequacy of that depiction, and contemporary pictures of Christ have sometimes purposely departed from it. Perhaps a new creative transformation will take place; and yet there are strong indications that the representation which has lasted for fifteen hundred years still remains potent.

Assimilation, rejection, and transformation have been going on constantly, and they still go on; hence, we come to another parallel between art and theology. Just as there is no final Christian theology, so there is no final Christian art. There is no style of art to which one can point and say, "This is Christian, and no other is." And yet Christian faith has exercised an enormous influence on art, and at certain times in the West practically everything that was painted was explicitly religious. There would seem to be some real sense in which one can speak of *Christian art.*

It must be repeated, however, that there has persisted in the Christian consciousness a strong suspicion of art, and the history of the church has been marked by recurrent reactions against it. The second commandment has not been forgotten. In the eighth century the Eastern Roman empire saw the rise of the Iconoclasts—Christians stimulated by the rivalry of Islam to do away with all pictures in churches. They were vigorously opposed by those to whom the pictures were dear, and a controversy occurred which stirred the entire East. Eventually there was a compromise which is reflected in the usages of the Orthodox Church to our own day. Pictures are permitted, since they can serve as symbols—the Greek word is *icon*—of spiritual realities; but sculptures are forbidden, since they offer too dangerous an invitation to idolatry.

Thus through the history of the Christian church—as through the history of Israel before it—runs a tension with reference to art. It is the reflection, of course, in the aesthetic field of a tension which runs throughout Christian faith between devotion to Creator and created, to God and his world.

2. THE CHRISTIAN ARTIST

If our observations are correct, two matters are now before us. Certain attitudes lie at the heart of historic Christianity, and these have received expression in art. Since the link between attitude and expression is obviously the artist, some attention must be accorded him. The task of tracing the inner workings of his creative acts is beyond the reach of our analysis—and probably beyond his, too. But it is possible to draw certain implications from the attitudes characteristic of Christian faith which have a bearing on the manner in which that faith has been expressed in art.

The positive attitude toward nature which is in keeping with the declaration concerning creation helps us to understand the manner in which the artist can be intrigued with things. These are precious, says the Christian, because God made them. The artist's treatment of them reflects a treasuring of the concrete particular, for its own sake, in all its uniqueness, a stone or a tree, a leaf or a bird. There may also be some attempt to intimate that which lies beyond nature, the very Reality from which each thing derives the sacredness of its uniqueness. When this is not present, art becomes preoccupied with the creature, and may well end in futility.

It is surely not strange for a being who is essentially creative to express himself in a way that justifies itself and which issues in things that exist for their own sake. Christian theology should have no difficulty with the thesis that art is expression. Herein lies the passionate concern of the artist for integrity; he must find himself so that he can be himself if he is to have a center from which to create. And yet, says Christian faith, that creation must find its place in a larger framework if it is not to be self-defeating. The saying of Jesus applies to the artist as it does to others: "Whosoever shall seek to save his life shall lose it; and whosoever shall lose his life shall preserve it." [15]

Christian faith proclaims that one of the ways by which God saves a man from self-preoccupation is by surrounding him with other human beings. Furthermore, as John Calvin put it, "God has made him [that is, our neighbor] his substitute" [16] and bids us love him. Art can be communication, and Christian faith is likely to see it so. But it is important to take into account that when the artist gives himself to others, he gives himself as artist, not as teacher or preacher. And the object through which he communicates is one which evokes a response which is primarily aesthetic in character.

Another means which God can use to save a man from his self-preoccupation is that of offering himself to him through his gifts.

---

[15] Luke 17:33, K.J.V.

[16] John Calvin, *Institutes of the Christian Religion,* John Allen, trans. (Philadelphia: Presbyterian Board of Christian Education, 1930), I, 625 (III, vii, 6). Reprinted by permission. A new translation of the *Institutes* has recently been made by Ford L. Battles (Philadelphia: The Westminster Press, 1960). References can be readily identified by book, chapter, and section, which are given in parentheses in each note.

Gratitude opens the spirit that is closed up within itself. The gospels tell us that the healing touch of the Christ upon the bodies of men would call forth a faith by which their very persons were made whole. God surrounds the artist with many things, and art is, in part, response. The artist whose sensibilities have been formed by the attitudes which belong to Christian faith will respond to many things. His eyes are open to nature, and he puts it on his canvas. He sees his fellow humans and paints them, too. Aware of the heights and depths of life, he may see in them what others do not: that which brings a brooding sadness to the eyes or an enigmatic smile to the lips. He is also aware of the social dimensions of their lives. He may portray the agony of isolation with sympathy. He may paint so that a picture, without ceasing to be art, becomes bitter social commentary on "man's inhumanity to man." He may see glory in simple acts of kindness or occasions of happy companionship.

Since God offers himself to men through mediators, the specific response of the artist may be to many things; ultimately, however, it is to God. In the end, says Christian faith, only God can save him from idolatry of himself, his fellows, or his world. Because he is able to respond, he can find freedom to express and to communicate.

3. TYPES OF CHRISTIAN ART

Deep within the spirit of man lie connections between worship and art. It is almost impossible to think of an act of worship of any amplitude at all that is not accompanied by artistic overtones. The impulse to worship carries over into an impulse to create things which will enhance that worship. As a result, there arises within a faith a body of art which owes its existence to the worship life of its people. This is usually called *liturgical art*.

Though the reference of the term is restricted by some to art directly connected with the Eucharist, "the liturgy" in the narrower sense, a broader usage is common and it will be convenient for our purpose. Liturgical art includes such items as communion silver and linens, tables and altars, pictures and carvings, hymns and anthems. It is very probable that much of the earliest Christian art which appears in the catacombs was of this character. The depiction of scenes which represented the mighty redemptive acts of God were intended to enhance services of worship in which those acts were celebrated. There is good reason to think that there were references to Daniel, Jonah, and Susanna, who were portrayed on the walls of the cells and passages, in rituals for the dying and the dead.[17] The scene of the baptism of Jesus as well as that of Moses striking the rock for water connected themselves naturally with the baptism of Christians. Several pictures show seven men seated at a table on which are loaves and fishes.[18] Along its lower edge stand baskets of left-overs. The loaves and fish as well as the left-overs are reminiscent of the stories of Jesus' feeding of the multitudes; the seven at the table appear to be those who were described in the book of Acts as having been selected that they might "serve tables." The reference to New Testament incidents is rather complex, but the connection of the subjects with the liturgical practices of the early Christians is not difficult to trace. Here was art intended to enhance the meaning of the celebration of the Lord's supper.

Perhaps few services in the modern church engage the richness and variety of art that is present in a wedding ceremony in a Greek Orthodox Church. The walls and ceilings of the church are adorned with paintings or mosaics, and icons are suspended on the screen. From time to time a deep male voice booms out some portion of the service. The bride's dress has been delicately fashioned. Small coronets, like haloes, are waved over the head of the bride and groom. And at one point in the service these two follow the priest around the chancel in a happy dance. While most churches do not call upon so many of the arts as this for the enhancement of their worship, there are few that do not use them at all. A bare, wooden-walled church standing at a country crossroad will have a bit of lovely linen or a bowl of flowers on its communion table.

There is a second body of art, closely connected with the Christian faith though not directly related to the life of worship. It includes references that are specifically Christian: such things as scenes from Biblical or ecclesiastical history, the portrayal of saints and heroes, or even representations of doctrines and ideas. Rembrandt painted Christ in many situations: as a babe, on the stormy sea, before Pilate, blessing bread at Emmaus. Michelangelo pictured God pointing a finger and bringing man into being. Dürer showed the Christian knight accompanied by death and the devil. Concert music is often composed for religious texts. The dance has frequently drawn themes from Christian

---

[17] Hans Lietzmann, *The Founding of the Church Universal*, pp. 184ff.
[18] See Roland Bainton, *The Panorama of the Christian Church*, p. 17.

MEDIEVAL CATHEDRAL The building of a cathedral involved a variety of arts: architecture, sculpture, and the fashioning of stained glass. Cathedral of Chartres (Courtesy of the French Government Tourist Office.)

heritage: the expulsion from the garden of Eden, the story of Ruth, the successive moods of a Psalm. This large body of objects and compositions can be described simply by the term *religious art.*

A third body of art deserves the adjective "Christian," though it contains no specific reference to matters of the faith. It is that art which reflects, in some significant way, the vision and attitudes of Christian faith. Its character has been suggested in the treatment of the Christian artist. Perhaps absolutes should not be applied to it. No man is completely Christian; why should a picture be expected to be so? It is perhaps best to say that a picture is Christian to the extent that it reflects Christian vision and attitudes. The presence of these will probably be more discernible in the art of a period than in any single work. And their absence will often be easier to detect than their presence. In theology it is easier to spot heresy than it is to be certain of orthodoxy. Similarly, in art, it is easier to say of a given picture or of the work of a certain period that it is clearly non-Christian or even anti-Christian than to say that it is positively Christian. However, the very fact that the negatives have a fairly clear meaning is some indication that there is significance in saying that there is Christian art even when there is no specific religious content. To such art may be applied the rather awkward term: *non-religious Christian art.*

So it is that works of art can be classified in terms of intentions reflected in their creation. But once an object comes into being, it may be used in a variety of ways. An afternoon at a museum will afford numerous illustrations of the way in which things created for liturgical use have become simply religious art. Any sizable art gallery will contain altar pieces and illuminated manuscripts. It may have a cathedral portal with an array of statuary. A major exhibit in the Boston Museum of Fine Arts is a medieval chapel from Spain which was dismantled and reassembled with incredible skill. An evening at a concert hall is hardly complete without some compositions drawn from the store of sacred music. On the other hand an hour in church will reveal the way in which religious art has become liturgical. The prelude may well be a composition which was not written for specific use in the service of worship and yet is definitely Christian in its feeling. *The Last Supper* of Leonardo da Vinci, painted for the refectory of Santa Maria della Grazia, in Milan, may be reproduced in a woodcarving over the altar. Thus there is mutual enrichment of art and liturgy.

A pathway runs between liturgical, religious, and non-religious Christian art. Along it there is passage in both directions.

4. THE CHRISTIAN CRITIC

Creation is not the only expression of Christian faith with reference to art. From earliest times Christian thinkers have offered interpretations of it. While no generally accepted name has been given to it, there is a discipline within Christian thought which might be appropriately called *the theology of art* or *theological aesthetics.* Like other aspects of theology it is concerned to distinguish and to relate. It tries, in the first place, to set forth that which is distinctive in Christian art. In doing this it tries to be self-conscious about the basic character of the faith. In the second place it seeks to relate Christian art to the whole field of artistic creation, and Christian ideas about art to other such ideas. In doing this it enters into conversation with those who have made art the center of their interest, those who have given themselves to the study of aesthetics. On the basis of study of the faith itself and conversation with many people there emerges a constantly renewed Christian theory of art.

Linked to the theoretical discipline is a practical one. Confronted by works or trends in art the Christian thinker may assume the role of a critic. Thus arises *theological art criticism.* Of specific things it asks, "Is it art?" and "Is it Christian?"

Since even works without specific religious reference can be the bearers of a Christian content, the critic may well address himself to them. In an essay in the little book called *The Christian Answer* Paul Tillich describes currents of faith that have moved in the life of Western Europe over the past few centuries and ways in which these have been related to the various aspects of culture: economics, politics, education, and various others. He gives special attention to art as a peculiarly sensitive instrument for reading the trends of the times.

> If we study the portraits of *Rembrandt,* especially in his later period, we confront personalities who are like self-enclosed worlds—strong, lonely, tragic but unbroken, carrying the marks of their unique histories in every line of their faces, expressing the ideals of personality of a humanistic Protestantism. To compare these portraits with *Giotto*'s pictures of St. Francis and his monks is to recognize the difference between two worlds. Giotto's Francis is the expression of a Divine power by which man is possessed and elevated beyond his individual character and personal experiences.[19]

---

[19] Henry P. Van Dusen, ed., *The Christian Answer,* p. 10. Reprinted by permission.

Paul Tillich is noting here the content of two types of art, both of them Christian, and yet different in important ways. In one example the specific reference to a saint is a matter of indifference insofar as its comparison with the other is concerned. The illustration of Rembrandt's work which accompanies the essay is his *Portrait of Jan Six*. Tillich also gives attention to the art of Titian and John Singer Sargent, drawing his illustrations from purely secular subjects. His essay shows the way in which theological art criticism, grounded in a Christian theory of art —which he has made explicit in other writings—can address itself to art even though it has no specific religious content.

Confronted by objects or movements in art which do have such content, the critic must begin by asking the questions which have already been formulated. "Is it art?" "Is it Christian?" The simple fact that a biblical hero is portrayed in color does not give a satisfactory answer. The background against which he is set and the manner in which he is depicted may deny the Christian vision and attitude. On the other hand, the critic may feel that his questions have received an affirmative answer and that he has before him an example of Christian art. Then he must proceed to a third question: "Is the portrayal adequate to the specific content of the picture?" An answer to a query of this kind can be drawn from a passage from a little book recently written by Willem A. Visser 't Hooft on *Rembrandt and the Gospel.*

> As Rembrandt deeply understood the mystery of the Incarnation he was able in the passion story to express the whole tension contained in the gospel between God's wrath and his mercy. Some painters have represented the crucifixion more eloquently. But their very eloquence is suspect. Rembrandt does not omit anything of the biblical story. In the second version of the *Three Crosses* we feel all the human and cosmic horror of Golgotha. But he does not add anything either; for we cannot add anything where 'all things are accomplished.' . . .[20]

It is clear that the author feels that an affirmative answer can be given with reference to the work before him to all three of the questions that may properly be asked of religious art.

Liturgical art calls forth the questions which have already been posed and adds another to them: "Is it appropriate to the use for which it is intended?" It ought to be good, Christian art, but a magnificent picture

---

[20] Willem A. Visser 't Hooft, *Rembrandt and the Gospel*, K. Gregor Smith, trans. (Philadelphia: The Westminster Press; London: S. C. M. Press, 1958), p. 37. Reprinted by permission.

may be liturgically poor because it does not achieve its objective. Some time ago *The Catholic Art Quarterly* carried a two part article by A. Durand with the title, "How Art Becomes Liturgical." It is obvious that the author's aesthetic sensibilities have been offended by some things he has seen; they are poor art. And it is clear that he is deeply aware of the nature of Christian theology and its bearing on art of all sorts, especially Christian. His analysis may be taken to illustrate the way in which a critic within the framework of one of the Christian communions treats the problem of the relation of art to liturgy. He points up the difference between the incarnation and the eucharist: in the former, divinity is concealed but humanity is visible; in the latter, both divinity and humanity are concealed. Hence, the problem of religious art in setting forth the incarnation is that of presenting the human and suggesting the divine. The specific problem of liturgical art is that of suggesting both. Liturgical art will use symbols (signs whose meaning is known to the faithful) rather than images (which point rather obviously to what they represent) because the liturgy conceals Christ as it reveals him—both his humanity and his divinity are concealed by the sacrament, which is a greater mystery than the Incarnation.[21] Christians of other communions than the Roman Catholic may well have other interpretations of the eucharist. And yet, in their own ways, they will have to answer the question, "What is the character of appropriate liturgical art?"

In making judgments concerning liturgical art, the critic may well be involved in the practical matters of the church. A decision may be in the making with regard to some specific object. But theory can never be far away. Theological art criticism and theological aesthetics are parts of a single whole. As everywhere in Christian faith, theology and decision are inextricably interwoven.

5. CHRISTIAN APPRECIATION

The ancient Hebrews were suspicious of art; for them it was connected with idolatry. There may have been intimations of a suspicion that included more than literal idolatry, however, something bound up with a characteristic of art that has been noted again and again. "Pure art" appears to exist for itself and to carry its own reward. Hence, the

---

[21] A. Durand, "How Art Becomes Liturgical," two-part article in *The Catholic Art Quarterly*, XXII, Christmas 1958, pp. 24-30; Easter 1959, pp. 56-60. Used by permission.

modern Christian may well reflect the suspicions of ancient Hebrews. Experiences that carry their own reward may easily make too large a claim. Indeed, a life devoted simply to them and their multiplication will end in futility.

However, the ancient Hebrews also treasured some forms of art and attributed their creation to the inspiration of the Spirit. And this, perhaps, is because they saw life as a totality lived before the presence of God, a whole made up of many parts. And the Christian, reflecting their faith, may look upon aesthetic experience as one of the goods which God has placed in life. At times, he can give himself to art because the whole of his life has another dedication. He has heard the apostle say to him, "All things are yours,"[22] and he gratefully accepts what is given. His appreciation can range over the entirety of art, for to him belongs art pagan as well as art Christian, primitive as well as civilized. And he is likely to be aware of more in art than that which speaks to his senses. For great art always intimates vision. Without that, it loses its own validity; with it, art itself has meaning.

In retrospect, the Christian can ponder the meaning of an experience enjoyed for its own sake. The creativity of God may have been at work enhancing the world he had made. He can walk by the seaside after looking at paintings by the Impressionists and see colors he had not seen before. The judgment of God may have been at work condemning his smallness of mind and insensitivity of spirit. He may recognize why he was disturbed by what he saw, why he wanted to slash a picture or smash a statue. The redemption of God may have been at work bringing him serenity in times of distraction. In a moment of despair, when all else seemed to proclaim the world meaningless, he may have found a grace which bound him to life through experiences enjoyed for their own sake. The whole of the Christian vision may have come to him with fresh meaning as art suggested what theologies had never successfully said.

To lay undue stress on the self-rewarding character of the aesthetic experience may lead one to overlook the interconnectedness of the various experiences of life; they flow into one another, modifying each other in various subtle ways. Hence, art can teach, though it does so without being pedagogical; it can preach, though it does so without being homiletical. It can affect our actions; though, if it is true to itself, it will do so without moralizing. Aesthetic experience may flow into that of worship; herein lies the possibility of liturgical art. Good religious

[22] I Corinthians 3:21.

art always calls us to itself, but points beyond itself. Its very character, that of being able to evoke a response which is self-rewarding, frees us from preoccupations of many kinds; its capacity to evoke a response to that which is beyond it frees us from our preoccupation with it. If it does not, false worship occurs. The danger of art lies in the very quality which gives it its glory.

God himself is the first artist; he it is who creates for the sake of creating; who expresses his very self in so doing; and also communicates his own goodness to his world and to his creatures through his world. He alone is to be sought by the whole of life for his own sake, and only by so seeking can man be saved. But that seeking is prefigured in art, which enjoys his world. One of the great Christian confessions affirms the conviction that "man's chief end is to glorify God and enjoy him forever."[23]

READINGS

From the Bible

1. The use of music in worship is clearly reflected in I Chronicles 25 and in many Psalms, as 145, 149, 150.

2. Dancing before the Lord is described in II Samuel 6.

3. Skill for the building of the tabernacle is attributed to divine inspiration in Exodus 35:30-36:1.

From Historic Christianity

1. Reproductions of pictures and works of sculpture from the whole range of Christian history are easily available.

2. A selection of hymns and tunes on various topics and from several periods of the life of the church can be made from any good hymnal.

---

[23] "The Westminster Shorter Catechism," A.D. 1647, Philip Schaff, ed., *The Creeds of Christendom* (New York: Harper & Brothers, 1877), III, 676.

3. Major musical works treat great themes of Christian faith: Franz Joseph Haydn's *Creation,* Johann Sebastian Bach's *The Passion According to Saint Matthew,* George Friedrich Handel's *The Messiah.*

4. Services in which music is integral to the worship will be found in various service books: some have been recorded.

FOR STUDY AND DISCUSSION

1. Study a composer or a composition, an artist or a work of art.
2. The problem of portraying Christ in our time is a formidable one. How much should the artist be bound by traditional notions? Has the Christ idea been distorted in the art of the last few centuries?
3. Lewis Mumford, *The Condition of Man* (New York: Harcourt, Brace & World, 1944) finds Grosz, Ernst, Dali, Van Gogh, and Picasso prophetic interpreters of the character of our time, which he describes in terms of "Barbarism and Dissolution," pp. 343-391. Other writers say similar things. What truth do you see in their assertions on the basis of study of the artists and their work?
4. What sort of dance, if any, might be worked out to interpret a theme of Christian faith? Would it be appropriate for presentation in a service of worship? Should it be performed in a church?
5. Study recordings of historical and contemporary musical settings of some service of the church: Morning Prayer, Communion, The Mass, Marriage.

XV

A COLLEGE CHAPEL

Courses in Christian thought do not normally involve laboratory work. And yet, if our reading of the faith is correct, a live theology is one which is involved in man's actual decisions. Hence, it seems appropriate to include here the description of a specific attempt to give expression to the vision and attitudes of Christian faith.

Some years back the generosity of a great number of people made it possible to erect a chapel on the campus of Hollins College, a school with a broadly Christian heritage. I was chaplain at that time and together with the choirmaster was invited to work with the trustees and administration of the college in the planning of the building. Valued suggestions came from colleagues and students, college chaplains and musical directors, clergymen and other friends. The planning itself was a labor of several years, and the building, when complete, was a large one. It comprised a main chapel seating some eight hundred and fifty, a meditation chapel seating fifty, a social room, conference room, choir rehearsal room, sacristy, several offices, and various other rooms; though nothing comparable to the educational unit of a church was constructed. In honor of a long-time friend of the college, the building was named the Jessie Ball duPont Chapel.

Some of the thinking that went into that building will be described in this chapter: the planning called for definition of the faith; some delineation of the relation of faith to culture, represented in miniature in the various facets of collegiate life; and the tracing out of relationships between faith and one of the arts, that of architecture.

1. ARCHITECT AND THEOLOGIAN

In building a church the conversation between thought and art becomes literal and personal; theology and architecture are related through theologians and architects. Any significant personal relationship in teamwork involves friendship. This fact creates problems as well as opportunities for cooperation. The theologian must fight the temptation to try to become an amateur architect and thus get in the way of the integrity of the aesthetic effort. And yet he must enter sympathetically into the architect's problems and even his inspirations, seeking to understand and encourage. There may be times when he will resist the impulse to speak to his friend because he knows that the architect is at a stage in his design work at which he must be left alone to think and work through in his own way.

The architect, on the other hand, need not seek to be a complete theologian. Certainly he is partly a theologian, all men are. He is not simply neutral in matters of faith. For him his art must speak of certain things, convey certain convictions. These must be sufficiently similar to the convictions of the theologian that the two can seek the same ends in the specific project before them. And yet the architect will recognize that there are ranges of theological insight of which he is not, as an architect, expected to be aware. The lines cannot be tightly drawn; they never can where personalities are involved. The personal problem in the relationship between architect and theologian is that of keeping an open and sustained mutual interchange and understanding. This is never an accomplished fact; it is a continuing process.

The present, it would seem, is a particularly auspicious time for conversation between theology and architecture, for there are indications that convictions of many architects bear strong resemblances to those of many theologians. Both are convinced of deep hungers of the human heart which have been denied by thought and life in the recent past. As we shall see, architects have in some cases sought to help satisfy these hungers through their own art. Furthermore, contemporary architectural forms have made possible an expression of historic insights of faith in rather remarkable ways. This is not to say that at long last there has emerged a Christian architecture. If the theses of this book are correct, there is no such thing nor can there be. Styles of architecture come and go, as do styles of thought and even of conduct. And the Christian faith has outlived many styles. However, there seem to be certain styles which open themselves more readily than others to the expression of historic Christian convictions about man, his world, and his God.

The pattern of conversation between theologian and architect might be described in the following way, though it obviously oversimplifies the issues considerably:

> the theologian confronts the architect with a theological demand for which he requires an architectural answer—the chapel should say X or Y; how can this be expressed in architecture?
>
> the architect confronts the theologian with an aesthetic demand for which he requires a theological answer—the chapel should have X or Y; what can this mean?

At an early stage in the planning of the Hollins College chapel it was suggested that a set of principles be formulated for the guidance of the project. As chaplain I drew up such a set, and it was approved by the college. When it was presented to the architects, they indicated their complete agreement, and the principles became a general guide for the work. It is obvious that they reflect an outlook which has been described in this book in terms of vision and attitude.

1. Whoever enters the chapel should feel a sense of awe, and, at the same time, a sense of welcome, of friendliness. The awe should not be forbidding nor the friendliness sentimental. The problem here is difficult. Indeed, it is one aspect of one of the most difficult problems in religious thought: that of taking account of the holiness and the love of God at once, though from a human point of view the two are in tension. The sense of awe should bring to our total campus life a sense of reverence, the sense of friendliness should remind us of the intangibles of grace and goodness which are ever in our midst.

2. Whoever enters the chapel should feel a sense of a brooding perfection—the perfectness of the divine. The building itself—its own integrity and beauty—should be a witness to the divine perfection, by being simply itself. Here is a pointer toward that urge to perfection which haunts our pursuit of truth, our devotion to beauty, our concern for rightness in personal conduct and social relations.

3. Whoever enters the chapel should feel anew the glory of the earth

which reflects its divine origination. Here is the vision which gives substance to our science—the study of the earth—and to our art—its celebration in beauty of color and form.

4. Whoever enters the chapel should sense that love which meets human sin and rebellion with its own forgiveness. Religion is no sweeping aside of the anxieties and frustrations of life, but the discovery of a peace which passes understanding. Hence, while the chapel enhances the glory of the earth and of human values, it always points away from these too.

5. Whoever enters the chapel should feel that the divine love which meets him in forgiveness unites him with others—in this place and beyond its walls. Our faith is to its very center social. The chapel must foster our sense of togetherness in worship, draw us out of our isolation. It must also carry our thoughts to concern for the sorrows and woes of the world and to the sharing of its deepest joys.[1]

2. THE PRIMACY OF GOD

All the attitudes of life must be determined by the attitude toward God; our reading of man and his meaning, of the world and its significance is determined by the vision of God; and He is the high and holy One who inhabits eternity—these are ideas which we have encountered again and again. Through the centuries and in our own time they have had enormous significance in the effort to give expression to Christian faith through architectural form. Negatively they have meant that a church must be, first of all, a house of worship and not an example of art for its own sake; that it cannot be an overgrown living room in which polite people sip tea and talk about trivialities; that it cannot be a purveyor of creature comforts which leaves men unaware of a disturbing peace which passes understanding. The means by which reference to the Holy has been expressed have been many, and they have varied with the years. I cannot forget opening a simple and utterly unpretentious little door and being confronted by the nave of Ely Cathedral. The simplicity of some New England meeting houses, with their rejection of all that might detract from the meeting with God as his word is read and preached, bears witness to it. In our time the tools of modern engineering and fabrication have placed at men's disposal new means of expressing their awareness of the holiness of God. Architects have

[1] The statement was sent by the architects to *Progressive Architecture* and appeared in the issue of November, 1956, XXXVII, No. 11, pp. 16ff. Reprinted by permission.

become aware in new and fresh ways of the awe-inspiring possibilities of space and light, of surface and angle, of texture and color. They are sensitive to the elemental power of simple substances—stone and timber and steel. The outright modernism of such a building as Eliel Saarinen's Christ Lutheran Church in Minneapolis has, for me at least, a measure of the power which characterized the great churches of the Middle Ages, without involving a romantic retreat into the past.

The high and holy One demands truth in the inward parts; here lies the basis of that sense of law which, as we have seen, informs religion. Its implications have been recurrently effectual in architecture. In simplest form it is the demand that a building, whether it is a church or anything else, must be honest, and that the man who plans it must possess aesthetic integrity. Often, I suspect, in the conversations between theologians and architects, it has been the latter who have insisted upon it; thus they have reminded theologians of an aspect of their faith of which they may have been unaware. At the least, it seems to mean that there should be no trickery in building, that religious symbols should not be toyed with, that cheap theatrical effects are as distasteful and dishonest in the church as they are in serious theater. Surely it does not mean that there is no place in life or in church for the expression of a sense of humor. In the Cathedral of Lincoln the face of an imp stares down from the loveliness of a fan-vaulted ceiling; he belongs there. And who would remove the gargoyles from medieval churches? The tumblers of God must have their chance to praise the Creator. The passion for sincerity on the part of architects who are true to their vocation is like that of any other artist. Earlier in this century it expressed itself through the formula that "form follows function."[2] Sometimes this was so narrowly defined that only rather obvious practical functions were envisioned. But when religious and aesthetic function are recognized, the formula may still be seen as a pointer toward that honesty without which art cannot exist and faith cannot survive. A church must be what it is, expressing faith in an architectural language in which yea is yea, and nay is nay.

However, the Holy One does not simply confront us with a demand; he offers us a gift. Christian faith affirms that the deepest revelation of the Holy shows it to be identical with love. It is only holiness re-

---

[2] Guiding principle in the work of Louis Sullivan. See Hugh Morrison, *Louis Sullivan* (New York: W. W. Norton, 1935), p. 251. It is important to note that Sullivan's functionalism "means something far more than mechanism and utilitarianism" (p. 253). Morrison quotes Sullivan: "'I value spiritual results only.'" (p. 253). Reprinted by permission.

Massive strength marks the work of Norman builders who constructed the walls of this nave; the Gothic arch and window at the far end came later. Ely Cathedral (Courtesy of the British Information Services)

An imposing site provides the opportunity for the massive thrust of the towers of this great church. Durham Cathedral (Courtesy of the British Information Services)

THE STRENGTH OF ELEMENTAL MATERIALS

Blocks of stone, panes of glass, and a squared tower of brick impart simple strength to this contemporary church. Christ Lutheran Church, Minneapolis. Eliel and Eero Saarinen, Architects (George Miles Ryan, Minneapolis)

Large planes of simple brick are broken by glass and stone in this contemporary church. Christ Lutheran Church, Minneapolis. Eliel and Eero Saarinen, Architects (George Miles Ryan, Minneapolis)

Hearing is most important in this church in the Puritan tradition, and a great pulpit where the Word can be read and preached is central; observance of the Lord's supper is important too, and a simple table is provided for it. The First Baptist Church, Providence, Rhode Island (Norman S. Watson, Providence)

Seeing the altar and celebrating the Communion Service at it are central in this contemporary church in the liturgical tradition; hearing is important too, so a large pulpit and a prominent lectern are provided for preaching and reading the Word. Christ Lutheran Church, Minneapolis, Minnesota. Eliel and Eero Saarinen, Architects (George Miles Ryan, Minneapolis)

vealed as love that we can bear, and it is only love known as holiness that confronts us with its full majesty. Here is a matter so delicate that it is difficult to say anything in a general way concerning it. Subtle intimations of grace come through treatments of approaches and entrances to the church and its interior, of the play of light and shade, of colors and materials. However, since Christian faith associates the disclosure of the love of God with events in history, it seems inevitable that reminders of those events will have their place in the church. In one way or another symbols pointing to God's redemptive acts are called for. Here is a point at which questions about architectural styles are of central significance; for some styles make it easy to give a focal place to such symbols, others make it very difficult. It is important to see, however, that different Christian groups treasure different symbols. Some emphasize symbols which appeal to the eye; the altar and the cross may be of prime importance. Perhaps among traditional styles they will find the Gothic most congenial; the New England meeting house will not easily adapt itself to their needs. Others emphasize symbols which are heard; to them the reading and the preaching of the word are the major purveyors of the assurance of grace. For them the New England Meeting House, with its conscious exclusion of specific visual symbolism and its attention to the high central pulpit will seem appropriate. Among modern churches some have been so constructed as to give prominence to altar and cross; others to the pulpit.

In the Hollins College chapel the attempt was made to focus attention on a few powerful symbols of the redemptive acts of God, significant for both the eye and the ear. At the center of the forward wall of the nave is a huge ebony cross. Behind it is a reredos with three simple symbols repeated within it: the bread, the cup, and the cross itself. Beneath it is a large but very simple communion table. To one side is a large lectern with a great Bible open on it. To the other is the pulpit, imposing in size and yet not so placed as to detract attention from cross and table. Thus the forgiveness of God is ever before the worshipper. The cross proclaims that "while we were yet sinners, Christ died for us"; [3] the table is one to which we do not come of our own worthiness and from which we receive the bread and wine which show forth the Lord's death; the Bible is there to tell of a grace that is undeserved; and the pulpit affords a place from which the word of reconciliation may be spoken.

Simple geometric forms intimate an infinite perfection while they seek

---

[3] Romans 5:8, K.J.V.

CHANCEL OF A COLLEGE CHAPEL In this college chapel a large, free-standing altar is central and is used for communion services in various traditions. The pulpit is prominent too, as is the lectern which holds a great Bible. Jessie Ball duPont Chapel, Hollins College. Frantz and Addkison, Architects (Deyerle Studies, Roanoke)

to embody its reflection in finite figures. Seen from the front the outside of the chapel is composed of two balanced triangles of unequal size connected by a low horizontal element from which a steeple is thrust upward. Within the nave of the main chapel is one great triangle, bounded by huge wooden arches; from its base piers spring upward toward an apex, but call the eye to pierce the roof.

It is the huge arches of the nave and the upspringing of the reredos which largely impart the sense of awe; color and texture break its austerity. Thus a feeling of friendliness suffuses the whole, leading toward the central symbols which speak of God's love in its utmost manifestation, that point at which love and holiness were revealed as one.

3. THE PHYSICAL AND THE SPIRITUAL

The high and holy One is the free Lord of all things and he is bound to none; this is a central conviction of Christian faith. It is an important one to keep in mind, for it reminds us that he can make his way to the spirit of man under any conditions. Sincere acts of worship are possible in the most unlikely places. And the finest setting cannot guarantee that he who is placed in it will be irresistibly drawn into relationship with the eternal Spirit. Architecture can be taken too seriously.

At the same time it is important to recall the conviction that this world is God's creation and that all within it is available for his redemptive uses. Specifically, there is no line between spirit and matter such that one is sacred, the other unholy. Nature within and without man is good, and can serve its Maker. This conviction sees a sacramental potentiality in matter and makes it possible for the vocation of the architect to find its place within the priesthood of all believers. Under his hand a material thing is fashioned that it may be a bearer of the power of the Spirit into the life of mankind.

The physical aspect of the building of a church is simply prodigious. There are surveys and core-borings, there are endless consultations with various engineers, and finally the appearance of page after page of blue prints. The respect of the theologian for the architect is bound to grow. It is amazing to see how a man can keep in mind an aesthetic effect that is desired and at the same time remember to make provision for convenient office space. It is all well and good to say that people should think of spiritual matters when they are in church, but clattering dishes in a misplaced kitchen can prove stiff competition for the most eloquent preacher.

The Christian life has a variety of expressions, and a church building will rightly seek to serve a multiplicity of concerns. However, that part of it which is often called *the sanctuary* is first of all a place of worship. Here is the function that determines its form. But in itself this is no simple thing. It involves, in the first place, attention to the general mood which is induced by any architectural feature. To this reference has already been made. It involves, in the second place, attention to the actual conduct of services. General planning in terms of types of services which are expected is essential. Members of the congregation have to be able to get into and out of the building; they must be seated where they can see and hear. Those who have part in the leading of worship—ministers and musicians—must have access to the places they need to be. Many cautions are negative: people must not move at times and places when their movement will divert attention from what is central at that moment in the service. Attention to acoustics is of central importance. The preacher must be heard; the choir and organ must be loud enough, but not too loud. The people must have a sense of being a congregation as they sing and enter into spoken responses. Lighting

There is room for a hundred singers, organ console, harpsichord, and a small orchestra in the spacious balcony at the rear of the chapel.

The Hollins Chapel Choir is ready to sing; above and behind it is the organ, designed for beauty of appearance as well as balance of tone.

MUSIC IN A COLLEGE CHAPEL Jessie Ball DuPont Chapel, Hollins College. Frantz and Addkison, Architects. The Allie Nash Young Memorial Organ designed and built by Walter Holtkamp. Choir directed by Arthur S. Talmadge (Deyerle Studies, Roanoke)

must be carefully planned so that attention is given to that which is important and drawn away from that which is not. In these matters the whole modern development of engineering techniques is of the greatest value. We need no longer build a church and simply hope that we shall hear without difficulty when we are within its walls. Knowledge of physics normally prevents the modern church builder from having his steeple crash because he has not calculated stresses correctly. The developments of modern science have made it possible for men to bring the material to the service of the spiritual in ways that exceed the possibilities of earlier times.

Much could be said about what the Hollins College Chapel owes to the study of books, the examination of churches, consultation with clergymen and others, and the ingenuity of architects and engineers. Such questions as "How far should this be from that?" may be of great importance when an actual service is going on. A year of experience with the chapel has proved that little time given to such questions was wasted. An ambulatory around the chancel, light switches with dimmers, a section at the rear of the nave which can be closed off with folding doors, an excellent sound system—these and other things have been helpful at many times. Perhaps the best illustration of the contribution of arrangements to the conduct of services, however, is to be seen in the provisions for music. At the rear of the nave of the main chapel is a balcony adequate in size for a large choir as well as a number of musical instruments. The acoustics of the building are such that these are well heard, and yet they do not conceal the altar nor distract attention from the chapel chancel with its significant symbols. The permanent instruments are a harpsichord, and an organ so built that parts of it are actually cantilevered over the heads of the choir. Stairways at the two sides of the balcony afford access from the main floor; at the turn of each stair is a light controlled from the organ which can be flashed to keep a marching choir on beat. Off one of these stairways is the choir library and office of the organist and choirmaster. Off the other is the choir rehearsal room, identical in floor arrangement with the balcony above. Ceiling and walls are acoustically treated; closets line the walls. Electric signals make possible communication between organ, choir room, and a hallway just off the chancel. The meditation chapel is provided with a small organ specially constructed for it. Recessed speakers in its ceiling make it possible to play recorded music into it, or even a service from the main chapel. A carillon of forty-seven bells in the steeple adds yet another dimension to the contribution of music to the worship of the entire college community.

4. MAN AND NATURE

Thus it is that through the eye and the ear impulses come which contribute to the experience of worship; the physical and the spiritual are parts of a single whole. But there is a part of the physical which has special significance; it can speak in a rather direct way of the Divine. Wood and stone and leaf can echo the words which the things of earth said to the responsive ears of Augustine: "We are not God," but "He made us." [4]

Builders sometimes obscured that witness; they fashioned things in such a manner that natural qualities were covered over. Wood was carved so that it imitated stone. Bricks and boards were overlaid with layers of paint which made it impossible for them to display the grain of a tree or the color of clay. Currents of attitude which found other expressions in the different aspects of culture were thus reflected through the media of the architect and craftsman. As we have seen, there were profound movements in the spiritual life of mankind during recent centuries which created a gap between man and the earth from which he was fashioned.

The past few decades, however, have furnished considerable evidence of an increasing sensitivity on the part of architects to the goodness of the natural world. Indeed, some have expressed a genuine sense of responsibility for helping to close the gap between man and his mother earth. Attention has been given to the settings in which houses were placed, and the very form of the domicile is sometimes determined largely by the contours of the land on which it is built. The line between outdoors and indoors has been, in some cases, almost obscured so that living space, lawn, and garden fade into one another. The use of materials reflects a new respect for their natural condition. In part this is a reflection of the passion for honesty to which reference has already been made. Rightly the question is asked, "Why should one thing be disguised in order to look like something it is not?" Perhaps Gertrude Stein was speaking of something like this in her enigmatic words about a rose.[5] At any rate many contemporary architects insist that "a board is a board is a board."

An architect sensitive to the significance of the world may well enter into congenial conversation with a theologian who is aware of the atti-

[4] *The Confessions of Saint Augustine,* translated by F. J. Sheed, p. 177. (X, vi).

[5] The interpretation here given was suggested in a conversation by Professor John Ballator of Hollins College.

Light floods the altar area from a large window in this contemporary church; the windows at the side of the nave are designed so that light falls forward through them. Christ Lutheran Church, Minneapolis, Minnesota. Eliel and Eero Saarinen, Architects (George Miles Ryan, Minneapolis)

Sunlight comes through the ceiling to accentuate the chancel with its cross, altar, and plantings. First Methodist Church, Midland, Michigan. Alden B. Dow, Architect (Bill Hedrich, Hedrich-Blessing, Chicago)

tude toward nature that is in keeping with the Christian vision. That such conversation has been going on in recent years is evidenced by trends in church architecture. In many churches that are being built today there is lavish use of natural materials, the opening of windows on close-lying lawns and gardens or even on sea and sky and mountain far off; plants grow inside the church and vines make their way up interior walls as well as those outside.

At this point one comment is needed; it has to do with symbolism. As we have seen, material things can take on meanings. Thus, in a church, wood or stone can be so fashioned as to bring to the remembrance of the worshippers the supper which Jesus celebrated with his disciples on the night in which he was betrayed. It may also stir the mind to thoughts of those millions who through the centuries and in our time have received bread and wine and in so doing have showed forth the Lord's death till he come. Thus wood and stone speak of the redemptive act of God. And their native beauty can enhance the acts of worship in which that act is celebrated. But at least in some parts of the church wood and stone should speak of something else, something that is not directly associated with historical events. If our reading of Christian faith is correct, the appropriation of redemption should carry with it an appreciation of creation. Wood and stone should be permitted to say simply, "God saw everything that he had made, and behold, it was very good." [6] To make every bit of wood or stone in a church bear a specific symbolic meaning is to drain away the meaning that is in its very self. To be sensitive to the preciousness that is in wood and earth and stone is to witness to the God who made them good.

In the building of the Hollins College Chapel a concern to make men feel the glory of the earth was a guiding principle. The large sanctuary reflects it on every side. The floor is of varicolored Vermont slate, the front of the chancel is Lynchburg greenstone, and beneath the altar is white Georgia marble. Great arches of pine support the ceiling. Pews are of oak, walls of soft brick; and woods of various sorts panel the chancel area. The grain of fir from the Pacific Northwest shows through the soft blue wash of the ceiling. In the Meditation Chapel again are stone and brick and wood; here a garden, where dogwoods bloom and a brook flows softly, seems to come in through the huge rear window and continue itself in the window box beneath it.

---

[6] Genesis 1:31.

5. PERSON AND GROUP

One of the most difficult demands with which the theologian confronts the architect is that of doing justice to a faith which proclaims the preciousness of the individual at the same time as it sets forth the significance of his relations to others. The adequate church should be such as to provide the setting for acts of private devotion and of public worship. It should afford support for the human spirit in moments when it seeks its solitary way to God. And yet the entrance of ministers, choirs, and congregations should not seem an intrusion. Rather should the church seem to be fulfilling a major function when its people are at worship within it. The requirements are not easy, and most churches are more successful in meeting one than the other; indeed, some types of churches are better adapted to the worship of individuals, others to that of congregations.

During the past several centuries, as we have seen, powerful forces have been at work in our culture emphasizing the individual to the neglect of his involvement in the community. Religious thought and action have responded to them in ways that have been noted. A premium has been placed on the religious experience of the individual, and religious architecture has reflected this concern. In liturgical churches the altar has been placed at the end of a long choir and sanctuary, while individual worshippers, not essentially related to each other, sit in rows to watch something happen. In churches where preaching is central, an imposing pulpit gives an individual opportunity to voice his religious convictions while his congregation passively listens. A small table for communion is on the floor below the pulpit and is a convenient stand for flowers and collection plates.

Contemporary theologians are not alone in being aware of the essentially social nature of man. Architecture has also been sensitive to man's need for fellowship, indeed of the need to transform some of the very patterns of his living if his isolation is not to destroy him. The fragmenting force of urban life is actively resisted in the planning of apartments and villages which make comradeship natural and almost inevitable. Ecclesiastical architecture has also responded to the rediscovery of the social dimension of faith. Pope Pius X called on Catholics to bring the altar out of the dim recesses of a deep sanctuary and build the church as a single room where the unity of priest and people might be felt.[7] Reformed churches enlarged the communion table and gave it a place alongside the pulpit. Some churches have placed the Lord's table at the very center of the building, arranging the seats in a circle or square around it. Thus, the congregation is conceived as a group, not a series of isolated individuals. It is the people of God who gather around his word or sit as a family around his table.

Concern for both the individual and the social dimensions of worship reflected itself in the planning of the Hollins College Chapel. The Meditation chapel invites the solitary to moments of reflection and also provides a meeting place for groups so small that they would be lost in a large room. The large chapel has its silent word for the one who goes to it alone. And yet awareness of the social dimension of faith was a fundamental principle in its planning, though no attempt was made to implement it by departure from the conventional arrangement of long pews in straight rows. Other values seemed to point to the retention of this form. But like many contemporary churches the chapel has a very shallow and broad chancel, one room with the nave of the church. Minister and people are together in a shared act of worship; the priesthood of all believers is recognized. The Lord's table is very large—eleven feet in length—and stands free. The choir is at the rear. No group of stellar performers sing for the entertainment of listening individuals. The choir is the part of the congregation which can sing better than the rest of us, but facing as we do, singing to our common Lord, it brings the rest of us into the beauty of its worship. Acoustics are such as to give those who sing and read together a sense of each other's presence. Thus in many ways the chapel seeks to help people in a time when lives are being driven to separation to rediscover that "no man is an island." [8]

But a chapel must do more than remind us that we are members one of another; it must point beyond human community. It is very easy for college worship to become a celebration of the spirit of a school. And it is easy for a college chapel to encourage obeisance before the idols of the collegiate forum. John R. Everett, then President of Hollins College, rightly rejected the suggestion to place the college seal in a central place in the chapel sanctuary.

Theology places a great demand before architecture in the building of a church. It must glorify the earth, but point beyond it to its Maker. It must help man discover the greatness of the human spirit while it points beyond it to the Reality before whom man hides his face. It must

---

[7] George E. Kidder Smith, *Switzerland Builds* (New York: Albert Bonnier, 1950), p. 131.

[8] John Donne, *Devotions*, p. 108.

recall to him the high meaning of his own intelligence while it reminds him that "reverence for the Lord is the beginning of wisdom." [9] It is no wonder that one of the architects who had a part in planning the chapel for Hollins College spoke of building a church as the "most difficult of architectural problems."

READINGS

From the Bible

1. Elaborate plans were made by Solomon for the building of the temple as it is described in II Chronicles 3-5. Most scholars hold this to be a very late account reflecting, in part, post-exilic attitudes.

2. The dedicatory prayer for the temple is given in II Chronicles 6.

3. Superstitious reverence for the temple is attacked by Jeremiah 7.

4. The joy of a Jew as he thinks about the temple is reflected in Psalm 84.

5. Concern for rebuilding the temple is a theme of Ezra and Haggai.

From Historic Christianity

1. Reproductions of churches from all periods of the church's life are available and may be studied with a view to their adequacy in witnessing to the totality of the faith.

2. Examples of church architecture reflecting various historic styles are present in most communities and afford an opportunity for analysis.

---

[9] Psalm 111:10. R.S.V. reads: "The fear of the Lord is the beginning of wisdom." I have used the phrase: "reverence for the Lord" which is used by J. M. Powis Smith in *The Bible, An American Translation* (Chicago: The University of Chicago Press, 1935). Reprinted by permission.

FOR STUDY AND DISCUSSION

1. Study some church in the light of your own principles, those of someone else, or those suggested here.
2. What is the arrangement of objects (altar, pulpit, etc.) at the front of the church? Why? Is it appropriate for services that are held in the church?
3. Is the provision for music adequate and appropriate? Is congregational singing easy and natural? Is the place assigned to the choir good acoustically, visually, and liturgically?
4. How adaptable is the church for special services: baptisms, the celebration of communion, weddings?
5. What is the historic significance of the style in which the church is built? Is the use of the church today in keeping with the use for which churches in the same architectural style were intended?

XVI

POETRY

Some years ago a theological faculty announced that all of its candidates for the B.D. and Ph.D. degrees—those who were preparing for the ministry or for teaching—were required to demonstrate their competence in dealing with the relationship of theology and imaginative literature.[1] This was not because the faculty wanted to make it possible for students to garner literary gems for the decoration of their sermons or lectures. They were convinced that the faith of the Christian people had been set forth in distinctive fashion in literature and that the student should become aware of this. With others in our time they saw a significant relationship between Christian faith and literary expression.

That relationship is the theme of two chapters. The first deals with its general character, then turns to the expression of faith in poetry. The second goes on to a consideration of stories and plays.

---

[1] The Federated Theological Faculty at the University of Chicago. Having been a member of the faculty which made the decision, I was involved in the discussion which preceded it.

1. LITERATURE AND THE RECOVERY OF FAITH

Awareness of the relationships between faith and literature has several facets. In the first place a reappraisal of the significance of the literary element in the Bible is going on. It is recognized, for example, that a certain type of "literary" approach to the Bible may hide rather than disclose its meaning. Students may enroll in a course on "The Bible as Literature," though they hope to evade the religious element in it. Even rhapsodic exclamations about the glory of biblical literature may simply divert the attention of people from the main thing. For what the Bible centrally talks about is the shock which men—individually and in community—experience when they are confronted by the Living Lord who is the Creator of heaven and earth. In his presence literature stops—as does everything else. For when he speaks, the only appropriate response is, "let all the earth keep silence before him." [2] And yet out of the confrontation emerge expressions, in words as well as in actions. What the expressions are like depends in part on the people who do the expressing. The Lord is no respecter of persons; he can confront the prosaic as well as the poetic. And the prosaic will give a prosy account of their encounter.

But the poetic will give a poetic account, and this is a matter of great significance. The fact is that there is a great deal that can be called literature in the Bible. And particularly do certain of those key passages which have had a critical effect in molding men's imagination to the Christian vision have literary quality. Some of these have been quoted or cited in the exposition of the great themes of the faith—the Creation, the primeval rebellion, the dream of the redeemer, the coming of the Christ. An issue among Christian thinkers of our time occurs just at this point. There are those who feel that the central themes of faith can be expressed with any adequacy only in some literary form. To set them forth in systematic and coherent fashion is to omit something essential and, actually, to distort them. Without entering into the quarrel at the moment, we may concede that the literary expression is, at least, appropriate.

A second aspect of contemporary response to the relations of faith and literature concerns historic Christianity itself. We, in our time, are seeing an awakening of interest in the specifically Christian contribution to the

[2] Habbakuk 2:20.

literary heritage of the West. At the time when Christianity exercised its greatest influence on the culture, other factors certainly played upon its literary expression. The heritage of Greece remained strong throughout the history of literature in Europe. And yet in men like Chaucer and Shakespeare and Milton a distinctively Christian element was at work. In recent centuries the Christian influence has waned. However, there has been considerable literature which has been Christian in name and intent. Our contemporaries see much of this as actually departing from the historic faith in rather serious fashion. Under the impetus of influences tending to equate faith with ethics there has emerged a literature in which the Christian is portrayed as the moral hero, saving himself. And under the impetus of the emphasis on religious experience there has emerged a considerable body of literature which dwells on inward feelings and subjective emotions. Often this descends to sentimentality of the worst sort. And yet even during the recent centuries there have been men of letters who have continued to be aware of the more profound strains of historic faith. Like their counterparts in other spheres of the Christian faith, they have formed a note of protest against the common temper even when that appeared to be Christian. Men like Hawthorne and Melville were sensitive to the more somber sides of the Christian gospel when their contemporaries were dwelling on its brighter aspects.

A third aspect of contemporary awareness of relations between faith and literature has to do with our contemporaries themselves. Some theologians are seeing in the literature of our time intimations of aspects of historic Christianity that have been long neglected. This is true even in the work of writers who are not, at least consciously, Christians. It is an evidence, perhaps, of the manner in which a faith remains in a culture and works in the depths even when it is not apparent on the surface. Often that which is said is critical and even hostile to our conventional Christianity. And it may be said in a way that is strange and even bizarre. But when we look at it carefully, we can see in it some affirmation that belongs to a historic Christianity from which we have been cut off. The ordinary Christian words may conceal rather than disclose the very affirmation the poet makes. In some cases, of course, the poet may be consciously and intentionally Christian. Some poets have felt profoundly the meaning of faith for their lives and for their expression. And yet they may feel that in order to give expression to the faith as they apprehend it, they must depart from the commonplace verbiage, and even, in some cases, from the traditional forms. The depths of anguish and the summits of grace require a language which is strange to the contemporary world.

2. FAITH AND LITERATURE: GENERAL CONSIDERATIONS

Significant literature always reflects a vision of the world and its meaning; it embodies a set of attitudes. For this reason it can be called *religious* no matter what its specific subject matter may be. The question, therefore, about the vision it reflects is germane to an appreciation and understanding of it.

That some literature reflects a vision and a set of attitudes so clearly as to be a veritable witness to these is implied in the very content of the Christian scriptures. The early church was convinced that a certain set of books could be singled out as normative for its thought and practice; and within these books were certainly bits of literature: there were stories and poems. The important thing about the stories was that they were told in a certain way; and the important thing about the poems was that they intimated certain responses to reality. Further, these stories and these poems emerged out of the events in which Christians believed God had disclosed himself to men. These pieces were imbedded in the Bible; there was for the Christians—as there have been for men of other faiths—*sacred literature*.

In this respect literature differs from other arts. In it, as we have noted, meanings are rendered explicit as they usually are not in other arts. And yet the meanings are not set forth in their bare didactic form. Attention is given to the connotative as well as the denotative dimensions of the meanings of the words which are used. The relation of literature to faith may not be closer than that of the other arts; it is, however, more explicit.

With respect to those characteristics which literature shares with other arts, its relations to faith parallels theirs. Since we have already dealt with these in some detail, we can simply review them briefly at this point. There are, thus, types of literature which have their analogs in other arts. There is *liturgical literature* growing out of an effort to enhance the worship life of the churches: prayers, sermons, hymns belong to it. There is also *Christian religious literature* in which a specifically Christian element is intended and apparent. And there is, finally, a third body of literature, difficult to define because its themes may be hard to discern; it reflects the Christian vision and attitudes but makes no explicit reference to these. It might be called *non-religious Christian literature.*

Within the domain of the theology of art there emerges a discipline dealing with the special problems of the relations of literature and faith. It proceeds at the general theoretic level discussing general questions about the nature of literature as this is seen from the viewpoint of Christian faith. It also proceeds at another level, addressing itself to specific literary works, types, and movements. Here it becomes *theological literary criticism.* Confronted by some literary phenomenon it asks questions similar to those we have noted in theological art criticism. Of any work it may ask, "To what extent is it Christian?" Of an explicitly Christian work it may ask, "How adequately does it present the theme it intends to set forth?" Of liturgical literature it asks, "Is it appropriate to the purpose it seeks to serve?"

The discipline of theological literary criticism is difficult and delicate. In an introductory study such as this, it is possible only to indicate its existence and delineate its general character. It is possible, however, to give some hint of its operation by illustrating the manner in which themes of Christian faith have received expression in works of literature. Those themes have been the subject of two major sections of this book. It may be helpful, however, to summarize some of the aspects of the Christian vision and attitudes which in rather obvious ways affect literary expression. Convictions about creation are reflected in the view that nature is appreciable as God's creation but is not to be confused with its creator; that man is a being with a significant margin of self-determination; that in his essential being he is good and lives in a good world; that he is essentially bound to other human beings so that he lives in a family and in economic and political and racial orders; that he is finite and must bear the burden of partial knowledge and power. At the same time he is not bound or fully determined by the creation or any part of it: he is not wholly the creature of his economic or political or racial situation, of the physical part of his own being, or even of his own past moral and intellectual decisions. Convictions about sin are reflected in the view that man's misery is not to be attributed to forces for which he is in no way responsible; that it stems ultimately from his alienation from God; that it is partly due to his involvement with others who are also sinners and to his participation in economic and political and racial structures which are infected by sin. Convictions about redemption are reflected in the view that man cannot save himself and will be driven to frustration if he tries to do so; that man can be redeemed in and from any situation; that his redemption comes as an act of God's love in a way that involves his self-determined decision; that his redemption may come in part through the relationships among which he is set and will reflect itself in these relationships. Redemption is no immediate transport into a never-never land where all "live happily ever after"; it contains a call to enter into God's redemptive and creative purposes within a world which is broken by sin. And yet it does bring love, joy, and peace.

3. A SONG FROM ANCIENT ISRAEL

A recital of requirements for authentic Christian literature reveals the high demand that is placed on the poet and also indicates why there is much poetry which seems at first to be Christian but on closer analysis turns out to be inadequate to express the fullness of the faith. That some of this poetry deceives "the very elect" [3] is evidenced by the fact that it is frequently read by well-meaning people as devotional material in services of worship. It is published for the comfort of troubled souls in the name of the Christian church. There is poetry that intends high praise of God and yet removes him utterly from his world; there is poetry that celebrates a god with whom we can be comfortable—even chummy—because he is not the Lord. Some verses betray us into a worship of nature which is the modern counterpart of baalism; others throw the solitary human figure into relief unsupported by any surrounding context of grace. We are challenged to deeds of moral heroism with the promise that thus we may be saved; we are called to the service of great causes that thus the world may be saved. We are given means to evade our fundamental uneasiness and to comfort us in our callous indifference to the sufferings of others and the plight of the world. We are shown a Christ who is the easy companion of our ways, who utters no word of condemnation and therefore speaks no word of forgiveness. We are offered love, joy, and peace on our terms, not God's.

We may be brought up short when we turn to the poetry of the Bible. In part this is due to the fact that thought-forms of other times meet us there, and that some of the ideas need transformation before they can be taken into the fullness of biblical faith. But even when we take these matters into account, we may find ourselves in a different world from that of much popular religious poetry when we come to terms with that which we find in the Bible.

We can meet the Hebrew mind, near the earliest stage for which there is written evidence, in a document which many scholars consider the oldest sizable piece in the Old Testament—the song of Deborah as it is

---

[3] Matthew 24:24. The exact reading of the K.J.V. is "shall deceive the very elect."

given in the fifth chapter of Judges. Here along with much that is primitive are a surprising number of the enduring themes which we have noted as characterizing the faith of both the Old and the New Testaments. The poem is a celebration of a victory which is described by a later writer in the preceding chapter, and it may well have been sung by Deborah herself, as the narrative says. It comes from the early days of the settlement in Canaan, a time when the Israelitish tribes were only loosely bound together and when their Canaanite neighbors were powerful adversaries, more advanced in civilization and in methods of warfare. The very fact that these neighbors had entered the iron age and were using horse-drawn chariots enters into the story. Jabin, a Canaanite king, and his general, Sisera, were oppressing the Israelites. A prophetess named Deborah arose and summoned a man named Barak to lead an army against the enemy. Soon after the battle was joined, a furious rain storm came up, and the chariots of the Canaanites were mired in the mud. Sisera sought refuge in the tent of a man named Heber, whose wife put a tent-peg through his head while he slept. Thus the Canaanites were routed, and the Israelites enjoyed a period of peace.

The poem which tells of these events begins with a triple celebration: of the might of Israel's God who came from Sinai to help his people; of Deborah, the "mother in Israel,"[4] who was inspired to rise to the situation; of the people who "offered themselves willingly"[5] to the Lord. It goes on to a vivid, sometimes humorous, description of the reaction of the various tribes to Deborah's summons for help.

> The princes of Issachar came with Deborah,
> and Issachar faithful to Barak;
> into the valley they rushed forth at his heels.
> Among the clans of Reuben
> there were great searchings of heart.
> Why did you tarry among the sheepfolds,
> to hear the piping of the flocks?
> Among the clans of Reuben
> there were great searchings of heart.[6]

Then the battle begins, and the great event which turned its tide is interpreted in cosmic dimensions:

> From heaven fought the stars,
> from their courses they fought against Sisera.

---

[4] Judges 5:7.
[5] Judges 5:2.
[6] Judges 5:15f.

The torrent Kishon swept them away,
  the onrushing torrent, the torrent Kishon.
March on, my soul, with might! [7]

The wife of Heber is praised and her act described. Then follows the final section of the poem, a bit of savage irony set forth with consummate skill. The mother of Sisera looks out of her lattice and talks with her ladies:

"Why is his chariot so long in coming?
  Why tarry the hoofbeats of his chariots?"
Her wisest ladies make answer,
  nay, she gives answer to herself,
"Are they not finding and dividing the spoil?
  A maiden or two for every man;
spoil of dyed stuffs for Sisera,
  spoil of dyed stuffs embroidered,
  two pieces of dyed work embroidered for my
    neck as spoil?" [8]

The poem is primitive. Its themes will be transformed by the musings of prophets and the experiences of countless people before they emerge as aspects of the Christian vision. But many of the themes are there: A God who works redemptively in history, who uses nature for his purposes, who vanquishes his enemies; men who are faced with difficult but important decisions which they themselves must make; a people who commit themselves by their own will to the Lord; a God who uses a committed people.

4. A MIRROR OF MEDIEVAL CHRISTIANITY

Some years back John Herman Randall, Jr. wrote these words: "The most important fact about what appears to our more sophisticated minds as the bandbox universe of the Middle Ages, was its essential purpose as the scene of the great drama God had prepared for the human race." [9] To him it seemed that the medievalist's vision was constricted by contrast to the modern man's envisioning of a world of almost unimaginable vastness in space and time. A few years later, however, it has come to

---

[7] Judges 5:20, 21.

[8] Judges 5:28-30.

[9] John H. Randall, *The Making of the Modern Mind* (Boston: Houghton Mifflin Company, 1940), p. 18. Reprinted by permission.

seem to many that the modern man's vision may be, in fact, more restricted than that of his predecessors. The man of the Middle Ages may have had a smaller universe in terms of its outward aspects. But as a home for the human spirit, it may have been more adequate than that of many moderns. It was set within a vast context of significance and meaning, and intimated heights and depths of the human spirit of which the sophisticates are only now becoming aware.

Dante was the poet of the Medieval vision, and in his *Divine Comedy* he set forth the ranges of faith as scarcely anyone has, before or since. That he himself was more sophisticated than those who take his poem literally can scarcely be doubted. His cosmology is interesting, indeed essential, for following the poem. But what the poem says about the world and its meaning is not tied up with his picturing of its place within the system of the stars. The fact that the poem speaks richly and unmistakably of vision and attitude is its link with our time.

Since the poem mirrors every other expression of Christian faith, it possesses unusual interest for us in illustrating the manner in which these can be related to one another. The very structure of the poem is theologically delineated—in a symbolic manner. Human reason, in the person of Virgil, the pre-Christian poet, can guide the traveller through hell and purgatory. The tour of heaven must be conducted by revelation —Beatrice—who leads the poet at the last to Bernard who opens his eyes to the beatific vision. There are from time to time sections of specific theological teaching; but the impregnation of the whole by theological concern is made most clear by the subtle references to points of doctrine—often in symbolic terms. The importance of action to the Christian life is so clear as to need no word; indeed, a question can be raised if Christianity is overmoralized. The several attitudes which are appropriate to the various relationships of life come out again and again. And the moral reflex of the faith is considered both in terms of private and personal goodness and in terms of the wider reaches of action in the economic and political orders. The church comes upon the pages of the book again and again. Its sins are castigated without mercy, its redemption is pictured in glory. But even where it is attacked, there is no hint of a transformation of faith in the direction of a churchless Christianity. Rather, the whole potential of the church is treasured. In particular, its worship life runs through the entirety of the poem. At a strategic moment the poet undergoes the purgations of the penitential sacrament. And the patterns of the liturgy are always in the background of the progress of the journey. Indeed, the whole of the action is an act of personal devotion. Its intent is the conversion of the spirit, and at its close comes the ecstatic vision, sweet beyond speech, imperfectly remembered and yet compellingly real.

The very success of the poem in reflecting the Christian vision as it was seen at one time raises difficulties for us, however, as we seek to range through the centuries of the faith. Serious questions have been raised, particularly among Protestants, concerning the degree to which the Christian emphases in the poem have been qualified by influences stemming from a variety of sources. Is the notion of love too strongly reminiscent of Plato and Aristotle to be unequivocally Christian? Is there a moralistic strain in the poem which is out of keeping with the Christian insistence that works grow out of faith? These are important questions. For our purposes, however, they may be set aside as we concern ourselves with the aspects of the poem which reflect the common concerns of Christians.

If redemptive love, springing from God and moving toward the creature to awaken a response in him, is at the center of the Christian vision, it is also at the center of Dante's poem. At the beginning he is wandering in a dark wood where fearsome creatures threaten; the proposed journey, even through hell, is intended to bring direction to his purposeless life.

We are more ready than men a few years back to read with understanding the journey among the lost people, for, as Nathan Scott has pointed out, the image of hell has come alive in the literature of our time.[10] Dante's *Inferno* is no stranger than the scene of Sartre's *No Exit.* A clue to the imagery of the book may be suggested by the insight of Augustine, that sin actually changes the person.[11] And beneath the somewhat lurid picturings of the circumstances of damnation are to be seen portrayals of the fate of the people themselves—in terms of the kind of persons sin has made them. People who have lived for money push weights which go nowhere and crash senselessly against each other. Paolo and Francesca have each other eternally, but nothing else, as Santayana saw.[12] Sins are noted which have their setting in all the areas of attitude at which we have looked. Despising nature or caring too much for her bounties: these alike are punished. Self-centeredness and self-destruction are both visited with vengeance. And Dante sees clearly

---

[10] Nathan A. Scott, Jr., *Modern Literature and the Religious Frontier* (New York: Harper & Brothers, 1958), pp. 74ff.

[11] *The Confessions of Saint Augustine,* translated by F. J. Sheed, p. 13. (I, xii).

[12] George Santayana, *Three Philosophical Poets* (Cambridge: Harvard University Press, 1947), pp. 117ff.

the social character of man's life. Because love binds man remorselessly to others, he cannot betray it. He must recognize the claims which God places on him through others in his personal dealings with them and in his action within the economic and political sphere, as well as in the church.

Many Christians, of course, deny outright any purgatorial punishments beyond this life. But they may well see in the *Purgatorio* of Dante a picturing of the place of discipline in the Christian life on this earth. Having discovered that an easy-going Christianity does not yield an adequate faith, they may read the Medieval poet with interest and understanding. Again it is important to note that divine grace is the initiator of the action: God acts and man responds. Only at the close is man crowned king and bishop—Lord over himself—the self-determining being who really wants the right things and from his own center of being does the right things. Then is he truly self-determined because he is wholly determined by God. The specific stages must be studied for themselves; here it is enough, perhaps, to note that at every point the discipline is set within a large context. In part, to be sure, it involves determinate decision; but it takes place in the midst of a sustaining community and includes acts of worship and devotion. At the end of the section is a vision of a good society on earth, a purged political order and a transformed church, each performing its own proper service to God.

The *Paradiso* is at once the richest and most difficult part of the Comedy. And it is, perhaps, the one least accessible to us. The vision of hell is easier for us to grasp than that of heaven. And yet it is the purpose and the objective of the poem. Here the sense for the wholeness of redemption comes before us in striking fashion. Accustomed as we are to thinking in terms of individual souls "washed in the blood of the lamb," we are not used to the Medieval poet's vision of the range of redemption. In his heaven man's intellectual, economic, and political life, as well as his moral and religious, have their place. In redemption the creative intent is realized. At the close is the vision of the redeemed church, a white rose, and a momentary glimpse of

> the Love that moves the sun
> and the other stars.[13]

---

[13] The famous final words of Dante's *Divine Comedy,* translated in several ways with slight variations.

5. A CONTEMPORARY LOOKS AT CHRISTMAS

No poet of our time is furnished even so imperfect a realization of the wholeness of historic Christianity for reflection in his work as was Dante. And yet men of our time have been aware of that faith. Bits of it are encountered here and there in verses written by our contemporaries, sometimes bringing to our remembrance matters which our conventional churches often overlook. Some poets are vividly aware of the wholeness of the faith and give an interpretation of the human situation in terms of it. Such a one is W. H. Auden, and it is to his work that we turn to illustrate the manner in which faith can find expression in poetic form in our own day. His dramatic poem called *For the Time Being* contains allusions to almost every aspect of the Christian vision and attitudes that have been our concern, and these are brought to powerful unity by the central theme of the poem. It focuses its attention on the coming of the Christ; it is subtitled "A Christmas Oratorio."

The work of Auden is peculiarly apt as illustration of the relations of faith and poetry because of the insistence of the poet on the strictly artistic character of his intention. He is aware of that quality of all art to which allusion has already been made: its right to exist for its own sake.

> Art is not life and cannot be
> A midwife to society.[14]

If the poet is right about himself, then, he is seeking to give us in his Oratorio a poem, not a sermon or a moral or religious essay. And, as we shall see, he believes that there is theological as well as aesthetic justification for his convictions concerning the integrity of the artist. Since poetry is our concern in this chapter, we shall disregard the dramatic aspects of the "Oratorio" and focus our attention on the poetic.

If our reading of the Christian vision has been correct, redemption stands at its central point. And in Auden's poem redemption is at the center. Its very heart, as he views it, is the incarnation. A poem about Christmas is, therefore, one which can be a gathering point for all the themes of faith. Mary, singing to her baby, bids him dream while he may, for the sorrowful way is before him. The cross and the resurrection

[14] W. H. Auden, "New Year Letter." (Copyright 1941 by W. H. Auden. Reprinted from *The Collected Poetry of W. H. Auden* by permission of Random House, Inc., New York, and Faber & Faber, London) p. 267.

are involved in the incarnation. But the accent falls on the embodiment itself, upon the incursion of Divine Love into human life. Here is the redemptive act. It is the "Infinite" manifesting "Itself in the finite," "the Unconditional" manifesting "Itself under the conditions of existence."[15]

The very difficulties of the poem are appropriate to the exposition of its theme. Its modernity is a vehicle for the setting forth of complex thoughts. There are strange juxtapositions of images and ideas. The incarnation was a specific event in time and space, the birth of a real person then and there; on this Auden insists. But it is also an event of universal meaning, hence the then and there opens upon the everytime and everywhere: "By the event of this birth the true significance of all other events is defined."[16] But the universal reference is not vague and general. The incarnation has a specific, even unique, relevance to the time in which we live. Christ is, as Kierkegaard said, our contemporary.[17] And those about him, in Auden's poem, are at once people of the first and the twentieth century: Joseph, Mary, the shepherds, Herod.

The incarnation appears against the background of the fall and of sin. Man is a bewildered being, estranged from true knowledge, true goodness, true love, true God. Auden comes close to erasing the line between creation and fall:

> even in
> The germ-cell's primary division
> Innocence is lost and sin,
> Already given as a fact,
> Once more issues as an act.[18]

So deeply does sin affect every area of man's existence that "there remained but one thing for him to know, his Original Sin, but of this it is impossible for him to become conscious because it is itself what conditions his will to knowledge."[19] The peculiarly modern bewilderment is poignantly described; suddenly, it seems, man has become aware of a wrongness that cannot be righted:

> We are afraid
> Of pain but more afraid of silence; for no nightmare

---

[15] W. H. Auden, "For the Time Being, A Christmas Oratorio," (Copyright 1944 by W. H. Auden. Reprinted from *The Collected Poetry of W. H. Auden* by permission of Random House, Inc., New York, and Faber & Faber, London), pp. 449f.

[16] *Ibid.,* p. 451.

[17] Søren Kierkegaard, *Philosophical Fragments,* David F. Swenson, trans. (Princeton: Princeton University Press, 1946), p. 74.

[18] W. H. Auden, "For the Time Being, A Christmas Oratorio," *The Collected Poetry of W. H. Auden,* p. 427.

[19] *Ibid.,* p. 450.

> Of hostile objects could be as terrible as this Void.
> This is the Abomination. This is the wrath of God.[20]

The winter of Christmastide is the symbol of the human condition.

> Alone, alone, about a dreadful Wood
> Of conscious evil runs a lost mankind,
> Dreading to find its Father lest it find
> The Goodness it has dreaded is not good:
> Alone, alone, about our dreadful wood.[21]

Man's sin does not erase the fact of his createdness; the wise men follow the star that they may become truthful, living, loving, and human. The spirit is haunted by the memory of the garden from which man was driven. On the one side this memory but increases the burden of his sinfulness. It also calls forth efforts at self-salvation. The primitive seeks his God among the forces of nature. The Greek tries to save himself by Wisdom. And each cherishes the illusion that his efforts at self-salvation will be successful. Modern man's efforts to save himself are set forth in a eulogy to Caesar in which each stanza closes with the refrain:

> Great is Caesar: God must be with him.[22]

With ironic wit Auden catalogs the kingdoms Caesar has conquered. Logic has replaced the wood-nymphs and river-demons, science has replaced religion, mathematics has made friends of the transcendentals, and economics has changed our neighbors into our customers. Technology has constructed the means by which the great forces of inorganic nature can be controlled—and it has put the weapons of destruction in our hands. Medicine has conquered the ills of the body. And the popular Soul has been conquered so that Caesar tells all others what is good and bad, what is true and false, what is laughable and what is wretched.

Because of man's sin-caused confusion, he cannot even guess the means by which God will bring him the redemption he seeks. In it "the Unknown seeks the known." [23] The incarnation is miracle; it is absurd. To it the appropriate response is faith:

> . . . you must believe,
> Be silent, and sit still.[24]

---

[20] *Ibid.*, p. 441.
[21] *Ibid.*, p. 411.
[22] *Ibid.*, pp. 432ff.
[23] *Ibid.*, p. 420.
[24] *Ibid.*, p. 424.

And yet in the act of redemption the essential dignity of the creature is not denied. Man is offered that to which he can respond with self-determination. Even Mary is not overwhelmed. Says Gabriel,

> What I am willed to ask, your own
> Will has to answer; child, it lies
> Within your power of choosing to
> Conceive the Child who chooses you.[25]

The Christ himself is truly human. Here is at once the reality of incarnation and the hope of mankind's renewal. When he comes, love is "No longer a pretend but true." [26] The various phantasms which man has conjured up in order to save himself have now been replaced by something real.

> O Living Love, replacing phantasy,
> O Joy of Life revealed in Love's creation;
> Our mood of longing turns to indication:
> Space is the Whom our loves are needed by,
> Time is our choice of How to love and Why.[27]

The significance of the incarnation can be traced further—to use the terminology of this book, which, of course, is not Auden's—in the transformation of attitudes which it effects. With reference to the first of the relationships within which we have viewed man the poet writes:

> There is one World of Nature and one Life;
> Sin fractures the Vision, not the Fact: . . .[28]

Particularly does the poet dwell on the dislocations of man's attitude toward the body as these are distorted by sin. The influence of Sigmund Freud is unmistakable here, and it is significant that Auden wrote of him as if he were a Virgil for the contemporary Dante, taking man "among the Lost People." [29] Sin expresses itself in passion, in childish curiosities, but also in moralistic repressions.

> When Eve, in love with her own will,
> Denied the will of Love and fell,
> She turned the flesh Love knew so well

---

[25] *Ibid.*, p. 420.
[26] *Ibid.*, p. 418.
[27] *Ibid.*, p. 447.
[28] *Ibid.*, p. 426.
[29] W. H. Auden, "In Memory of Sigmund Freud." (Copyright 1940 by W. H. Auden. Reprinted from *The Collected Poetry of W. H. Auden* by permission of Random House, Inc., New York, and Faber & Faber, London), p. 165.

To knowledge of her love until
Both love and knowledge were of sin: . . .[30]

But the incarnation brings wholeness to the life of the body.

He is the Life.
Love Him in the World of the Flesh;
And at your marriage all its occasions shall dance
for joy.[31]

The relations of man to his own self were such at his creation that he was whole and free. Now his faculties of intuition, feeling, sensation, and thought are dissociated.

We were himself when
His will was free,
His error became our
Chance to be.[32]

And yet they can peep over the wall of the garden from which he has been driven, bringing him suggestions of what he surrendered there. But they cannot take him into it. He longs for an "immortal and nameless Centre" for his being,

The well of our wish to wander, the everlasting fountain
Of the waters of joy that our sorrow uses for tears.[33]

In the incarnate One is man whole, and in him is the hope for the wholeness of others. He sets free the creativity of the human spirit: reason is redeemed so that "the continuous development of science is assured"; freedom is given so that history becomes a reality. Further,

> Because in Him the Flesh is united to the Word without magical transformation, Imagination is redeemed from promiscuous fornication with her own images. . . . Because in Him all passions find a logical In-Order-That, by Him is the perpetual recurrence of Art assured.[34]

Here is the theological reason which can be set beside the aesthetic—indeed, the reason which makes the aesthetic finally meaningful—for the integrity and significance of art.

---

[30] W. H. Auden, "For the Time Being, A Christmas Oratorio," *The Collected Poetry of W. H. Auden,* p. 419.
[31] *Ibid.,* p. 466.
[32] *Ibid.,* p. 414.
[33] *Ibid.,* pp. 412f.
[34] *Ibid.,* pp. 452f; history is treated on p. 452; science on pp. 453f.

Man's relations to others are transformed with his relations to himself and nature. The incarnation is the embodiment of love. To the *I Am* which had long before been disclosed, it added a "THOU ART."[35] It made man an object of the divine love as it also offered him an object to love. And in the disclosure of love as the appropriate relation between human beings, it disclosed the possibility of an apprehension of others in their uniqueness and particularity.

> The singular is not Love's enemy;
> Love's possibilities of realisation
> Require an Otherness that can say *I*.[36]

Love is therefore the foe of all tendencies to reduce the person to the status of an individual within a mass. Auden, like others of our time, is deeply sensitive to the threats to personal life that are present in contemporary society.

> . . . darkness and snow descend
> On all personality.[37]

Political groupings in particular come before his attention. Herod broods over the strange circumstance which makes it necessary for him to order the killing of "an artisan's child" for the maintenance of public order.[38] And yet the political order is not as such the enemy of the Christ.

> . . . all societies and epochs are transient details,
> Transmitting an everlasting opportunity
> That the Kingdom of Heaven may come, not in our present
> And not in our future, but in the Fullness of Time.[39]

Other themes, too, appear in the poem. But our concern here has simply been to point up some of those which appear to be characteristic within historic Christianity. It would be a mistake, however, to think of the poem as simply a transcription of theology. The subjects are not treated in order as they have been set forth here. Certainly the poet is learned in theological lore. But he is not simply setting forth theology in fancy dress. He is learned in psychological lore, but his work will not displace textbooks in psychology. If we treat him as a poetical theologian, we do violence to his work. And we fail to see the faith in its wholeness. Christianity is a total faith. One of its expressions is poetry; another is

---

[35] *Ibid.*, p. 451.
[36] *Ibid.*, p. 447.
[37] *Ibid.*, p. 407.
[38] *Ibid.*, pp. 454ff.
[39] *Ibid.*, p. 435.

theology. And these are distinct. We must listen to ancient Deborah, medieval Dante, and contemporary Auden as poets. To do so is to be authentically Christian. For it is to attend to the unique and the personal in the creative capacities of our fellows.

READINGS

From the Bible

1. The book of Psalms is an inexhaustible store of poetry on the whole range of faith.

2. The Song of Solomon contains beautiful love poetry.

3. The book of Nahum is a poetic celebration of joy over the fall of Nineveh.

4. In the book of Lamentations are poetic expressions of grief over the fall of Jerusalem.

From Historic Christianity

1. Books of religious verse are easily available for study.

2. A selection of significant hymns on various topics and from various periods of the life of the church can be made from any good hymnal. A theme might well be followed through chronologically, for example, the conception of God or of Jesus, the attitude toward nature, or sin, or the individual.

3. Major poems on Christian themes are John Milton's *Paradise Lost* and *Paradise Regained*, Dante's *Divine Comedy*.

FOR STUDY AND DISCUSSION

1. Name some poems which commonly pass as good Christian poetry which do not qualify.
2. List ten hymns which are of good literary quality and adequately reflect their themes.
3. Study a poem from the Bible.
4. Study a poem with Christian content from the past, such as Robert Browning's "Saul" or Francis Thompson's "The Hound of Heaven."
5. Study a contemporary poet like W. H. Auden, T. S. Eliot, or Allen Tate.

XVII

STORIES AND PLAYS

Anyone who has attended Sunday School regularly during his childhood tends to think of the Bible as a book of stories. He knows of the wanderings of Abraham, of Joseph in Egypt, of Moses and Joshua, and many others. This is natural enough. The Bible is full of stories. The faith it reflects finds fitting expression in the telling of tales. And the faith it has continued to inspire has found expression again and again in the telling of tales. Stories from the past and stories from our present are imbued with the vision and attitudes of the faith of the Christian people.

1. MORALITY OR REDEMPTION

The Sunday School pupil is apt to think that at the close of every story in the Bible there is a moral. There are at least two good reasons for his thinking so. One is that his Sunday School teacher may have tried to find morals to go with the stories. The other is that for many stories morals were relatively easy to find. As we have seen, there is a strain of thought running through the Old Testament in which God is conceived as a lawgiver who tells his people what to do; if they obey him, he will reward them; if they disobey, he will punish. Perhaps no more striking stories illustrating this way of thinking can be found than those in the book of Daniel. The hero and his friends are true to their faith in spite of all; and, though they are not presumptuous, their fidelity finds its reward in the care of God for them in desperate circumstances.[1]

In the Old Testament, of course, the commands of God are not simply moral. Daniel and his friends perform the correct ritual actions of pious Jews. It is these, as much as their moral actions, which express their obedience to God. But once the Christian church had discarded the ceremonial practices of Judaism, it often looked at obedience to God in predominantly moral terms. Hence the exhortation, "Dare to be a Daniel," means to the youngster in Sunday School, "Dare to do what is morally right, and you may expect something in return." Even on a more sophisticated level, there appears within Christianity a literature of stories which find moral heroism the center of faith. And this sort of story is felt to be a rescript of Biblical faith, the ancestral heritage of the Christian church.

At its very beginnings, however, the Christian church went through a crisis over the place of morality in religion. Its specific form was a quarrel over the requirements of the Jewish law and their applicability to Gentile converts. But men like the Apostle Paul saw the farther reaches of the struggle. And in his letters to the Romans and the Galatians, in particular, Paul wrote unequivocally of the centrality of faith rather than moral or religious goodness as the basis of man's right relations with God. To take the story of redemption through moral heroism as a proper account of Christian faith is, therefore, to reject that outlook which is clearly set forth in Apostolic literature.

The Old Testament had already faced the problem. We have seen that Paul appealed to his ancestral faith as substantiating his own view of religion. For him there was a strain of Hebrew religion which centered in law and morality; it had been provisional. It had been antedated, and, with the coming of Christ, it was to be superseded by a view of religion in which trust was the central attitude appropriate to man. God was a loving Father, not a lawgiver, and the whole of man's response to him was to be predicated upon this conviction. Paul pointed particularly to certain key verses in the Old Testament to illustrate his point. A great prophet had announced that "the just shall live by faith,"[2]

---

[1] Note that the three heroes defy the king and affirm their intention of remaining true to their faith whether their God delivers them or not. See Daniel 3:16-18. The late Edwin E. Aubrey once spoke of their words as "the bravest" in the Old Testament.

[2] Romans 1:17; Habbakuk 2:4, K.J.V.

and Abraham, the father of the faithful, had "believed God, and it was counted unto him for righteousness."[3] He could have pointed to many stories in the Old Testament which are told in such a way that it is clear that God takes the initiative, that human action is response to his acting.

In one of the greatest of the Old Testament books, from a literary point of view, the question of the adequacy of the moral view of life is at the very center. This is, of course, the book of Job. It is a complex, and there are several strains of ideas which run through it. But if we attend to the poetical cycle of speeches which runs from chapter three through some twenty chapters, as William A. Irwin suggests,[4] we may see one answer which the book gives to the problem of its hero. The cycle is a series of exchanges between Job and the three friends who have come to reason with him in view of the calamity which has overtaken him. The friends represent the view of life which makes moral rectitude central, and their constant word is simply this: Job is suffering, therefore he must have sinned. He should confess and repent. But this is just what Job will not do. He bitterly attacks his friends and their viewpoint. In doing so, however, he cuts himself off from a significant part of his own ancestral faith, from the community of believing in Israel. The friends are aware of this, for they cite ancient wisdom on their side.

Job's bitterness, then, is in part his isolation. And it terrifies him. He simply does not know where to turn. Enough of his faith is left so that he will not commit suicide. And he knows that there is a Reality somewhere with whom he has to deal. It is the character of that Reality which is his central problem. If God is not a moral arbiter, what is he then? At times, at least, it seems as if he is sheer arbitrary power. But this is just the idea which enrages Job. He simply cannot believe it. Hence his veritable attack on God himself. He wishes there were an umpire between him and God, some just court where he could plead his case. But everything points to a Reality who simply crushes him, who curdles him "like cheese,"[5] who gives him dreadful dreams at night, who terrifies him. And yet he does not really know where to find him.

Resolution finally comes. He gets to the point where he utters the words, "I know that my Redeemer lives."[6] And a bit later he contrasts

---

[3] Romans 4:3, K.J.V.

[4] See the article "Job and Prometheus," in *The Journal of Religion,* XXX, 90-108, April, 1950.

[5] Job 10:10.

[6] Job 19:25.

the notion of God as power with the God whom he has, at the last, encountered:

> Would he contend with me in the greatness of his power?
> No; he would give heed to me.[7]

Here the Old Testament is enunciating themes central in the Christian vision. And its break with the essentially moral way of looking at life comes clear.

The exclusively moral story is apt to be poor literature for a very simple but important reason. The moral perspective calls everything to serve itself, and it is likely to insist that the real function of literature is to exhort, to influence behavior in some rather direct fashion. At such a notion the artist himself ever rebels—and he may be driven into anti-moralistic attitudes as he does so. The exclusively moral story also tends to an oversimplification of the human situation and to a superficial delineation of character. It sees the real problem of life as the separation of the "good guys" from the bad, and the subtleties of human life are overlooked. The exclusively moral story is also out of character with Christian faith. It misreads the world, the nature of man, and the character of God.

To deny that the moral vision of life is adequate is not, however, to deny that literature deals with moral matters nor that these are a matter of indifference to faith. Much great literature is about morality, and the Christian vision is inclusive of moral concern. The difficulty is that of seeing the moral within its proper perspective. Just here literature may be of signal significance for faith. Amos Wilder writes:

> The urgency today of a re-examination of Christian codes and moral attitudes is pressing. The great masses of men are baffled by the issues of conduct and decision. They are caught in new circumstances for which older prescriptions offer no guidance. They feel themselves under constraints whose authority they no longer recognize, and caught in social patterns which dwarf them and which breed hostility and frustration. Literature often uncovers these tangles more discerningly than moral theology.[8]

Literature affords means of apprehending the setting within which perceptive moral thinking takes place. And it is in part the capacity of literature to intimate that setting which gives it its significance for the understanding of Christian faith.

---

[7] Job 23:6.

[8] Amos N. Wilder, *Theology and Modern Literature* (Cambridge: Harvard University Press, 1958), p. 115. Reprinted by permission.

2. STORY AND HISTORY

The ex-Sunday School pupil is right in thinking of the Bible in large measure as a book of stories. And one of the great contributions of that school to his life is to bring those stories to him and make them part of his life. He is mistaken, we have seen, if the stories are simply taken as tokens of a moral way of looking at life. Through them he may come to some glimpse of another way of looking at life: what has here been called the Christian vision. Now the story is a peculiarly appropriate means by which an understanding of that vision can be conveyed. Emil Brunner writes that the relation between God and men "is an event, and hence narration is the proper form to describe it. The decisive word-form in the language of the Bible is not the substantive, as in Greek, but the verb, the word of action." [9] The Bible tells of the confrontation of God by men in specific historic situations where personal decisions were called for—hence the interest in the unique and the personal.

By contrast, a view of life which sees man's obligation to God as calling for disdain of the present world does not yield itself to interpretation in terms of the story. One of the able prose writers of the eighteenth century was the mystic William Law. He wrote deftly and sometimes brilliantly in calling men of his time to a life of Christian perfection. A literary device which he often employed was that of describing a character who would typify some virtue or vice. Critics have pondered the question concerning why his bad people are likely to be interesting, while his good characters are invariably dull. The reason seems to be this: that his "view of religion . . . leaves the world out altogether, one good person is exactly like another. A pious physician is acceptable to God as pious, but not at all as a physician." [10] In the Bible men are not types of virtue or vice; they are people in their own right who come before us in their concrete situations.

The interest of the Bible in stories goes back to an interest in history. Though there are some stories in the Bible which are intentionally fictional, for the most part it tells of real people. Its writers may, of course, have been mistaken about the historicity of what they told; but their intention was to set forth events "as they really happened." [11] We have

---

[9] Emil Brunner, *The Divine-Human Encounter,* p. 47. Reprinted by permission.

[10] Henri Talon, *William Law* (New York: Harper & Brothers, n.d.), p. 38. Reprinted by permission.

[11] The phrase of Leopold von Ranke is often quoted: "wie es eigentlich gewesen." It appears, for example, in George P. Gooch, *History and Historians in the Nineteenth Century* (London: Longmans, Green and Company, 1920), p. 78.

OLD TESTAMENT STORIES AS SUBJECTS OF ART The virtuosity of a Renaissance artist is displayed in his treatment of incidents from the Bible. The sequence runs from left to right, row by row.

Creation and Fall	Cain and Abel
Noah and the Flood	Abraham
Isaac, Jacob and Esau	Joseph and His Brothers
Moses at Sinai	Joshua at Jericho
David and Goliath	Solomon and the Queen of Sheba

"The Gates of Paradise." Doors of the Baptistry in Florence. Lorenzo Ghiberti (Alinari Photo)

already looked at the oldest sizable document in the Bible, the Song of Deborah, and have noted some of its themes. We may now turn our attention to the oldest sizable prose document in it. Like the Song of Deborah it is imbedded in later materials, and its specific delineation is the work of modern scholars. Upon careful examination of the books of Judges, First and Second Samuel, and First Kings, they discover a strand of narrative having a character of its own which can be distinguished from the remainder of the materials there. It describes the background of the setting up of the kingdom of David and ends with the accession of Solomon. Its author may well have been a member of David's court so that he was an actual eye witness of much that he relates. Recently printed as a continuous narrative, it has been titled "The Hebrew Iliad" because it invites comparison with the Greek epic. A few words written by its translator, Robert H. Pfeiffer, give some clue to its significance:

> Ahimaaz, or whoever wrote the early source of Samuel, is "the father of history" in a much truer sense than Herodotus half a millennium later. As far as we know, he created history as an art, as a recital of past events dominated by a great idea. In this sense, history did not exist at the time. . . . David's biographer was a man of genius. Without any previous models as guide, he wrote a masterpiece, unsurpassed in historicity, insight, literary style, and dramatic power. . . . The style of the early source of Samuel . . . is unsurpassed in the whole range of Hebrew prose literature. The author's expert use of syntax and appropriate idiomatic expressions, his classic Hebrew, ranging from the noblest to the coarsest expressions, his vivid descriptions and characterizations, and his lively dialogues have seldom if ever been surpassed in the literature of mankind.[12]

A reading of the text reveals some of those themes which were to be central in the Christian vision, presented in simple and often primitive form. A sense of the numinous pervades the whole. God imparts to that which he sets aside a sacred quality which must not be violated. From this source come the stories with which we have illustrated the idea of sin as violation of the holy: Jonathan eating the honey, Uzziah touching the ark. The king is the anointed of the Lord, and even when David is at odds with him, he will not lay a hand on the man God has chosen. The Lord is an active, aggressive, even "militant"[13] Reality,

---

[12] *The Hebrew Iliad*, trans. by Robert H. Pfeiffer with general and chapter introductions by William G. Pollard (New York: Harper & Brothers, 1957), p. 10. Reprinted by permission.

[13] *Ibid.*, from the Introduction, William G. Pollard, p. 20.

moving in the midst of human events. He also is "no respecter of persons"; [14] through his prophet even the king is brought to admit his guilt in the murder of Uriah and the adultery with Bathsheba. But he is a God who restores his own to himself after their defection. He is the one who has taken David out of his troubles.

So it is that in the earliest prose portions of the Bible the faith is set forth. When we turn to the New Testament, we are also confronted with story and with history. The Christ comes before us in the events of his life, eating and drinking, meeting with men, weeping and laughing, suffering and dying. He also tells stories, for through them he can give to "those who have ears to hear" an interpretation of the meaning of the kingdom. Much of the Christian vision is transmitted to us in the simple tale of the prodigal son.

The Bible is largely history and story; and this is because of the character of the faith that is in it. Frequently Christians have overlooked this fact. And when they have, they have missed something the Bible is talking about. At the same time they have overlooked the significance of literature within the wholeness of Christian faith.

3. THE CHRISTIAN VISION IN *BILLY BUDD*

It is essential to the character of the Christian vision that it emerge out of history, and it is not unnatural that its emergence should be assisted by stories of a fictional character. It is not strange, either, that it should reflect itself in storytelling once it had captured the imaginations of men.

We have already noted some of the requirements which the Christian vision and the attitudes consonant with it impose on the storyteller. These need not be repeated here, though it might be worth while to recall them at this point. They place a high demand on the storyteller. They have made themselves felt, with varying force, in relating stories, sacred and secular, in the West. Literary criticism at best is a very difficult discipline, and it is no easy thing to say unequivocally of any story, "This is Christian." And since the Christian vision plays over the ambiguities and uncertainties of existence, the uniquenesses of human life, the uncertainties of motivation and the almost inextricable interconnections of good and evil, that vision itself is not easily discernible. The

---

[14] Acts 10:34, K.J.V.

religious story as such is likely to be too obvious to be true to it, the secular story too subtle to be easily recognizable.

There are, however, stories which numbers of critics point to as having significant connection with Christian faith. Among these is Herman Melville's short novel *Billy Budd.* Unless, as one critic argues, it is ironic throughout,[15] filled with double meanings penetrable only to the careful observer, the story is strongly suggestive of a Christian interpretation. Nature, the sea upon which the drama is played out, is good. And human life is basically good. Its goodness has the opportunity of shining through in such a character as the young hero, Billy. "He showed in face that humane look of reposeful good nature which the Greek sculptor in some instances gave to his heroic strong man, Hercules." [16] Innocence was his enduring character; he thought evil of no one, and faced by evil, could not speak. But upon the basic good of life, Melville saw evil imposed. He seems almost apologetic as he quotes the Biblical phrase, " 'mysteries of iniquity,' " [17] as if his contemporaries will think him a bit strange if he speaks of it; however, he hints at a significant meaning in the notion. Civilization sometimes seems to be evil in his eyes: the requirements of justice are such that in some circumstances evil must be done. At any rate war is evil; the chaplain is an anomaly: "He is the minister of the Prince of Peace serving in the host of the God of War—Mars." [18] And evil sometimes is embodied in individuals, as it is in Claggart. Melville is careful to point out that in him there is a sort of evil that is not in every man. It is innate, a badness that seems to come out of nowhere, which infects the man it seizes in such a way that the very goodness of others drives him into opposition. Thus it is that Billy's innocence brings forth a reaction of sin on the part of Claggart, and the latter accuses him to the Captain.

The Captain's character is drawn with sympathy and understanding by the author. In the situation of ambiguity he is forced to render a decision. He sees that the blow with which Billy strikes Claggart is a judgment of God. It is struck by an angel, "yet the angel must hang." [19] The justice of the fleet—is it the justice of sinful war?—requires that

---

[15] Lawrence Thompson, *Melville's Quarrel with God* (Princeton: Princeton University Press, 1952), 355ff.

[16] Herman Melville, *Shorter Novels* (New York: Horace Liveright, Inc., 1928), p. 238.

[17] *Ibid.*, p. 267.

[18] *Ibid.*, p. 316.

[19] *Ibid.*, p. 293.

Billy be condemned. And so he is. But as he goes to his death, innocent Billy, clear of voice, says simply, "God bless Captain Vere." [20]

> The hull, deliberately recovering from the periodic roll to leeward, was just regaining an even keel—when the last signal, the preconcerted dumb one, was given. At the same moment it chanced that the vapoury fleece hanging low in the East, was shot through with a soft glory as of the fleece of the Lamb of God seen in mystical vision; and simultaneously therewith, watched by the wedged mass of upturned faces, Billy ascended; and ascending, took the full rose of the dawn.[21]

Afterwards the sailors cherished even the chips of the spar on which he was hanged, as though "it was a piece of the Cross." [22] And on his deathbed Captain Vere murmured over and over the name of Billy Budd.

Critics differ in their interpretation of the story. One has found in it the belief "that though good goes to defeat and death, its radiance can redeem life." [23] And another says that "it was as if, Billy being a type of the Christ, faith in Billy and his atoning death were the power of God unto salvation to everyone that believeth." [24]

4. TENSIONS OF ATTITUDE IN *THE CASTLE*

Melville lived in the nineteenth century, a representative in literature of those who brought a reminiscence of the wholeness of historic Christianity, with its discernment of a deep evil against which a difficult good suddenly emerges, into a world which for the most part regarded reference to original sin as a mark of primitive thinking. Our time sees the world more somber. And it is particularly in the sense of need, the awareness of the void, that we find a feeling for aspects of historic faith. There is, so to speak, in much of contemporary literature, a witness to the faith in reverse, an insistence that this is what we want, even though many of us cannot find it. The human situation in its depth is analyzed

---

[20] *Ibid.*, p. 318.
[21] *Ibid.*, p. 319.
[22] *Ibid.*, p. 327.
[23] F. O. Matthiessen, *American Renaissance* (New York: Oxford University Press, Inc., 1941), p. 514. Reprinted by permission.
[24] Randall Stewart, "The Vision of Evil in Hawthorne and Melville," Nathan A. Scott, Jr., ed., *The Tragic Vision and the Christian Faith* (New York: Association Press, 1957), p. 261. Reprinted by permission.

in terms reminiscent of faith, but the solution to the problem is not readily discovered. It is as representative of this searching spirit that *The Castle* by Franz Kafka may come before us. In the judgment of W. H. Auden its author comes closer than any other contemporary artist to having the sort of relation to our age that Dante, Shakespeare, and Goethe had to theirs.[25]

The story concerns the adventures of a man simply designated *K,* who arrives in a village on a snowy evening.[26] His right to be there is soon challenged, and he affirms that he has been summoned by the Count to act as a land-surveyor. The Count lives in the Castle nearby, and that Castle owns and controls the village. On a morning walk K sees it shimmering in bright sunlight, but when he walks toward it, the castle recedes into the distance.[27] Indeed, the Castle is always just so: it is there, but it is in the distance. Its whole relation to the village is strangely ambiguous. To it the villagers owe their allegiance, but they are never sure of their relations to it.

At the risk of reducing phantasy to prosaic systematic statement, we may look at K's predicament in terms of the attitudes we have examined. We have seen that Christian faith insists on the primacy of one's relation to God while it does not deny one's relations within the world in which he lives. The problem lies in the adjusting of the claims which this double set of relationships impose. In Kakfa's novel it is clear that everything depends upon K's relation to the Castle: it is always there in the distance. But he never leaves the relationships of the village to lose himself in a unilateral relatedness to the Castle. On the other hand he cannot simply ignore the Castle and live serenely as if the village alone existed. The relationship of K and everyone else to the Castle is so ambiguous that it is impossible for him to define what his relations to the village should be. In two spheres of life in particular does the ambiguity affect his life. He cannot fully give himself over to his vocation; nor can he abandon it. His claim to a place in the village depends on it. At the very beginning it is not clear if his very claim to be a land surveyor is a fiction of his own invention. The servant of the Castle who phones his superior to check K's claim receives two phone calls which contradict each other.[28] The second sphere of life which is ren-

---

[25] See J. Hillis Miller, Jr., "Franz Kafka and the Metaphysics of Alienation," Nathan A. Scott, Jr., ed., *The Tragic Vision and the Christian Faith,* p. 281.

[26] Franz Kafka, *The Castle,* Edwin and Willa Muir, trans. (New York: Alfred A. Knopf, Inc., 1947), p. 3.

[27] *Ibid.,* p. 21.

[28] *Ibid.,* pp. 5-7.

dered problematic by his relation to the castle is that of the home and the family. He would gladly settle down in the village; but the best he can do is to have an irregular relationship with a village girl which can never eventuate in the establishment of a home with some recognized status.[29]

Thus Kafka writes with a haunting sense of a vision once known. To read *The Castle* and the book of Job together is to gain understanding of both. Neither K nor Job forfeits his awareness of God; but through tortures of the spirit they speak of the difficulty of attaining to some clarity in their relations to him. K is unwilling to become a mystic, swallowed up in the ocean of divine being; neither will he become a secularist affirming that the village alone exists. So does K embody a poignant longing for salvation as a modern man feels it, and as one standing within the Judeo-Christian heritage defines it.

5. DRAMA

No book of the Bible was written for presentation on the stage. The Hebrews had no drama, and the early Christians were suspicious of the theater. The Greeks, on the other hand, had developed the writing and production of plays to a high degree of expertness and sophistication by the fifth century before Christ. Moreover, Aristotle, "the master of them that know," [30] had written a theory of the drama which set forth with clarity and reasonableness the character of comedy and tragedy. His *Poetics* have exercised an enormous influence over the writing and criticism of plays ever since. Some have felt that he set forth principles of universal validity which cannot be improved; others have felt that his canons were too restrictive for them. Many plays have been written which purposely conform to the principles he enunciated; some dramatists have consciously broken away and written in ways that do not comport with his ideas. Among those who have been critical of regarding the principles of Aristotle as statements of universal validity have been some who feel that he wrote from the specific perspectives of Greek culture, and that Christianity, for one thing, introduced certain ways of looking at life into the culture of the West which profoundly influenced the writing of dramas. Thus Søren Kierkegaard, in the middle of the nineteenth century, affirmed that a play written in accordance with

[29] *Ibid.*, pp. 54ff.
[30] Dante, *The Divine Comedy*, "Inferno," IV, 132.

the Aristotelian canons could not take into account the meaning of Christ or Spirit as Christian faith conceived these.[31]

Preston Roberts is among those who see in Aristotle's work a reflection of the specific outlooks which characterize Greek culture along with much that must be taken into account in the serious treatment of drama in any time or place. He has suggested that a Christian poetics ought to be essayed and has sketched an outline of what one might look like.[32] This would take into account the effect which Christian faith has had on the form as well as the content of plays. His work therefore offers us an illustration of theological literary criticism. It exhibits theology as a conversational venture, ever probing into the specific nature of Christian faith itself as it enters into dialogue with those who do not speak for the faith. Mr. Roberts sets his discipline within the framework of literary criticism on the one hand and within that of Christian theology on the other. Centering his attention on tragedy, he examines his materials in terms of components which Aristotle pointed out: protagonist, tragic flaw, recognition scene, reversal, and catharsis. He finds three basic types of drama in the West, though he warns that most specific plays are complex in character. The three are the Greek, the Christian, and the modern.

Mr. Robert's criticism has been directed, for the most part, to dramas which belong to the classification of nonreligious literature, as this has been described in an earlier chapter. He seeks for Christian—or non-Christian—motifs in plays which have no specific religious reference. That such plays should display Christian motifs is surely not strange. Serious drama throws the matters which give life meaning into relief, the desperation into which a man may be thrown, the resources which may come to him in times of stress, the grace which may sustain him when all else fails.

There is, of course, drama which is explicitly religious in theme, and the reappearance of such drama in our time is one aspect of the recovery of historic Christianity which is going on. Mystery and morality plays are being given, playwrights are choosing themes from the Bible and religious history. Concerning such dramas the critic must ask, "Are they Christian?" and "Do they justly present the theme they intend to portray?"

It is important to see, too, however, that drama itself can be liturgical

---

[31] Søren Kierkegaard, *Either/Or*, I, pp. 113ff.

[32] Preston T. Roberts, "A Christian Theory of Dramatic Tragedy," *The Journal of Religion*, XXXI, no. 1 (1951), pp. 1-21; "The Sequence in Religion and Art," *The Divinity School News*, XXI, no. 1 (February 1, 1954), pp. 1-9.

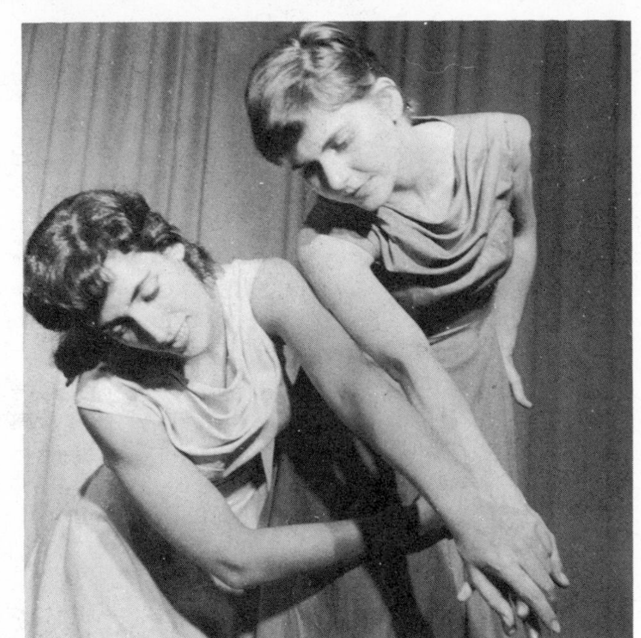

The singleness of spirit of Ruth and Naomi is the basis of Ruth's decision to go with her mother-in-law. *The Book of Ruth.* The dancers: Carol Wallace and Julia Hurd. (Goodsell, Hollins College)

Maidens of Bethlehem glean in the fields of Boaz to the music of Israeli melodies. *The Book of Ruth.* The dancers: members of Orchesis, Hollins College dance group. Choreography by Paula Levine. (Goodsell, Hollins College)

OLD TESTAMENT STORY AS SUBJECT OF DANCE DRAMA

literature. It may be written and presented quite purposely to serve an act of worship. It may, even, be written for presentation in a church. Then it enters into the life of worship itself; its express intention is that of evoking a response which is not simply aesthetic. It intends to change the spectator of art into participant in prayer. In this respect drama differs from other literary forms—except for poems which are intended for use as hymns. There is a real reason for the potentially liturgical character of drama; it lies in the dramatic character of liturgy. Here is at once the high possibility and the low for both drama and liturgy. If the latter becomes simply aesthetic—stagey—it ceases to be serious worship. If the former tries to exceed itself and enter into those aspects of liturgy which are not properly within its sphere, it loses its character as drama and at the same time dilutes the significance of aspects of the service of worship.

Not only can the drama become liturgical; it has a way of drawing other arts to itself. Thus an act of worship in which drama has a part is likely to be one into which many arts enter. Thus at the close of our consideration of worship, art, and literature, it may be fitting to note the manner in which all of these can be summoned to a single setting. A chapel service held one year in the Little Theatre of Hollins College was called "A Celebration of Christmas in Dance." In it were hymns and prayers, instrumental music, as well as dances. At its close a poem, written by a member of the college English faculty, set to music by a member of its music faculty, was sung by the chapel choir. Very simply the ancient drama of birth and shepherds and wise men unfolded in the rhythms of the dancers, ending with a suggestion of benediction from the Christ-child.[33]

---

[33] The service was planned co-operatively by the Reverend Alvord M. Beardslee, my successor as chaplain at Hollins College, and Miss Paula Levine, Professor of Dance. The hymn, "Upon a Night," was written by Professor Jesse Zeldin and set to music by Professor John Diercks. The choir was directed by Professor Arthur S. Talmadge.

READINGS

From the Bible

1. The reading of whole stories in the Bible is sometimes prevented by our attending too much to chapter divisions. A new appreciation of the old heroes, Abraham, Jacob, Joseph, and others can be gained by reading the whole of their adventures in a version of the Bible which prints them as consecutive narratives, or, at least, by reading them in such a way in one of the conventional versions. Read Genesis 12:1-25:11 as a whole; or Genesis 25:19-36:43; or Genesis 37-50.

2. Several books of the Bible are complete stories: Ruth, Esther, Daniel, and Jonah.

From Historic Christianity

1. John Milton, *Samson Agonistes*, portrays a biblical hero seen through the eyes of a Puritan with a strong sense for the Greek heritage.

2. William Shakespeare, *King Lear*, has often been cited as having clear Christian implications.

3. William Shakespeare, *The Tempest*, may be read as a drama about sin and forgiveness; it certainly contains viewpoints from other than Christian sources.

FOR STUDY AND DISCUSSION

1. Study a story in the Bible.
2. Do you agree that Melville's *Billy Budd* can be interpreted as a Christian novel?
3. Do you think that K is redeemed in *The Castle*?
4. Study Sophocles' *Oedipus Rex*, William Shakespeare's *King Lear*, and Tennessee Williams' *A Streetcar Named Desire* (New York: New Directions, 1947) in the light of Preston T. Roberts' analysis of types of plays.

XVIII

ACTION

The familiar words of Hamlet's soliloquy speak eloquently though not explicitly of the relations of action and faith. The prince ponders

> Whether 'tis nobler in the mind to suffer
> The slings and arrows of outrageous fortune,
> Or to take arms against a sea of troubles,
> And by opposing end them? [1]

But before he raises the question of whether he should act or not, he has set the context within which the action can be understood:

> To be, or not to be,—that is the question.[2]

Because that is the question, the prince must decide about the meaning and worth of his life before he can turn his attention to action. And because the meaning of his life is problematical, it is easy for resolution to be "sicklied o'er with the pale cast of thought." [3]

Hamlet implies what many Christian thinkers have said: that action takes place within the context of a conception of life's meaning. Questions about morality point to questions about faith. If we use the terms

---

[1] William Shakespeare, "Hamlet," Act III, Sc. 1, *Works*, p. 688.
[2] *Ibid.*
[3] *Ibid.*

of this book, we might say: What a person does depends on a vision of man and his significance, of his world and its meaning; it goes back to basic attitudes which determine his being. If we turn the matter the other way, we may say that vision and attitude imply deeds. More simply: Christian faith expresses itself in action.

In the broad sense, of course, praying, painting, and even thinking, are forms of action. In this chapter, however, we are concerned primarily with what may be called direct action—dealing with the man next-door, giving to the poor, voting in an election.

1. FAITH AND ACTION

Hamlet dies in the fifth act of Shakespeare's play; but after the curtain falls, he gets up to ponder again whether or not to kill the king. The man who plays his part is in a different situation. Faced with the situation in actuality which he portrays on the stage, he must make a decision and accept the real consequences of his action or inaction. And he must face the question of his life's significance, of his world's meaning.

The fact that the decision for actions of moment involve decisions about life's meaning indicates the relation of ethics to religion. Even small actions are indicative of fundamental attitudes, and large actions make these attitudes explicit. Furthermore, certain decisions are inescapable; hence, it is in the situation of such decisions that the question of faith is inescapable. One can read literature, see a play, or look at art and be aware of certain religious overtones in them. But faced with a decision for action, one must make up his mind about what to do and hence about what one believes about life and its significance. It is for this reason that Christian thinkers have often spoken of the importance of ethical decision as a focal point for faith. Indeed, it is questionable if anyone really knows what his faith is until he has been forced into a situation where an important decision must be made. There are some thinkers who so emphasize this point, that it would appear that only in such decision is faith fully embodied. While we do not need to go so far as to say this, it seems perfectly clear that unless there are some situations in which faith is related to important decisions involving the totality of one's life, the meaning of that faith has not been rendered explicit. Action is peculiarly a focal point of faith, and a faith which never focuses in action is simply not the real thing.

The New Testament repeatedly speaks of the importance of action. The words of Jesus were a call to sincere and resolute deeds of love toward other people. He who does not act has no right to the name disciple. "Why call ye me Lord, Lord, and do not the things which I say?" [4] For all of Paul's harsh words against a religion of works, he certainly knew of no faith that was not active in love.[5] For him to be in the Spirit meant to "walk in the Spirit," [6] to bear the burdens of others and thus fulfill the law of Christ. And John placed the matter bluntly by declaring, "he who does not love his brother whom he has seen, cannot love God whom he has not seen." [7]

Back of the New Testament is the Old. Jesus quoted the great commandments from it and remarked that "on these two commandments hang all the law and the prophets." [8] The ten commandments of the older tradition together with the various codes of laws that are imbedded in the Pentateuch are ethical to the core. And from the prophets come the great declarations which have stirred the conscience of Western man through the years:

> What doth the Lord require of thee,
> But to do justly, and to love mercy, and to walk humbly with thy God? [9]

And

> Let justice roll down like waters,
> and righteousness like an everflowing stream.[10]

There is an imperative to love and righteousness in faith itself; it lies in the nature of God and the character of man. God is love, and man was made in his image.

But man is a frail creature, and his imaging of the Divine has been fearfully distorted. There is, therefore, a basis for understanding something more than the imperative to action; the Bible gives clues to the difficulties. Man does not know what to do in every situation, even when he wants to do right. His moral resolution is weak. Further, the world in which he lives is, as Hamlet saw, "out of joint." [11] Hence, to do the deeds of love is often to invite anxiety, to do that which is met by a cross rather than by acclamation or even appreciation.

---

[4] Luke 6:46, K.J.V.
[5] Galatians 5:6.
[6] Galatians 5:25, K.J.V.
[7] I John 4:20.
[8] Matthew 22:40, K.J.V.
[9] Micah 6:8, K.J.V.
[10] Amos 5:24.
[11] William Shakespeare, "Hamlet," Act I, Sc. 5, *Works*, p. 679.

And yet he must act; here is the pathos of his situation; even inaction is also action. Time is real, and history is real; they are realms of decision. Into them man has been thrust, not by his own choosing. But it is just in the situation of decision that the faith may somehow come clear as nowhere else. Christianity places a question mark over the effort to see "life steadily" and see "it whole." [12] It may be in the unsteadiness of finite decision that a man is granted a glimpse of the wholeness of life. It is but a glimpse and can never be more, but by it, says the Christian, he can live. John's gospel in particular links action and insight. "If any man's will is to do his will, he shall know whether the teaching is from God." [13]

And yet it must not be forgotten that if action can be a focal point for faith, it is only because there is a faith to focalize. Action does not produce faith—it comes from it. The very attempt to derive faith from action is a symptom of the bondage of sin; we cannot save ourselves by morality. Furthermore, when faith is misplaced, action is corrupted. We have already noted Paul's analysis of the human situation as he sets it forth in the first chapter of Romans. When men had begun to worship the creature rather than the Creator, "God gave them up" [14] to all kinds of uncleanness. Action without faith is meaningless; its context of significance is lacking. Faith does not depend on action; but it inevitably eventuates in it.

2. PERPLEXITIES OF THE PRESENT

The Christian of today finds it easy to sympathize with Hamlet. He knows what it means to be caught between the impulse to act and the paralysis of not knowing what to do. He does not want to let things drift to awful catastrophe, but he finds it hard to discern how to keep them from doing so. Perplexities press upon him both in the sphere of his personal life and interpersonal relations and in the broader area of his involvement in the orders of society.

There is widespread confusion about the nature and even the basis of personal morality. The college freshman who says rather plaintively in a discussion group that at home he knows what is expected of him, but here everything is different, may be met with a laugh. But the laughter

---

[12] "Who saw life steadily, and saw it whole." Matthew Arnold, "Sonnet to a Friend," *Poetical Works of Matthew Arnold* (London: Macmillan & Co., Limited, 1913), p. 2.

[13] John 7:17.

[14] Romans 1:28.

of the group only thinly disguises the fact that all within it share the problem. If he seeks for a theoretic basis on which to build a morality for himself, he may well confront the current relativism whose counsel received classic statement in the words of the sociologist William Sumner: "The mores can make anything right." [15]

If the confused Christian turns to the church for guidance, he may or may not receive relevant help. It is possible that he will find available to him both understanding and sound counsel; a treasury of wisdom from the past may be coupled with wisdom from the present. On the other hand, he may find in the church a rather rigid though unwritten codification of certain moral patterns from the past identified as "Christian morality." These may be imposed on him with a ruthlessness and insensitivity which completely disregard his personal integrity. He may be driven into hostilities which tear him to pieces.

If the Christian seeks to define his responsibilities in the broad areas of public life, he may find his confusion growing. The very complexity of problems which call for decision is staggering. Seemingly inexorable forces press toward dehumanization and crush out matters of religious concern. At the same time there is a haunting cry from educators and scientists, politicians and economists for attention to value. But the values are almost impossible to define and their status in reality is problematical. On what basis, for example, can a group of nations try so-called "war criminals?" If what they did was in accord with the outlook of their own people, who is to say that they were wrong?

> There is nothing either good or bad,
> but thinking makes it so.[16]

Within some churches the Christian confronts a tradition which affirms that religion has to do only with private morality and interpersonal relations. Sometimes this is explicit in the outlook of a certain group; often it is implicit even in churches which think of themselves as concerned about larger issues. The reaction of the churches to the recent developments in the field of race relations illustrates the point. Many people sincerely feel that the role of religion is to develop and maintain friendly personal relations between people of various races; and, indeed, that in the past such relations did exist even where civic privileges were denied to segments of the population. But they believe that religion

---

[15] William G. Sumner, *Folkways* (Boston: Ginn and Company, 1906), p. 521. Reprinted by permission.

[16] William Shakespeare, "Hamlet," Act II, Sc. 2, *Works*, p. 684.

has nothing at all to do with the legal effort to secure equality of political and economic and educational opportunity for people of all races. That is held to be beyond the sphere of personal relationships which is defined as the area of religious concern.

In other churches the Christian may be confronted by a long tradition committed to searching out the implications of Christian faith for public life. These have entered into the heritage of the Social Gospel and continue to feel the force of its ideals. It has been difficult for them, however, to escape a sense of disillusionment about their hopes for effective action in the world, and even about the possibility of defining what Christian action ought to be. During the nineteen-twenties one of the most characteristic emphases of such churches was on peace. They believed that mankind stood on the threshold of a warless world, and one way of inducing men to step over that threshold was to declare in the name of Christianity that they would have nothing to do with war. It seemed obvious to them that when "the Prince of Peace" counselled men to turn the other cheek, he was setting forth a proposal which could guide the behavior of nations. But when Hitler began to overrun France and to bomb English cities, the question arose whether it was more in keeping with Christian faith to let him do it—in the name of peace—or enter into the struggle—in the name of justice. Many took the latter alternative. But when men have seen what atomic bombs did to Hiroshima and Nagasaki, when they have imagined what even more powerful bombs could do now, what should be their course of action? Should they favor the building up of reservoirs of force, or seek to speak peace to power? [17]

Even as the Christian counts the causes of his confusion, however, the matters which call for action multiply. Standards of personal morality appear to be deteriorating. Crime and delinquency increase every year. There is widespread starvation in parts of the world at the same time as there is stupendous overproduction in others. Racial discriminations continue. And there is an imminent threat of atomic annihilation.

3. THEORY AND PRACTICE

The musings of Hamlet are memorable because they are the work of a supreme poet. He was not the first, however, to question what he

[17] The phrase was suggested by the title of a pamphlet, *Speak Truth to Power*, prepared for the American Friends Service Committee and published by them in 1955. The pamphlet explores alternatives to war in the present situation.

should do and why. From early times men considered the significance of their actions. As their thinking became systematized, it found its place within the context of philosophy. The discipline of ethics became recognized. It has been defined in various ways, depending on the viewpoint of the one who defines. Most thinkers would agree, however, that it could be described as the discipline which seeks to define what men ought to do and why, or what sorts of acts are good and how these differ from acts that are bad.

Into a world in which ethical thinking had been going on for some time the Christian faith entered. Within it was a heritage from Judaism which it modified in terms of its own insights. As it encountered ethical thought of Greeks and Romans, it dealt with this thought as it had dealt with their art. Christian thinkers rejected outright some of what they found; some they assimilated; some they transformed. At some points they introduced creative ideas. Thus Christian ethical thought emerged, and it expressed itself—again, as was the case with art—both within the church itself, on explicitly Christian grounds, and as an influence in secular ethical thought within the culture.

The confusions of the present have called for serious efforts to reappropriate the ethical heritage of the faith. There has been a vigorous effort at the discipline of *Christian ethics*. It is that part of Christian theology which focuses attention specifically on the problem of how Christians ought to act and why, or what sorts of actions are good or bad from a Christian point of view. Rather naturally the discipline divides itself into two main areas: that of personal morality and interpersonal relations; and that of the larger relationships of life—economic, political, and international affairs. The latter part is often referred to as *Christian social ethics*.

Christian ethics may proceed at a very practical level, seeking to define courses of action with reference to fairly concrete situations. In the New Testament there appear tables of duties addressed to husbands and wives, masters and servants, as well as people in other categories.[18] Early in the second century a North African thinker named Tertullian wrote on a variety of practical matters, giving advice about stage entertainments, behavior in the market place, and the veiling of virgins. He even addressed a treatise to his wife about the proper conduct of widows.[19] At the present time almost every denomination has groups as-

---

[18] For example Ephesians 6, Colossians 3 and 4.

[19] Lucius Waterman, *The Post-Apostolic Age* (New York: Charles Scribner's Sons, 1900), p. 302.

signed to the problem of studying out the significance of issues which are before its people, and interdenominational agencies are at work on similar matters. At its meeting in Evanston in 1954 the World Council of Churches gave serious consideration to such subjects as "the responsible society in a world perspective," "Christians in the struggle for world community," and "the churches amid racial and ethnic tensions." [20] Religious journals comment on matters of current concern, seeking to set forth some Christian understanding of their implications. A glance at *The Christian Century* or *Commonweal* in any given week will reveal Protestants and Catholics addressing themselves to the happenings of the day, appraising them from an avowedly Christian point of view.

Always implicit and sometimes explicit in statements on specific issues are questions about the fundamental bases of Christian ethics: What sorts of deeds ought Christians do? what sorts of actions can be called good? When these problems are pursued, a discipline of theoretic Christian ethics emerges. The attempt is made to set forth the fundamental character of the Christian life and the relation of action to the totality of faith.

Christian ethics, like any other theological effort, may be essayed in purely kerygmatic fashion; that is, the ethical thinker may simply seek to set forth what the Christian conception of action is. He may turn to the Bible, the creeds, or to confessional statements, and there find the basis on which to erect his structure of thought. Such effort is of peculiar significance today for several reasons. By many people, even church members, it is taken for granted that Christian ethics is merely a rather simple sort of code. Faith is the sanctioning of rather common-place conceptions of decency and honor. Christianity is summed up in the phrases "love thy neighbor," with no sense for the dimensions which the words suggest when they are placed in their full setting. By others Christian ethics is conceived to be distinctive; it places demands on those who would call themselves Christians. But upon examination these demands turn out to be rather inadequate, if not perverted, renditions of the commandments imbedded in the historic faith. At the worst they are simply local customs which have been erected into universal patterns. The study of the sources of Christianity for the light they have to throw upon ethical problems of our time cuts through both of these conceptions of Christian morality; it is being carried on in many areas. William G. Cole has recently published a study on what the Bible says

[20] William Visser 't Hooft, ed., *The Evanston Report* (New York: Harper & Brothers, 1955), pp. 112ff.

about sex, love, and marriage; [21] Everett Tilson has probed the teachings of the scriptures with regard to race.[22]

Christian ethics may also proceed in conversational fashion. The thinker is concerned to come to terms with what people outside the faith are thinking. This sort of inquiry is also of special significance today. The Christian may be reminded of aspects of his own heritage which he and others have neglected. He may encounter what Amos Wilder has called "a kind of secular conscience." Of it he writes,

> This secular conscience itself rests back upon the religious tradition, although the critic may not be aware of it. The modern agnostic writer is often unconsciously appealing to a living religious tradition against one that is moribund.[23]

The Christian thinker may also discover insights that are current in the intellectual world about him which can illumine certain traditional Christian viewpoints, and even, in some cases, help to free them from perversions. Thus Mr. Cole, whose kerygmatic work has been mentioned, becomes conversational in a treatment of *Sex in Christianity and Psychoanalysis*.[24] He derives help from both traditional Christian sources and contemporary psychoanalytic studies in the formulation of Christian attitudes within a contemporary setting. Conversation is also of importance at the present moment because of the fact that often Christians are at work side by side with non-Christians in the field of practical action. It is necessary for them to be able to define the terms on which they can seek the same goals as others and the points at which they must state their objectives differently. Thus the question for Christians today is not simply, "How can we in the churches act in the face of present international tensions?" but "How can we and people who disagree with us very fundamentally on many matters come to some agreement on what to do just now?"

4. ACTION AND ATTITUDE

Theological Liberals have often accused those who are concerned to recover historic Christianity in our time of counselling inaction at a

---

[21] William G. Cole, *Sex and Love in the Bible* (New York: Association Press, 1959).

[22] Charles E. Tilson, *Segregation and the Bible* (New York: Abingdon Press, 1958).

[23] Amos N. Wilder, *Theology and Modern Literature,* p. 115.

[24] William G. Cole, *Sex in Christianity and Psychoanalysis* (New York: Oxford University Press, Inc., 1955).

time when action is desperately called for. Walter Marshall Horton describes the tension between American activists and Continental quietists at a church conference in Stockholm in 1925.

While we were singing,

> Rise up, O men of God,
> His kingdom tarries long,
> *Bring in* the day of brotherhood,
> And end the night of wrong.

it seemed as though our Continental critics were telling us,

> Sit down, O men of God,
> His Kingdom He will bring,
> Whenever it may please His will;
> You cannot do a thing! [25]

And it certainly is true that those who have delved into the past for their guiding conceptions of Christian faith have been sober in their hopes. Karl Barth vigorously attacked those who sought to build a Tower of Babel on this earth.[26] And other thinkers have agreed with him in pointing to the limitations of that which can be achieved by human effort, and even of the capacities of the human imagination to delineate an order of society that is in accordance with the will of God. The word "realism" appears often in the writings of contemporary ethical thinkers. And they are keenly aware of the qualifications that must be given to all human hopes by the ugly fact of sin.

We should be mistaken, however, if we interpreted their outlook as one indifferent to the ethical dimension of faith. Differing at many points, and on many issues, they still see the Christian as a responsible being set within a context of life in which he must act. If they repudiate certain liberal interpretations of the social gospel, they yet see the gospel as having inescapable relevance for society. Their hopes are tempered by a profound sense of the depth of sin and of its effects in personal and corporate life. They do not expect healthy actions of sick people living in a sick society. They know that there are situations when that which can be done is far less than the best that could be hoped, when the dilemma seems to be that of choosing the action which has the least bad consequences because none can be chosen which can issue in some unequivocal good. And yet they are aware of a grace

---

[25] Walter M. Horton, *Contemporary Continental Theology* (New York: Harper & Brothers, 1938), p. XVI. Reprinted by permission.

[26] Karl Barth, *The Word of God and the Word of Man,* p. 25.

which enables man to acknowledge his sin, and as a forgiven man receive courage to act. They agree with the Liberals that a faith which does not issue in the works of love cannot deserve the name Christian.

Books on Christian ethics are apt to be thick, and even the digest of one of the thinner ones is beyond the scope of this work. However, it is in keeping with our purpose to give some attention to the basic character of the discipline of which they speak. Having looked at the manner in which they may proceed, we may now turn attention to some of the most general characteristics of action that is in keeping with Christian faith. We can do so by drawing some of the implications of the attitudes that have been described. Actually much has already been said about Christian ethics in the very description of the attitudes. This is inevitable, because action is the most obvious and direct expression of attitude. If we love our neighbor, we may pray for him, think of him, perhaps even paint his picture; we shall surely act for his good. It is not too much to say, perhaps, that action is the final test of the sincerity of attitude.

We have seen that Christian faith sees one attitude as basic—that toward God. Its nature is indicated by the first commandment of the two cited by Jesus—"Thou shalt love the Lord thy God with all thy heart, and with all thy soul, and with all thy mind, and with all thy strength" [27]—and by the first commandment of the ten given in the ancient writings of the Hebrews—"I am the Lord thy God—Thou shalt have no other gods before me." [28] Christian ethical thinkers have repeatedly insisted that all thinking about conduct begins with concern for the will of God. To start by seeking to define the good for human life or the ought for human action by speaking of the search for pleasure or the desire for self-fulfillment is to confuse the issue at the start. The beginning of Christian action, like the first concern of Christian prayer, is "Thy will be done." [29]

However, the God whom man is commanded to love is the very God who loves man utterly. The redemptive act of Christ reveals him so. Here his attitude, so to speak, is made known in an act. And it is that act, ever made new in human experience by the work of the Holy Spirit, which is the actual generator of Christian conduct. "We love, because he first loved us." [30] The action comes before the definition, before the

---

[27] Mark 12:30, K.J.V.
[28] Exodus 20:2f, K.J.V.
[29] Matthew 6:10.
[30] I John 4:19.

theories. These may come later, and, indeed, they will come; for Christians will raise the question, "What is the nature of the love with which I am to love my neighbor?" But the life of the Christ, the creation of the community of love—these are the beginnings of Christian ethics. Acts precede theories, and ethical theorists try to transcribe the meaning of redemptive love as it is known in the Christ. Hence, Christian thinkers do not proceed as some ethical thinkers do, seeking to set forth a set of principles which are rationally self-coherent. They begin with the acts of God in human history and derive the theories from them.

The human being is confronted by the demand of God, by the law which says that he must love God and his neighbor. But this may be simply a disruptive force in his life, driving him to anxiety and hopelessness. He must also be confronted by the disclosure of God's redemptive love, and be convinced that he is the object of that love, before he can come to wholeness within himself. Action done from constraint is not good action; only the act freely done is truly good. And Christian moralists have laid great stress on the significance of motivation. "A sound tree cannot bear evil fruit, nor can a bad tree bear good fruit." [31]

Motive cannot, however, be separated from conduct. Well-meaning is not enough. The wounded man lies at the roadside and the good Samaritan must do what he needs. Because love of the neighbor, in his concreteness, in his creaturely uniqueness, is the central thrust of ethical action, principles cannot be made central in any delineation of ethical thought. Men are not bidden to love principles, they are commanded to love people. Indeed, some of the most selfish deeds can be cloaked in a hypocritical love of principle, and in an outward conformity to even high moral standards. Hence, the attack of Jesus on the Pharisees and of Paul on the legalists. The good of the neighbor is first; he is to be loved as he is and where he is.

The nature of the love with which the neighbor is to be loved has been disclosed in the Christ. It is utterly self-giving and calculates no return. The Christian does not act for what he can get out of it. He is not good even because of the hope of heaven. His actions spring from himself; they are not done for himself. "Love your enemies, and do good, and lend, expecting nothing in return. . . . Be merciful, even as your Father is merciful." [32] The love of the neighbor is, then, redemptive in its quality. It does not ask what the neighbor deserves; it inquires

[31] Matthew 7:18.
[32] Luke 6:35f.

what he needs and seeks to supply it. Here some of the great problems of Christian ethical thought occur. The love commandment appears utterly unrealistic. The man who lived by it finished his life on a cross, and he promised his followers that they would be shamefully treated too. Is an unrealistic ideal relevant to actual conduct? Problems arise also in conversational Christian ethics with reference to the love commandment. How is it related to the ethical wisdom that appears outside the Christian heritage, to conceptions of goodness and justice and love that occur in the philosophies and religions of the world?

Difficulties in defining the commandment are most complex, perhaps, in the sphere of the relation of the Christian to the groups in which he participates. Some of these are large and far-reaching. And Christian faith interprets this fact as part of the creatural situation of man. Hence, it is never satisfied if action is confined to interpersonal relationships. Man must act responsibly within the groups of which he is part; he must live out his faith in the racial, economic, and political orders. But what does it mean to love in these relationships? And how is love to be related to justice?

A man's interpretation of love for his neighbor and proper regard for himself will be significantly affected by his attitude toward nature within and outside himself. If he is concerned for his fellow's spiritual and mental well-being and unconcerned for his bodily and economic welfare, that is one thing; but if his love is to include the totality of his fellow's good, that is quite another. As we have seen, the question about whether the world was God's creation or not was not simply a matter of theoretic concern to the early Christians. Men who denied the goodness of matter set forth codes of conduct which condoned asceticism or libertinism. By contrast, the Christians were concerned for a statement of faith which proclaimed the world good while it denied its ultimate worth. From that conviction has arisen the tension which runs through ethical thought about man's relation to nature. On the one hand is the tendency to fear the world and the body to such an extent that men become "puritans"; on the other is a tendency to eschew legalism to the extent that men throw off all restraints. Through the centuries Christian moralists have tried to help men find the way toward such definitions of action as would do justice to both the goodness of nature and to the primacy of the Creator.

So it is that all the attitudes which are consonant with Christian faith have their ethical implications. Attitude without action is incomplete; action without attitude is futile. Attitude and action are part of a massive whole, the totality of the faith.

5. ACTION AMONG THE EXPRESSIONS OF FAITH

A serious moral decision has a religious dimension. Hamlet's question of whether or not to do involved him in the question of what it meant to be. There is a direct relationship between ethics and faith, for an ethical decision can become a focal point for faith. If this is true, all the expressions of faith other than the ethical can be related to it; indeed, they can also be focused upon the point of ethical decision. This is the case because all the expressions of the faith reflect the same vision and attitudes. Thus the ethical can be, so to speak, a means by which the adequacy of the other expressions can be measured; and the ethical can be a focal point upon which they converge. They can enhance the significance of ethical decision, give range to its meaning, provide a context for its execution. Of any of them the Christian moralist may ask, "Does it take account of the ethical dimension of faith?" Concerning any moral decision, he may ask, "How does it look within the context of the various expressions of faith?"

Thus, of any act of worship, private or public, the Christian moralist may ask, "Is it ethically adequate?" As we have seen, the most private and personal act of Christian worship has reference to others and their good; the God who is worshipped is the Father of all men. No strictly private beneficence may be sought from him. The genuine act of private devotion will place the relations of the worshipper to his fellows in the context of their common relation to God. He should gain a perspective and a poise which make it possible for him to meet situations calling for decision with equanimity and honesty. In the act of sincere prayer his own motives are tested and may be transformed. Again and again Christian writers have stressed the importance of earnest prayer as a precursor of significant decisions. Adequate public worship will also contain references to the living of the good life. The Bible, with its load of ethical import is read; prayers and intercessions are offered on behalf of all men; the sermon seeks to clarify the human situation in the light of the gospel and to exhort men toward obedience to the will of God; acts of dedication express the resolution of the worshippers. However, worship is not simply carried on for the sake of action. Like all personal communion, it carries its own reward. But like acts of explicit avowal of friendship within the relations of human beings, if it is genuine, it will find its issuance in action.

In his role as moralist the Christian thinker does not make judgments concerning the aesthetic worth of an art object. He does, however, seek to define the place of aesthetic expression and appreciation within the total life of faith. He may also be concerned to ask of a picture if it gives adequate and accurate portrayal of the moral situation of man. He will not make narrowly "moralistic" judgments concerning art, but this is quite as much because he seeks to do justice to the nature of Christian faith—which is not "moralistic"—as it is that he tries to deal honestly with the aesthetic realm. The appreciation of art may well increase the range of his own sensibilities and render him sensitive to reaches of the moral problem which otherwise he might overlook.

The Christian moralist will approach literature as he does any of the other arts. Since, however, meanings are explicit in it as they are not elsewhere, he may find it especially important. He will recognize the moral force which literature may exercise. He may turn to it also to seek for understanding of the human situation as it holds "the mirror up to nature." [33]

A constant conversation will take place between the moralist and the theologian. The moralist will remind his colleague of the rootage of Christian faith in concrete ethical decision and of the ranges of insight which are afforded when the situation is such that significant action involving risk is called for. He will keep his own mind sensitive to the fullness of Christian thinking as the theologian seeks to take it into account so that his own preoccupation with the ethical will not lead to a distorted view of the faith.

The moralist will also seek to make sensitive the conscience of the church, helping to clarify its thinking on moral issues and to render it alive to its responsibilities. But he will ever speak from within it, recognizing himself as its child—even when he tries to correct his mother.

The sermon is peculiarly a point at which action and the other expressions of faith may come together. In some ways it is the most immediate expression of Christian ethical thought, of theology turned toward problems of actual living. It occurs at a specific time and place and seeks to declare what ought to be done then and there. It tries to clarify the minds of the people with reference to the relevance of the gospel to concrete issues of the day. But it also exhorts to action. And yet, it is not bare exhortation; it must be at the same time a declaration of grace. And the grace it declares is set forth also in the context of worship within which the sermon is placed. Concern for literary style is not lacking; music, art, and architecture contribute to the setting. And the

[33] William Shakespeare, "Hamlet," Act III, Sc. 2, *Works*, p. 689.

sermon is preached to the church assembled, the people of God who come to find his forgiveness and to seek guidance for the mediation of his redeeming love to the world in which they live.

If action is taken out of its setting within the whole of the expressions of faith, it is perverted along with the faith itself. When all of one's faith is absorbed into ethical concern, even ethical concern suffers. Action is stripped bare of the graces that should surround it; it turns crabbed and insensitive. The most passionate concern for action—and there must be such concern in Christianity—drives men beyond action itself, to the fullness of faith, and to acts which are not their own, the actions of God.

READINGS

From the Bible

1. The final chapters of Romans 12-15 (omitting concluding greetings) speak of the actions which flow from the faith Paul has described in the earlier part of the book.

2. Job 31 presents a rounded description of a good man, as the author pictured him.

3. The book of James insists on the necessity for faith to find expression in action.

4. The prophets pour contempt on the substitution of "religious" observance for right living: Amos 4, Micah 6.

From Historic Christianity

1. John Bunyan, *Pilgrim's Progress,* describes the obstacles in the way of living the Christian life.

2. Thomas Aquinas, *Summa Theologica,* First part of the second part, questions 49-67, treats of the several virtues and their relations.

3. Søren Kierkegaard, *Fear and Trembling,* Walter Lowrie, trans. (Garden City, N.Y.: Doubleday & Company, Inc., 1955) analyzes the relation

of faith to ethics through a study of God's commandment to Abraham to sacrifice Isaac.

FOR STUDY AND DISCUSSION

1. Describe an actual or imaginary situation in which the Christian attitude toward each of the following might make the difference in what you would do: nature, self, others, groups.
2. Address yourself to a specific problem in personal morality or social life. What factors are involved in arriving at a decision? What are the relevant considerations arising from Christian faith? How do Bible study, private prayer, congregational worship bear upon it? What should Christians as individuals do about it? What should the attitude of the church be? Do art and literature contribute in any way to your understanding of it?

XIX

THE CHURCH

One of the earliest controversies about the person of Christ, we have seen, was over the question, "Did he have a true human body?" A group of men called Docetists were seeking to reconcile the Christian affirmation that God had come to man with a philosophy which denied the goodness of matter. They were willing to concede that a divine apparition had occurred, but it was that and nothing more. Someone who looked and sounded like a man had come from God, but there had been no incarnation of the Divine in human flesh.

The church countered with the affirmation that Jesus Christ had been "born . . . suffered . . . died . . . was buried." [1] He was truly human in body as in all else. And yet that which gave his body its unique significance was the Person to whom it belonged.

A view which might be called "docetism with regard to the church" has appeared repeatedly during the Christian centuries. Some have wanted to equate Christianity with the persuasive spirit of Jesus in its gentleness and beauty while they have denied any essential relationship between that spirit and the actual church. These have often been men

---

[1] The Apostles' Creed.

of deep sensitivity and earnestness who have been appalled by what they felt to be the intellectual ineptitude, the social indifference, and even religious obtuseness of the church and its people.

Contemporary theologians, on the other hand, are convinced that Christian faith is no disembodied essence. A recovery of historic Christianity is, in part, a recovery of the church. Just here, however, a formidable difficulty arises. For deep within the traditions of the various communions are divergencies concerning the nature and the structure of the church. And while some of these may be due to specific historic situations which called them into being, others reflect conscientious attempts to do justice to aspects of the Christian vision. The recovery of a sense of the church has been accompanied by honest and searching discussions of these differences.

As we have looked at the church within the context of vision and of attitude, much that is important for a consideration of it as an expression of faith has already been said. Here we turn more specifically to the church in its organization. We shall note the manner in which organization reflects vision and attitude, and how the church is related to other expressions of faith. We shall also give attention to some of the broad lines of difference of interpretation as these have been carried within various Christian communions.

1. SPIRIT AND BODY

Some of those who are docetics with reference to the church are not particularly critical of it; they are simply indifferent. They may be for religion, or even for Christianity, but they do not see any point in connecting it with the church. They reflect, in part, currents of attitude which we have been noting from time to time, currents which have tended to diminish the sensitivity of men to the vision and attitudes of historic Christianity. These have all had their effect on men's attitudes toward the church; they have often had effects also within the lives of the churches themselves.

People who think of religion in primarily individualistic terms do not see any essential connection between it and a fellowship. They feel no need to receive any of its graces through others, and they also feel no need to communicate them. The man who says bravely

> I am the master of my fate:
> I am the captain of my soul,[2]

[2] William E. Henley, *Poems* (London: Macmillan & Co., Limited, 1926), p. 84.

does not see any need to relate himself to others at the profound levels of life. The person who sees education as a means to making him independent of others will feel that to admit the need of others for his spiritual welfare is to betray his very goal in life. Those who have found a satisfying religion in nature would rather go for a walk in the woods on a Sunday morning, or spend it in the loveliness of their garden of flowers than to attend the worship of the church. Others who have lost their sense of reverence for things natural will be unable to readjust their emotional attitudes to a service in which bread and wine are somehow purveyors of spiritual good. Those who have lost their sense for ritual in any phase of life[3] will not easily seek it in the service of the church.

Some who have become docetists with reference to the church have done so by reason of deep conviction. To them the church is simply out of step with the character of the faith it is supposed to proclaim; indeed, at many points, it is simply different from the church which is described in the New Testament and in classic writings of the Christian centuries. A student a few years ago read a paper about the church in one of her classes. Reflecting the writings of contemporary theologians, she presented a moving account of the nature of the church and of its essential place in the realm of faith. At the close of her presentation she was asked if she had ever seen the church she had described. After a few moments' hesitation she replied that she had not.

We have already had occasion to set forth some of the central matters with reference to the character of the church as it is viewed within the context of historic Christianity. If our delineation of the faith is correct, the church is an aspect of the very vision of faith; and it is one of those groups which must be attended to if we would take account of all the relationships with which the Christian is concerned. It is a fellowship of those who respond to God's redemptive acts; who sense their corporate need of forgiveness; and who, as forgiven sinners, seek to mediate the love of God to others.

The church itself often seems to be something very different from this. It does not recognize the dignity of man's mental powers; rather, it stifles creative intellectual effort and discourages the questioning spirit. It does not meet sin with redemptive love; rather, it imposes moral codes and treats all offenders without sympathy or understanding. It does not recognize "the beauty of holiness"[4] but is tied to mediocrity if not

---

[3] Amos N. Wilder, *Modern Poetry and the Christian Tradition* (New York: Charles Scribner's Sons, 1952), p. 51.

[4] Psalms 96:9, K.J.V.

downright ugliness. It does not concern itself for the rule of love in all of life, but is callously indifferent to economic injustice, racial discrimination, and political evil. All these things and others like them have been said over and over. They have led many to wonder if there is something about the church as an organization that inevitably betrays the faith. Is the spirit incompatible with the flesh?

The answer to this question is not simple; it must take into account certain tensions which we have had occasion to note again and again. It is important to see that there is in the very core of Christian conviction that which asserts the freedom of God over against any organization, any finite thing. He is not bound, and he can work in his own ways. Further, any organization can become a kind of law, holding men under it in bondage. They come to feel that they must have it; that it is necessary for salvation. Hence, there is again and again that spirit within Christianity which breaks through particular organizations, which dispenses with things which have been hallowed by time. Paul wrote to the Thessalonians, "Quench not the Spirit." [5]

The evils of organization come in part when organization is expected to do what only spirit can. And they come also from the tendency to deify the finite, to idolize that which is time-bound. They come, further, from the sinfulness of people who are members of organizations. But it would seem to be out of character with faith itself to speak of organization as such as evil. To those who desired anarchy in Corinth Paul wrote, "God is not a God of confusion but of peace." [6]

The recovery of the church in our time is not simply a call to people to come to church. It is coupled with a realization that the church itself is summoned to repentance. If it is to be that which in Christian vision it is seen to be, it must come penitently before the high and holy Lord whom it has again and again betrayed, seeking his forgiveness. Then it can be a mediator of his forgiveness, not a purveyor of its own shabby moralities. And the recovery is not simply that of the church by itself. The whole massive fullness of faith must somehow come alive again. Men who are used to thinking in individual terms must come to think in corporate terms; those who worship nature must come to see some sense in entering a historic community. But the fullness of faith does not come alive without the church. There is no disembodied Christianity. Indeed, the church is one of the focal points from which all other expressions of faith may proceed.

---

[5] I Thessalonians 5:19, K.J.V.
[6] I Corinthians 14:33.

2. THE CHURCH AS FOCUS OF THE FAITH

The analogy of the body is a singularly apt one for the church, because a body is a center from which actions emerge. Similarly the church is a center from which the several expressions of faith begin. It can take its place with each of the others as a natural focal point for Christian faith. Some writers would make it the one focal point, and there is a reasonableness in their contention. Every Christian act can be regarded as a function of the church.

The most adequate corporate worship among Christians is that of the church. Here all the groupings of which man is a part are represented, and man's social life is seen in its ultimate reaches. Even the solitary who goes to his devotions alone will probably use the church's Bible and its prayers; he will include the church in his intercessions.

The classic literature of Christianity emerged in the church; it was written by churchmen for the benefit of others like themselves. Much of the New Testament was written directly for the purpose of being read to congregations, the familiar letters to the Romans, the Corinthians, and others. The choice of the Old Testament as Christian scripture was based, in part, on the conviction that the Christians entered into and continued the life of Israel and that the ancient oracles were spoken to them. These writings had come out of the historic experiences of the Hebrew people. They had been directed to them for their inspiration and instruction, and they had been chosen by them with the conviction that they were a message from God to his people. Hymns and liturgies were a direct literary product of the Christian church; and poems, stories, and dramas in Western culture bear their character in part by reason of the church to which many of their authors have belonged.

The church is also the mother of Christian art. The earliest paintings, as we have seen, were directly related to the liturgical as well as the common life of the Christian people, giving expression to their hopes and their convictions. One art in particular, that of architecture, has a special debt to the Christian people. Hymn tunes, preludes, and anthems have also been composed in order to give musical setting to acts of worship.

Ethical actions can also be traced to the focal center of the church. Vicious men have come under its ministrations and been changed into saints. Motives for conduct have been discovered in its common life. Exhortations to action have been enunciated in its liturgies and sermons.

Organizations for the elimination of abuses and for the reformation of society have come into being under its auspices. It has maintained by its very existence certain traditions about the character of the good life which have profoundly affected all ethical thought and action in the West and also in other parts of the world.

Theology is unthinkable apart from the church. It exists for the very purpose of helping the church to understand itself. The theologian is the church's servant. And the church in council comes to decisions about the character of its faith in doctrinal terms.

It may seem strange to add that the church is a focus from which its own organization comes, and yet this is the case. The New Testament points to the Spirit as the creator and guide of the church in the matters of its leadership, its unity, and its organization. These are given in concrete situations for the needs which are present. We shall have to see a little later how Christians have viewed the New Testament church with respect to whether its patterns were to be retained unchanged through all time. It is clear, however, that within the most primitive times the organization of the church developed and that this development was regarded as normal and necessary. Needs in the church, and inspirations to action, have repeatedly called forth organizational structures. There have been mission boards, educational societies, social action committees, and other groups for specific purposes throughout the history of the church.

Furthermore, the organized life of the church has affected the life of the society around it. Men who are Christians are bound to transfer, to some extent, the manner in which they think of the church to the manner in which they think of other associations of which they are a part. Hence the church has brought about effects not simply in its own organization, but in the organization of society at large. Thus the church parallels other expressions of faith in that there is a churchly element not only in the church itself, but in the culture around it.

3. THE EXTENT OF THE CHURCH

Few have been so insistent on the centrality of the church for Christian faith as a North African bishop of the middle of the third century. His name was Cyprian. He acted prudently during periods of persecution, even calling forth the accusation of cowardice by leaving the city of Carthage during a particularly severe time; but when the issue of his life was clearly joined, he accepted the death of a martyr with

CHURCH AND CULTURE The Medieval Cathedral was a center for worship, religious discipline, art, education, and ecclesiastical administration; castle and town were nearby. Durham Cathedral (Courtesy of the British Information Services)

dignity and honor. Perhaps his training as a lawyer helped to form a mind that formulated ideas clearly and expressed them trenchantly. At any rate, he created some of the neatest phrasing that has ever been set forth for the conviction that the church is essential for faith. "You cannot have God for your father," he proclaimed, "unless you have the Church for your mother." [7] His position can be summarized in words that have become classic: "Outside the church there is no salvation." [8]

Something like this had certainly been implied in the New Testament. If Christ is the source of life, then one must be part of his body to have a share in his vitalizing power. John uses a figure that is similar to that

---

[7] Cyprian, "The Unity of the Catholic Church," S. L. Greenslade, trans. and ed., *Early Latin Theology* (Philadelphia: The Westminster Press; London: S. C. M. Press, Ltd., 1956), pp. 127f. Reprinted by permission.

[8] Quoted by Arthur C. McGiffert, *A History of Christian Thought* (New York: Charles Scribner's Sons, 1947), II, 31.

of the human body—which is Paul's—in order to picture the character of the church and its relation to Christ. He speaks of a vine which has branches; if these do not remain in living relationship with the vine, they wither.[9]

The words of Cyprian are likely to be met with skepticism today. Many feel that the church can make no claim to be indispensable for living the Christian life. In the past, too, there has been a rather constant note of protest even within Christianity against any absolute identification of the actual church with the company of those who are to be designated as Christians. And yet on the whole there has been a feeling that the church is essential for Christian faith, a feeling which has significant connection with the vision and attitudes which are characteristic of Christianity. It could probably be said that Christian thinkers would agree that "outside the church there is no salvation" if enough latitude is given to the definition of "the church."

One way in which a measure of latitude has been introduced into the definition of the extent of the church has been to make a distinction between the visible and the invisible church. Most Christian thinkers—perhaps all—would deny that the number of the redeemed can be equated with the company of members of the church. The sayings of Jesus repeatedly point up the notion that those who consider themselves to belong to God may discover that they do not.[10] And there is a simple and clear word of an apostle: "The Lord knows those who are his." [11] The invisible church, as it is commonly understood, is composed of those who are truly God's children. Calvin speaks of it as the church

> which is really such in the sight of God, into which none are received but those who by adoption and grace are the children of God, and by the sanctification of the Spirit are the true members of Christ.[12]

Thus for him the invisible church is within the visible. During the past few centuries, however, partly under the influence of the spirit of toleration that grew up with the enlightenment, the term "invisible church" has often been used in a broader sense, to refer to those in any time or place who share in the spirit of Jesus:

> All Christly souls are one in Him
> Throughout the whole wide earth.[13]

---

[9] John 15:1-11.
[10] Matthew 7:21-23; Matthew 25:31-46.
[11] II Timothy 2:19.
[12] John Calvin, *Institutes of the Christian Religion,* II, 229. (IV, i, 7).
[13] John Oxenham, "In Christ there is No East or West," *Christian Worship and Praise,* no. 488.

Many Christian thinkers are suspicious, however, of an undue emphasis on the invisible church: it can easily lead to what has here been called "docetism" with regard to the church. There is a tendency to think of the invisible church as an ideal, floating about somewhere, in contrast to which the actual church is rather a shabby copy. Calvin certainly had no such intention; for him the concept of the invisible church simply guarded the freedom and omniscience of God. Like other theologians through the centuries, he took the visible church very seriously. If it could not be identified completely with the true church, it was yet the normal place in which the Spirit could be expected to operate.

Two tendencies have competed through the centuries in attempts to define the extent of the visible church. There have been, on the one hand, those who have sought to be very strict about the matter of membership. They have insisted that only those with certain qualifications of a rather high order should be counted. Sometimes these qualifications have been experiential in character: only those who have undergone a certain type of religious experience should be admitted to the church. Sometimes combined with the experiential has gone a ritual requirement: the converted person must be baptized. Often combined with these two, but sometimes found where these are not insisted upon, is an ethical requirement: the church is the company of the pure, defined in terms of certain moral qualifications. This tendency was present very early in the history of the church and has come to the fore on many occasions. In our time it is particularly associated with such groups as the Baptists.

The other tendency is to make the basis of church membership rather broad. Minimal requirements there must be, of course, but to seek to probe too far into man's experience or conduct is to court the danger of basing the church on human goodness rather than divine grace. The church leaves to God the determination of those who are his; it seeks to educate those who belong to her in knowledge of their faith and in their Christian responsibilities. But it is ready to accept the fact that "in this church are included many hypocrites . . . persons who are ambitious, avaricious, envious, slanderous, and dissolute in their lives," [14] as Calvin put it. Those who represent this tendency have repeatedly cited the parable of the tares sown among the wheat.[15] The owner of the field was instructed to let the two grow side by side until the harvest, lest a premature attempt to separate them might damage the good grain.

---

[14] John Calvin, *Institutes of the Christian Religion,* II, 230. (IV, i, 7).
[15] Matthew 13:24-30, K.J.V.

This tendency is found in Roman Catholicism as well as in many Protestant denominations.

Conversations are going on today among representatives of the two tendencies who are concerned to come to some common understanding of the nature of the church. On many matters it has proved feasible for churches of both kinds to cooperate in common ventures. It is important that both agree that the church should act as a mother to those who intend to have God as their Father.

4. THE MARKS OF THE CHURCH

Closely bound up with the question of the extent of the church is that of the manner in which it is to be defined. As every beginner in logic knows, the extension and intension of a term are interrelated; if there is uncertainty about the one, there will be lack of clarity concerning the other. And so it is with the term "church." As people have disagreed about its extent, so have they been at odds about its definition. The variety of views represented in the many denominations of Christians cannot here be reviewed. Three major approaches to the problem of definition may, however, include most of them. These are not mutually exclusive.

One approach to the definition of the church may be suggested by the phrase *the communion of saints,* which comes just after the word *church* in the Apostles' Creed and is intended to amplify its significance. It stresses the fellowship of people. One expression of it is to be seen in a phrase often used by Congregationalists: "the gathered church." The conception of the church held by the Anabaptists of the sixteenth century, as this has been made available to us through the research of Franklin H. Littell,[16] includes much that is typical of it. These people intended to restore the church to its original condition as it was disclosed in the New Testament; they were going behind even the earliest developments which went beyond that Book. They insisted that the church was composed of baptized believers, people who as responsible adults had made profession of their faith. These were bound together in a common discipline; something could be expected of every member, and he might be cited before the congregation for failing in his duty. The church must not be identified with the political order; its members belonged to it by voluntary choice, not by birth. And all were responsible for the work of the church and for the spread of the gospel through-

[16] Littell, *The Anabaptist View of the Church,* p. 11. Used by permission.

out the world. Others have disagreed with the Anabaptists on some of these points; but they have agreed with them in stressing the notion that it is the people by which the church is to be defined.

A second approach to the definition of the church stresses the notion that it is a locus of action. This is often connected with a tendency noted in the preceding section, that of avoiding any over-precise delineation of the church's membership. This approach is reflected in such a statement as that of John Calvin. He speaks strongly against the person "who voluntarily deserts the external communion of the Church where the word of God is preached, and the sacraments are administered." [17] Luther was of the same mind. As Gustaf Aulén points out, "However sharply and violently he criticizes Rome, he can nevertheless say that the Roman church is 'holy,' because in this church there still remain 'baptism, sacrament, the word of the Gospel, the Holy Scriptures, the churchly office, and the name of Christ and God.' " [18] It is interesting that in Saint Thomas Aquinas' summation of the Christian faith *Against the Gentiles,* he has no chapter on the church at all. He passes directly from the treatment of the Incarnation to the Sacraments, treating the church incidentally. Obviously the church is essential for the faith, but it is thought of as the place in which the sacramental life of the Christian is carried on.

A third approach to the defining of the church is suggested by a formula which has been current in the church for many centuries: here it is affirmed that the church is "one, holy, catholic, and apostolic." It stresses the continuity of the church in time and its universality in space. It derives much from such men as Cyprian, who, in the treatise already quoted, compared the church to the seamless robe of Christ which cannot be torn. The church for him was bound together, and defection from it was treachery to Christ. "If anyone could escape who was outside the ark of Noah he also may escape who is outside the church." [19] Later Augustine was to argue against those who separated from the Catholic church to set up a congregation of the "pure," that they had broken the bond of charity, they had sinned against the Holy Spirit—which he defined as the love of God which binds things together. People who argue for this conception of the church usually deny that its holiness is to be defined in terms of the actual purity of its members; to define it so would

---

[17] John Calvin, *Institutes of the Christian Religion,* II, 240. (IV, i, 19).

[18] Gustaf Aulén, *The Faith of the Christian Church,* Eric H. Wahlstrom and G. Everett Arden, trans. (Philadelphia: Muhlenberg Press, 1948), p. 338. Reprinted by permission.

[19] As quoted in McGiffert, *A History of Christian Thought,* II, 31.

be to make a human quality the mark of the church. Rather, say they, does its holiness consist in God's choice, in his action through preaching and sacraments. The catholicity of the church is its universality throughout the world. The apostolicity of the church is its continuity with the church of the first followers of Jesus, the twelve who were especially chosen by him and who furnished leadership in the primitive Christian community. A church is apostolic if it stands in continuity with them—though the terms of this continuity may be differently defined by various groups. For some it means fellowship with the churches founded by the apostles, for some actual succession through the centuries by the laying on of hands, for some fidelity to the apostolic understanding of the faith. Many Christians, some of whom differ rather fundamentally in their conception of the Christian faith, affirm their belief in a church which is "one, holy, catholic, and apostolic."

The several approaches to the definition of the church are not, we have seen, mutually exclusive. Some groups hold to more than one of them. In *The Book of Common Prayer* of the Episcopal Church all three can be found. Thus, in the "Articles of Religion" which are printed at the back of the book, "The visible Church of Christ" is defined as

> a congregation of faithful men, in the which the pure Word of God is preached, and the Sacraments be duly ministered according to Christ's ordinance, in all those things that of necessity are requisite to the same.[20]

Services of worship include the use of the Apostles' Creed, in which the people affirm their faith in "the church, the communion of saints," as well as the "Creed commonly called the 'Nicene,'" which has the words, "I believe one Catholic and Apostolic Church."

5. LEADERSHIP

A passage in the epistle to the Ephesians describes the Christ ascending into heaven from whence he gave gifts to men. When the gifts are identified, they turn out to be leaders for the church.

> And his gifts were that some should be apostles, some prophets, some evangelists, some pastors and teachers, for the equipment of the saints, for the work of ministry, for building up the body of Christ.[21]

---

[20] *The Book of Common Prayer,* p. 606.

[21] Ephesians 4:11f. The late Professor William Owen Carver's interpretation of this passage in his classes is unforgettable.

The writer is stating a common Christian conviction, that leadership in the church is intended by God and even provided by him. In some way the ministry of the church is regarded as a redemptive thrust by the Spirit toward the church.

Just how the ministry links the Spirit and the church has been a matter of difference among Christians, however. There are many degrees of opinion with regard to the matter, and these are reflected in the life of the various communions. At the one extreme, perhaps, is a viewpoint like that which is held by the Roman Catholic Church. Here the priest is viewed as being given a special and indelible character at his ordination. Because of it he has specific authority to announce to the penitent that his sins are forgiven. As a successor to the Apostles he can enter into the promise of the Christ to them; "If you forgive the sins of any, they are forgiven."[22] At the celebration of the Mass he is able to say the words at which God works the miracle changing the substance of bread and wine into that of the body and blood of the Christ. At the other extreme is a viewpoint one might encounter among some Baptists and Congregationalists. They would agree with the Roman Catholic that leadership for God's people was a gift of the Spirit. They might well also feel that there were times when the presence of a minister might be of the greatest help in making it possible for a penitent to come to the conviction that his sins were forgiven. And they would hold that for the sake of order in the church it is well that someone be set aside to lead in the celebration of the Lord's supper, and even hold that such a one should be ordained by the laying on of hands. But they would insist that no change took place in the elements, that nothing that this particular man could do would affect the benefit that worshippers might receive from partaking of bread and wine. And no word that he spoke could bear authority in declaring forgiveness. Between the extreme positions fall a great many others closer to one side or the other.

It is obvious from the very names by which various groups of Christians address their clergy that they differ in their identification as well as their understanding of the offices of their leaders. From a great variety of usages we may note a few. By the time of Cyprian a set of gradations of the ministry had developed which he accepted and helped to promote. At the beginning of the second century even, a Christian martyr named Ignatius had written a series of letters in which he espoused them. Without three offices, he said, there is no church.[23] At the head of the church

---

[22] John 20:23.

[23] Ignatius, "To the Trallians," 3:1, Cyril C. Richardson, trans. and ed., *Early Christian Fathers,* p. 99.

was the bishop, the very representative of Christ himself. Associated with him was a group of elders—the Greek word is "presbyters"—and below them in importance were the deacons. Gradually the custom developed of having one bishop in a central location, usually a city, of assigning presbyters to the oversight of individual congregations, and of using the deacons as administrative officers. The bishop came to be looked upon as the complete priest, the successor to the apostles, able to pass on to others through the laying on of hands certain graces of the Spirit. The presbyter came to be called *priest,* empowered to conduct the Eucharist and to exercise other ministerial functions. The deacon served in various capacities of helpfulness in the life and work of the church. Each office could be a preparation for that above it. This pattern persists in Roman Catholicism and in other churches of episcopal polity. In it the Spirit is generally thought of as working first through the bishop, then through the lesser clergy, and then to the people.

The threefold office has been rejected by some groups of Christians on the ground that it does not appear in the New Testament. They admit that the terms *bishop* and *presbyter* are to be found there, but hold that these refer to the same office. Thus they feel impelled to recognize within the church a minister—who might be called *bishop* or *presbyter*—who has oversight over a local congregation and a group of deacons who serve with him in the guidance of the affairs of the church. How the officers are named and exactly what their duties are may differ from group to group. Thus Presbyterians and Baptists both seek to model their church life after that which is presented in the New Testament, but there are significant differences in their modes of procedure.

Some Christian groups have tried to find their leadership in a different way from either of the preceding, and yet one that is certainly present in the New Testament. Sometimes called *charismatic,* this leadership is provided as men are especially endowed by the Spirit. Sometimes it is marked by prophetic utterances and by ecstatic behavior. At other times it is followed by a community with a considerable degree of discipline. Thus in the Quaker meeting of our time no one is designated to lead. Silence is maintained until such a time as one, anyone, feels a constraint to speak. At a Quaker wedding all those present sign a certificate of marriage. The entire congregation has acted in the capacity of minister. Here a conception of specific endowment by the Spirit is combined with a conviction about the complete democratization of church life.

Concerning leadership, then, there are wide divergencies within the traditions now alive within the various Christian communions. So are there divergencies of opinion with regard to the extent of the church and even to its very nature. And yet there are wide areas within which Christians can and do cooperate on common ventures. There are also numerous movements looking toward unifications within the church. Groups within denominations have joined together, as in the case of Methodists and Lutherans. Whole denominations have merged: the Congregationalists and the Evangelical and Reformed communion have come together to form the United Church of Christ. And after years of study and discussion Anglican, Congregationalist, Methodist, Presbyterian, and Reformed churches have joined to become the Church of South India.

The formation of the World Council of Churches in Amsterdam in 1948 marked the climax of efforts which had been carried on over many years. Movements for cooperative effort among Christians in student work, missions, social responsibility, and theological discussion lay behind it. While some groups have not entered into it, feeling that to do so would be to surrender something which they feel to be essential to the gospel, it has been a meeting ground for many Christian communions, some of them very different in structure and outlook. The list of member churches at the time of the first Assembly covers six pages of the official report.[24] There are points on which the member churches disagree and cannot see a way to overcome their differences. It has not proved possible so far to hold a single communion service to which all could come. And yet they have a medium through which they can discuss their disagreements as well as a means by which they can witness together to the convictions they share.

The prayer of the Christ in John 17 includes the petition that his followers may be one. The words have haunted the church through the centuries and they are disturbing today. Sometimes critics ask, "Why cannot the churches forget the little things they are always disagreeing about and attend to essentials?" There are two answers to the question, and neither can be neglected. The "little thing" which some specific group cherishes might be essential; it might, however, be some triviality to which a group clings because of its pride. To dissociate the answers is most difficult. But many churchmen of our time are penitently and honestly trying to do so. They feel that they must if a church is to emerge which will do some justice to the facets of faith which are grasped by the various communions without at the same time being divided into impotence.

---

[24] Willem Visser 't Hooft, ed., *The First Assembly of the World Council of Churches* (London: S. C. M. Press, Ltd., 1949), pp. 230-235.

READINGS

From the Bible

1. The notion of a covenant by which the children of Israel are constituted as a people of God runs through the Old Testament.

2. The Book of Acts is the first chapter in the story of the Christian Church.

3. The early Christians thought of themselves as the people of the new covenant: Jeremiah 31 is quoted in Hebrews 8 and 12.

4. Leadership in the early church is mentioned in I Corinthians 12:4-11, 27-31; Ephesians 4:11, I Timothy 3, 5.

5. The unity of the church is a theme of John 17 and I Corinthians 1. It is contrasted to the previous divisions of mankind in Ephesians.

6. The notion of the church as the body of Christ is found in I Corinthians 12 and Romans 12, as the vine in John 15.

From Historic Christianity

1. Cyprian, *On the Unity of the Church,* is a strong statement of the importance of the church, of its bishops, and of its oneness.

2. John Calvin, *Institutes,* sets forth his idea of church and ministry in accordance with biblical teachings in Book IV, chapters 1 and 3.

3. Dante, *Divine Comedy,* "Purgatorio," Canto 29, pictures the ideal church in the earthly paradise.

4. Richard Hooker, *The Laws of Ecclesiastical Polity,* argues for attention to tradition in the formulation of the life of the church. Book 3.

FOR STUDY AND DISCUSSION

1. What is the form of organization of your church and denomination? Is it based on the Bible, tradition?
2. Is your church under- or over-organized? What organizations would you add? What organizations would you drop?
3. Evaluate: denominations are a good thing. They keep any one group from becoming too powerful. They fit into our American way of life.
4. What is the attitude of your church and denomination toward efforts toward Christian unity? Is it contemplating union with any other group at the present time? If so, what are some problems involved?
5. Study the development of The World Council of Churches. What major Christian groups do not belong to it? Why?

XX

THOUGHT

The mind is a curious reality. It arises within a living being; and yet it is able to contain that being in its own thought. It includes in thought that which includes it in actuality. It is even able to think about its own thinking. But all the time it is within the living being.

The use of the mind in religion exhibits the curiosity which has been noted. Thought arises within the life of faith. And yet it makes faith its object. But all the time it is part of the life of faith.

If our analysis of the faith has been correct, any of its expressions might have been reserved for final treatment. Each can be a focal point for all the others; it could have been accorded a final place toward which all else pointed. Thought has been selected for that place for a very simple reason. This entire book is an exercise in thinking about the faith. Now it is time to look at the implications of that faith for the thinking itself. In looking at them we shall bring into review all the matters that have come before us. We shall look at what faith has to say about thought. First and last, we shall look for a moment at what thought might be expected to contribute to faith.

1. FAITH AND THOUGHT

We have already had occasion to notice some of the ways in which thought contributes to the life of faith. Each of faith's expressions calls for its own interpretation; there is a branch of theology parallel to it. The church has to define itself and its mission in the world. Worship involves understanding if it is to be meaningful. And central in Christian worship is preaching, the proclamation of good news. From one point of view the very central task of theology is that of seeking to delineate what ought to be preached. Action, likewise, calls for definition; how should the Christian and the church conduct themselves within the world? What are their responsibilities in the familial, racial, economic, and political orders? Literature and art also call for acts of discrimination. Disciplines develop which have as their primary objective that of giving guidance to each of the expressions of faith.

These disciplines are interrelated; they have a meeting point. Central kerygmatically, seeking to set forth that which is distinctive in Christians ought to believe and why. This is the very heart of theology. Its concern is to examine those guiding ideas which belong to faith in any of its expressions. It seeks to discern what Christians mean by their convictions about creation, rebellion, and redemption. It may proceed kerygmatically, seeking to set forth that which is distinctive in Christianity; it may go about its task conversationally, seeking to relate the ideas that belong to faith to ideas from other sources. Since theologians have usually tried to set forth their ideas in some sort of connected fashion, it is often called *Systematic Theology*.

To this point we have been looking at thought which is intentionally directed toward the service of the life of faith. It corresponds to that sort of thought which contributes in rather direct fashion to the well-being of the human organism. But in the living being thought may have purposes that are not strictly utilitarian. Men do not think only that they may secure food or shelter, or even that they may enjoy music or art. They think for the sake of thinking. They undertake researches which have no practical end in view. Indeed, they think about thinking itself for no ostensible reason. Hence thought attains a status in life that is similar to that of art; it simply is for its own sake. Some such thought is directed toward the gathering and interpretation of information; this occurs, of course, in the various natural sciences, in the social studies, in history. In a very rough sense, we may speak of this as *scientific*. Other thought is directed toward the most general ideas. It seeks answers to such questions as "What are causes?" "What is real?" "How do we know anything?" This sort of thought is called *philosophy.*

In the West science and philosophy developed within a culture where many were Christians. And they were carried on by men of Christian conviction, as, indeed, they are today. Men have studied astronomy to think God's thoughts after him. They have become absorbed in psychological studies to know what will help them in the cure of souls. They have studied sociology because they have been profoundly convinced that their faith demands expression in the social order. In these studies they have often been concerned for astronomy, psychology, and sociology *per se.* But they have carried into their studies certain Christian convictions. These do not, they believe, distort their studies; rather, they contribute significant insights at certain points. Christians have also pursued the study of philosophy. They have sometimes used the old words of Anselm, *fides quaerens intellectum,* "faith seeking understanding," [1] as a description of their undertakings. They have been concerned with philosophy itself—not necessarily with philosophy as an aid to theology—but they have been interested as Christians, and they have honestly believed that their Christian convictions contribute to philosophic understandings. There have been, then, intellectual efforts carried on in the West which have been purposely *Christian science* and *Christian philosophy.*

Thus there is explicitly Christian thought just as there is explicitly Christian art. But the parallelism between thought and art can be carried one step further. There is also scientific and philosophic thought in the West which is not explicitly Christian; nevertheless, it carries the impress of Christian affirmation and conviction. In our study of attitudes toward nature we have already noted that this is the case in the natural sciences. Christian faith has been a determinant in the subjects of observation, in the attitudes of observers, in the canons of interpretation that have characterized thought in the West with reference to the natural and biological sciences, psychological and sociological studies, the writing of history, and the analysis of culture. It has also been a determinant in thought about general ideas, philosophy, in its interest in nature, its concern for values, its perennial problems about the meaning of life and the world. There is a Christian element in science and philosophy as these have been carried on in the West.

---

[1] Anselm, "An Address (Proslogion)" Preface, Eugene R. Fairweather, ed. and trans., *A Scholastic Miscellany,* p. 70.

2. THOUGHT AND THE CHRISTIAN VISION

"Wisdom is the principal thing; therefore get wisdom: and with all thy getting get understanding." [2] So spoke one of the writers of the Old Testament. He was echoing an outlook which was held by many. The notion of wisdom loomed large in the thinking of Israel, at least in certain periods of her historic life. One writer personified her and presented her as speaking of herself:

> The Lord created me at the beginning of his work,
> the first of his acts of old.
> When he marked out the foundations of the earth,
> then I was beside him, like a master workman.
> By me kings reign,
> and rulers decree what is just;
> by me princes rule,
> and nobles govern the earth.[3]

The context indicates that the writer does not think of an impassable gap between divine and human wisdom; by the work of the human mind, reverently used, man can trace the divine ways and can live his own life in harmony with the everlasting Will.

There is also another strain in the thought of Israel, however, a deep scepticism about all human thought and contrivance. The story of the garden of Eden reflects it; the promise of the serpent is knowledge, knowledge of good and evil. God is pictured as resisting the human effort to know, thwarting it before it leads to other excesses of the human spirit. Man must be stopped before he reaches for the fruit of the tree of life and attains immortality.[4] The same resistance of God to the overweening efforts of human thought is present in the telling of the ancient story of the tower of Babel. Men's efforts to erect a building that will reach to heaven are effectively nullified by an act of God.[5] In a series of poetic stanzas God speaks to Job out of the whirlwind and reminds him of the limitations of human wisdom. Again and again in the Old Testament man is reminded of his smallness, of the frailness of his mind. "Canst thou by searching find out God?" [6]

---

[2] Proverbs 4:7, K.J.V.
[3] Proverbs 8:22, 29f., 15f.
[4] Genesis 3.
[5] Genesis 11:1-10.
[6] Job 11:7, K.J.V.

The New Testament reveals the same doubleness of viewpoint. Here the creation does not come into view so prominently. It is the greatness of God's redemptive act that beggars all human thought and imagination.

> Where is the wise man? Where is the scribe? Where is the debater of this age? Has not God made foolish the wisdom of the world? For since, in the wisdom of God, the world did not know God through wisdom, it pleased God through the folly of what we preach to save those who believe. . . . The foolishness of God is wiser than men, and the weakness of God is stronger than men.[7]

And yet the redemptive entrance of God into human life is described in terms of thought: Christ is "the wisdom of God." [8] Further, receiving the message is in part a mental response. The word which is normally used for repentance in the New Testament means "change of mind." When Paul, having described what God has done for men in Christ in the early chapters of his letter to the Romans, turns to a consideration of the response which is appropriate on their part, he tells them to be "transformed by the renewing of your mind." [9] And when he seeks to restrain the Corinthians from an over-emphasis of emotional excitement in their worship, he says, "I will pray with the spirit and I will pray with the mind also." [10]

The double valuation of wisdom which we find in the Old and New Testaments appears throughout the history of Christian thought. Already in the second century the figure of the Christian philosopher appears. Justin Martyr taught in Rome, wearing a philosopher's cloak, and proclaiming that the very *Wisdom* which had been incarnate in Jesus had earlier been the inspirer of Socrates and Plato. By contrast, not long thereafter the North African Christian named Tertullian asked disdainfully, "What has Jerusalem to do with Athens?" [11] In our own time there are those who feel that Christian proclamation involves a full-scale attack on the pretentions of human reason while others seek to bring reason to the service of the Christian cause. Having seen the parallel to the double valuation of reason in Christian attitudes toward art, worship, literature, and morality, we are not surprised to encounter it again when we come to a consideration of thought. Here once more is the tension that has been noted over and over: because the mind is God's creature, it is, in some real

---

[7] I Corinthians 1:20f., 25.
[8] I Corinthians 1:24.
[9] Romans 12:2, K.J.V.
[10] I Corinthians 14:15.
[11] Tertullian, "The Prescriptions Against the Heretics," S. L. Greenslade, trans. and ed., "Early Latin Theology," p. 36.

sense good; because it can join in man's rebellion against his Creator, it can become a center of sinfulness; because God redeems the whole of his creatures, it can participate in man's redemption. The implications of the Christian vision for human thought apply to it whether it seeks to serve faith as theology or simply is exercised for its own sake in researches or philosophical thought.

The significance of the double valuation is, perhaps, more clearly discernible when it is disregarded than when it is attended. Utter abandonment of rationality opens the church to any and every form of superstition in religious thought. The discrimination of Christianity from Gnosticism was a work of the mind. On the other hand, emphasis on thought can deliver Christianity to any philosophy that happens to be persuasive at a given time even though that philosophy acts as a solvent of all that is precious in the faith. Used in another way, thought may bind faith to a specific set of ideas which are inadequate to it. Some given theology becomes finalized, even though it contains much that is time-bound. Being a Christian may also be identified with adherence to a certain set of ideas; then, the personal character of faith is betrayed.

To say just what is the place of thought in faith is no easy thing, however. Certain broad principles can be derived from the Christian vision. In the first place, no thinker nor any thought can be taken as final. All are at the level of creatural life and cannot be given a status that is proper to the divine. This negative judgment applies to thought whether it is carried on for its own sake or seeks to serve faith in direct fashion. It is true of philosophical systems as well as for canons of evidence in the sciences. Indeed, the Christian vision would seem to be in accord with that view of the nature of science which takes it to be an ever-corrected enterprise, always open to new evidence and even to the revisions of its methodologies. The negative judgment must be applied also to efforts to set forth the ideas that belong to the Christian faith. No theological system is final, no statement of the faith is in itself infallible. Paradoxically, the Christian faith contains a principle which denies that any statement of that faith can be final. Every statement is made by creatures, and even if it be held that they are led by the divine Spirit, their finiteness cannot be overcome.

On the other hand, it is not strange to one looking at the intellectual life from the viewpont of the Christian vision to see in it that which points toward God. It is not strange that the character of things should suggest to an observer that the world had a Creator, or that the nature of thought should suggest to a thinker that truth has an Ultimate Source. The Christian is not surprised that proofs for the existence of God should emerge within the history of thought. Nor does it seem strange that wisdom should be able to add to the goodness of life, that it should prove helpful for the guidance of conduct.

However, human thought can essay too much; it can identify its idea of God with the everlasting God who is Lord over all; it may confuse its guidance for the conduct of life with that which appears only when men in humility and trust seek for a way that they have not found. There is in Christian faith a scepticism about man and his efforts of thought. So easily does he make himself the "measure of all things," make his own ways, his own culture, his own intellectual attainments the center of life, that his intellect cannot be trusted too far. He is a rebel and his rebellion reflects itself in all that he does, even the thoughts that he thinks.

And yet the mind of man is not simply denied. Redemption comes. It comes supremely in a personal life, not in a set of ideas. But that personal life appears against a heritage which bears, among other things, great guiding ideas. It transforms those ideas and is generative of others. It calls for a "renewing of the mind"; it results in making a new creature who uses his mind, as all else in the service of his Lord. He seeks to bring "every thought to the obedience of Christ." [12] Thus his mind, given by God, is released for God's service. Yet, it remains a human, limited mind. But even the discernment of the limitation is itself, in part, a work of the mind.

3. THOUGHT AND THE CHRISTIAN ATTITUDES

The relationships in which a man stands and his interpretation of them will affect the character of his thought, and the implications of the Christian vision are rendered more precise as we trace the implications of the Christian attitudes. These, too, involve thought whether it seeks to serve the faith or whether it simply arises for its own sake. The attitudes determine the thinker, his thoughts, and the objects about which he thinks.

Thus the Christian attitude toward nature has profoundly affected all thought in the West. There has been a careful avoidance of tendencies to deify nature itself, and these have sometimes led Christians to a spirit of disdain toward nature. Repeatedly Christian thinkers have expressed themselves in ways which bordered on the Gnostic denial that matter is good. Indifference to the study of the natural world was the spirit of even so great a mind as that of Augustine, and his influence was deeply felt throughout the medieval centuries. However, even he did not think of

[12] II Corinthians 10:5, K.J.V.

matter as positively evil. And he did set forth the idea of a dependable God who ruled all things. And this idea, when it became coupled with an attitude of positive appreciation of the world, was one of the germinating forces in the development of science. Nature followed God's laws, said Christian thinkers. And though God could intervene, he did not ordinarily do so. His world was dependable, as he was.

Christian faith reminds the thinker to consider himself, too, as he thinks of nature and her ways. Made from the good earth, he still bears the marks of his origin. He is no disembodied mind, able to dissociate himself from a particular point in time and space. His body determines to a degree his own interpretation of that which is significant for life. He, like others of whom he thinks, is subject to drives of hunger and sex, and these are matters of which his thought must take account.

The Christian view of man's relation to himself reminds the thinker that he can never leave himself out of account in what he thinks. The thinker and the thoughts cannot be separated. Even his thinking is itself personal decision; it reflects his anxieties and involves him in risks. It can never transcend the broken human situation in which he is involved. It is the thought of one man in a specific situation, caught by his finitude and yet reflecting also some glimpse of that which exceeds his situation.

He cannot forget that others are like him. No account of the world can overlook human decision. The world cannot be a machine in which persons are simply cogs; it cannot be a mind in which persons are simply thoughts. It is a reality which, in some strange manner, contains beings who live by meanings and who express them in decisions which are their own.

That he encounters others as groups as well as individuals is important for him too. He can never get outside of the group relationships within which he stands. They limit him. And yet they afford him insights which he would not possess otherwise. His involvement in the life of the family gives him a group of people for whom he feels special responsibility. It is almost inevitable that he will favor them, seek to give them security and status, and that in so doing he will be unfair to others. However, at the same time, he may know the heights and depths of life in ways that he simply cannot if he ever stands outside the responsibilities of family involvement. He is involved in economic and political groupings which he is apt to want to preserve insofar as they minister to his needs. It is hard for him to look favorably at types of thought which tend to undermine his position. At the same time, he cannot be indifferent to the economic and political ingredients in all thinking—even theological.

He will be sensitive, too, to the group life of mankind, past and present. The Christian is an historical thinker, knowing his own involvement in history, and concerned that others remember the significance of history. No non-historical view of reality will be adequate for him. Indeed, Christian faith has been one of the forces that has constantly called for the development of philosophies of history.

That the attitude toward God is involved in all thinking will be clear to him. Thought inevitably points toward a central source. And yet that Reality does not in itself deny the existence of all else. Science is important, psychology rightly studies the human creature; sociology appropriately examines the behavior of men in groups; history traces the course of their life; philosophy properly probes meanings and seeks their interrelationships. The adding of all these together cannot span the gap between creature and Creator. But in their exercise will be intimations of that Reality which is the source and ground of all meaning.

4. THOUGHT AND THE EXPRESSIONS OF FAITH

Because thought, arising in the life of faith, can stand outside of faith, make it an object, thought is able to derive something from and contribute something to the other expressions of faith. Generally speaking Christians have held that thought must ever remain in dynamic connection with faith's other expressions. But at times, as we shall see, it can contribute to them by standing—for a time at least, outside of them. There is a time to think—even for the man of faith—a time when he does not worship, or act, or engage actively in the church. And if that time is permitted, thought can make its most significant contribution to worship, action, and the church.

Thought must ever take into account that which is experienced in worship. The high and holy One confronts man, and overcomes the chasm that lies between them. He brings man love, and joy, and peace. No system of thought that takes the Christian vision seriously can overlook this. It must be remembered even at times when thought carries on its cool analytic work. But that cool work can make its contribution to worship, too. For thought, as we have said, distinguishes and relates. It seeks to set the true experience of worship apart from obeisance before false gods. And it seeks to trace out ways in which the experience of worship can be related to the rest of life.

The fellowship of the church is the matrix within which Christian thought normally arises. There the thinker has met the redemptive love which has been borne through the centuries since the decisive act of disclosure. The theologian is no solitary who goes, like Descartes, to sit and think by himself, spinning ideas out of his own consciousness. He is responsible to the church; he recognizes its problems and is engaged in the task of seeking to find a word that will be relevant to it. And yet the capacity of thought to stand outside that in which it lives makes it possible for the thinker to carry on his constructive and critical thought with reference to the church. He can compare her action with the vision she carries, confront her with the gospel she proclaims, compare her with the ideal described in the classic books of faith. Indeed, thought that comes from outside the church may become God's word for her. Those who are driven from the church, who bitterly resent her behavior, may have something true to say to her. Rufus Jones wrote a book with the significant title, *The Church's Debt to Heretics.*[13]

The call for action in the concrete situation is apt to call to the attention of the thinker that which he easily forgets. It has been almost a disease of philosophical thinkers to have tended to oversimplify the ethical situation. Ideals are presented, but the difficulties of choices in situations where risks are real, where knowledge is less than complete, where ambiguities appear, are overlooked. The Christian imperative of love, to be expressed here and now, without waiting for the ideal moment to arrive, gives the thinker difficult material with which to deal. On the other hand, the cold and hard-headed analysis of issues, the gathering of information, the weighing of ideals can contribute significantly to effective action. Without them love is apt to be blind indeed.

The arts and literature present the thinker with material which may cause him difficulty. So concerned is he for precision of expression that he is apt to be impatient when ideas are simply suggested or clothed in the language of phantasy. It may be—and many have said that it is—true that the things of greatest concern in faith simply cannot be expressed in cold prose. At any rate, it seems that much is to be gained by a careful attention to their poetic and artistic expression. Doctrine may fail to say what a story or a picture can convey. The parables of Jesus are difficult to contain in prosaic utterance. On the other hand, not to seek accuracy of expression where it is possible may be to betray religion. The distinctions will be overlooked; the true and the false will not be set apart.

A personal question is involved in the preceding analysis. Can there be Christian thinking where there is not involvement of the thinker in the

---

[13] Rufus M. Jones, *The Church's Debt to Heretics* (New York: George H. Doran Company, 1924).

life and worship of the church? It is a difficult question indeed. Some consideration of it belongs to the final section of the book. For here we come to the nature of Christian thinking and its relation to Christian living.

5. THOUGHT AND FAITH

We have now completed our survey of the setting within which Christian thinking takes place. Theology has been viewed from the standpoint of the Christian vision; it has been examined in terms of the Christian attitudes; it has been seen in relationship to other expressions of faith.

That the task of Christian thinking is never ended is implied in all that has been said. As the Christians of the early centuries had to define their faith and relate it to ideas they encountered in the culture about them, so does the modern church, so do modern Christians. The definitions at which they arrive will stand in some real continuity with those of the past; but they will be products of the present.

Thought again is needed to distinguish the faith of the church. The bases which have been chosen by the church in the past come before us for examination again. What do the ancient creeds mean, and how should they be interpreted? What is the message of the Bible? What part does the tradition of the church play in the determination of the theology of the present? What is the place of religious experience in the determination of belief? What is the function of reason in the life of faith?

As in the earliest days of the church, so today there are ideas all about it in the culture. With them Christian thought must enter into a never-ending conversation. It has the task of relating the faith, which, as we have seen, is inseparable from that of distinguishing it. The natural sciences are developing ideas about matter and motion, energy and existence, time and space. Conversation can clarify the relation of these to Christian convictions about God and the world. Psychologists are making discoveries concerning the behavior of human beings. Teamwork is actually going on at the practical level between ministers and psychologists. Conversations are being carried on at the theoretical level about the relations between the theories and discoveries of the psychologists and the convictions of Christians about the nature of the human being. Sociologists turn their attention to the nature of man, to the significance of his life in culture, to his religious behavior in particular. Here again actual teamwork is in progress between church groups and social workers for the alleviation of maladjustments in the social area. And conversation is being carried on at the theoretic level between theologians and social scientists about the nature of man as a social being. Philosophers are continuing the age-long search for wisdom, the analysis of the basic ideas which emerge in the mind of man. And the conversation which has been carried on through the centuries between theologians and philosophers still goes on. The question of the relations between faith and reason is opened again and again. How much can be discovered by reason? What is the relation of that which faith believes and that which the reason holds to be true? Is it possible to prove that God exists? If so, what is the relation of the God so proven to God as disclosed in the Christian revelation? Out of the conversations come new definitions. Thought distinguishes, then relates, then distinguishes again.

We return now at the last to the two groups for whom this book is written. They were compared with people coming to the examination of a work of art. One who is a student of history may be concerned with a certain picture because of what the examination of it may contribute to his understanding of the century in which it was painted. Its artistic merit is a matter of indifference; its aesthetic effect on the student himself does not matter. He may be moved by it or not. As a student of history he wants to understand a certain century, and the picture can help him do it. A second student may be deeply moved by a picture and undertakes a study of it in the effort to derive a fuller and richer appreciation of it than he now has. He studies its colors and contours, he reads about its creator, about trends in artistic production, about symbolism, about aesthetic theory—indeed, he studies everything that he can lay his hands on which will help him to appreciate the picture.

Similarly two people can engage in thinking about faith. This is true because of the nature of thought. Arising within life, it can yet stand outside of life. Once religious ideas have arisen, they can be examined, so to speak, from the outside. For the student of Western culture it is important that he understand the nature of the Christian vision, of the attitudes involved in it, of the expressions it has found. To identify it is an academic exercise of significance for the intellectual enterprise in which he is engaged.

Another thinks for the sake of his faith. For him the study of it becomes a source of religious enrichment. His thought is not detached. The affirmation of the mind is carried into the service of worship and illuminates its meaning. It is carried into the arena of action and becomes a determining factor in a decision that is to be made. It affects appreciation of art and music, of poetry and prose. It finds its place among the binding forces which relate him to others in the fellowship of the church.

But, because he has a mind, he can be imaginatively on the outside even when he is actively on the inside of the life of faith. This is important, because it means that thought can exercise its critical functions. The conversation with various philosophies and religions goes on within him. Even the conversation of faith with doubt is not excluded; he can repeat words once used in response to Jesus, "Lord, I believe; help thou mine unbelief!" [14]

The problem of personal faith is critical today. The individual may find that resources and supports which were available to men in times past offer little help to him. And yet if he is like some others in our time, Christian faith may come alive for him. Its vision of the world and its meaning, of man and his significance may present him with a compelling interpretation of his own life and the context within which it is set. Its attitudes may bring wholeness to his living. And its several expressions may sustain him.

He enters into the life of the church; but this may be in a problematical situation. It often appears to be far from that which can bring a surrounding context of wholeness to the people within it. Its status within the present situation is not clear; it is cut off from parts of its own past. And yet it is rediscovering its heritage, and the recovery of one part contributes to the finding of another. Marvin Halverson points out ways in which interest in religious drama today is connected with a renewal of the liturgical life of the church; both are connected with a reappropriation of theological understandings.[15] Further, a new consciousness of the character of the church and of its role in the contemporary world is arising. A new wholeness is coming to realization within its life.

The wholeness of the individual and that of the church are torn, however, by the fragmentation of our culture. Sober analysts of our present speak of dislocations and disturbances with little hope of any healing soon. Whether changes will come which will radically change all that we are accustomed to, or if there will be transformations of a more gradual sort into some kind of stable order, or, indeed, if annihilation of life as we know it is in store, we cannot know. The Christian is not untouched by all this. He cannot find religious fulfillment by withdrawal from life and the world. He may feel that he has seen a vision which presents the kind of wholeness that any worthwhile culture must possess. He may also treasure realizations of that wholeness as they are remembered within the culture of the past. And he may see, scattered and dissociated, the bits of a cultural vision even among the dislocations of the present. So he may in

---

[14] Mark 9:24, K.J.V.

[15] Marvin Halverson, ed., *Religious Drama, I* (New York: Meridian Books, Inc., 1957), p. 5.

imagination project some image of what a significant culture might be like. But he will be bound neither by the past nor by his imaginative thoughts concerning the future. For his is a faith which envisages a Reality transcending particular cultures, a Reality both creative and redemptive in his relations with all of his world.

READINGS

From the Bible

1. A high valuation is placed on wisdom in some passages in Proverbs: 8 and 9, for example.

2. Scepticism about wisdom is voiced in Job 28, Ecclesiastes 2.

3. Christ is identified as the wisdom of God by a number of New Testament writers: John 1, I Corinthians 1.

From Historic Christianity

1. Justin Martyr, *The First Apology,* relates the revelation in Christ to the wisdom of the Greeks.

2. Anselm, *An Address* (Proslogion), is an illustration of "faith seeking understanding" about the nature and existence of God.

3. Søren Kierkegaard, *Philosophical Fragments,* chapter 3, presents the central affirmation of Christianity as "The Absolute Paradox: a Metaphysical Crotchet."

FOR STUDY AND DISCUSSION

Re-examine the statement of Christian affirmations you made at the beginning of the study. What would you add? What would you subtract? Why?

BIBLIOGRAPHY

SOURCE MATERIALS FOR THE STUDY OF HISTORIC CHRISTIANITY

Collections

John Baillie, John T. McNeill, and Henry P. Van Dusen, general editors, *The Library of Christian Classics* (Philadelphia: The Westminster Press; London: S. C. M. Press, Ltd.).

Editorial Board headed by Roy J. Deferrari, *The Fathers of the Church* (New York: Fathers of the Church, Inc.).

Johannes Quasten, editor, *Ancient Christian Writers* (Westminster: The Newman Press).

Alexander Roberts and James Donaldson, editors, *Ante-Nicene Christian Library* (Edinburgh: T. and T. Clark). American Reprint of the Edinburgh Edition, Revised by A. Cleveland Coxe (New York: Charles Scribner's Sons).

Philip Schaff, editor, *A Select Library of the Nicene and Post-Nicene Fathers* (New York: The Christian Literature Company).

Available in Paperback Editions (Code numbers should be used in ordering. A key to publishers follows this list.)

Anonymous	*Little Flowers of Saint Francis.* D69-Im and L91-Pen
Anselm, Saint	*Proslogium; Monologium; An Appendix in Behalf of the Fool by Gaunilon; & Cur Deus Homo.* P54-Open
Aquinas, Saint Thomas	*The Pocket Aquinas.* W575-WSP
	Providence and Predestination. 6064-Gate
	On the Truth of the Catholic Faith (Summa Contra Gentiles). Five vols. D26-, D27-, D28a and b-, D29-IM

Augustine, Saint	*On Christian Doctrine.* LLA80-Lib *The City of God.* D59-Im and M101-Ungar (Selections) *Confessions.* W245-WSP and D101-Im *The Enchiridion on Faith, Hope and Love.* 6065-Gate *Of True Religion.* 6042-Gate *Augustine Synthesis,* Erich Przywara, ed. TB35-Torch
Boehme, Jacob	*Personal Christianity.* 502-Ungar
Bonaventura, Saint	*Mind's Road to God.* LLA32-Lib
Butler, Joseph	*The Analogy of Religion.* M115-Ungar *Five Sermons.* LLA21-Lib
Calvin, John	*On the Christian Faith.* Selections from the *Institutes, Commentaries,* and *Tracts.* LLA93-Lib *On God and Man.* M103-Ungar *On God and Political Duty.* LLA23-Lib *Institutes of the Christian Religion.* (2 Vol. Set) Eerd
Channing, William Ellery	*Unitarian Christianity and Other Essays.* AHS21-Lib
Donne, John	*Devotions.* 30-AA *Sermons of John Donne.* LA17-Mer
Meister Eckhart	*Meister Eckhart: A Modern Translation.* TB8-Torch
Edwards, Jonathan	*Nature of True Virtue.* 37-AA
Erasmus, Desiderius	*Praise of Folly.* 23-AA
Erasmus–Luther	*Discourse on Free Will.* M114-Ungar
Feuerbach, Ludwig	*Essence of Christianity.* M109-Ungar and TB11-Torch
Francis de Sales, Saint	*Introduction to the Devout Life.* D13-Im
Harnack, Adolf	*Outlines of the History of Dogma.* BP49-Bea *What is Christianity?* TB17-Torch
Hegel, Friedrich	*On Christianity: Early Theological Writings.* TB79-Torch
Hilton, Walter	*The Ladder of Perfection.* L74-Pen

James, William
The Varieties of Religious Experience. C71-Dolp and MT320-Ment
Will to Believe and Human Immortality. Dov.

Saint John of the Cross
Dark Night of the Soul. D78-Im and M110-Ungar

Kant, Immanuel
Religion within the Limits of Reason Alone. TB67-Torch

Kierkegaard, Søren
Christian Discourses. 49-GB
Edifying Discourses. TB32-Torch
Fear and Trembling and *Sickness Unto Death.* A30-Anch
Purity of Heart. TB4-Torch
Selections from the Writings of Kierkegaard. A210-Anch

Luther, Martin
Christian Liberty. Muhl
Three Treatises. Muhl

Locke, John
Letter Concerning Toleration. LLA22-Lib

Mather, Cotton
Selections from Cotton Mather. 20-Haf

Mirandola, Pico Della
Oration on the Dignity of Man. 6040-Gate

Newman, John Henry
Apologia Pro Vita Sua. D37-Im and B10-RivEd
Essay on the Development of Christian Doctrine. D105-Im
Grammar of Assent. D19-Im

Rauschenbusch, Walter
A Theology for the Social Gospel. E7-Apex

Schelling, F. W. J.
Of Human Freedom. P73-Open

Schleiermacher, Friedrich
On Religion: Speeches to Its Cultured Despisers. TB36-Torch and 507-Ungar (Abridged)
Soliloquies. P77-Open

Thomas a Kempis
The Imitation of Christ. PL5-PB, D17-Im and L27-Pen

Wesley, John
By John Wesley. 542-Refl

Woolman, John
Journal of John Woolman and a Plea for the Poor. AE2-Ctdl

Key to code letters of publishers

AA Ann Arbor Paperbacks, University of Michigan Press, Ann Arbor, Mich.
Anch Anchor Books, Doubleday & Co., Inc., 575 Madison Ave., New York 22, N. Y.
Apex Apex Books, Abingdon Press, 201 8th Ave. S., Nashville 3, Tenn.
Bea Beacon Press, 25 Beacon St., Boston 8, Mass.
Ctdl The Citadel Press, 222 Park Ave. South, New York 3, N. Y.
Dolp Dolphin Books and Dolphin Masters, 575 Madison Ave., New York 22, N. Y.
Dov Dover Publications, Inc., 180 Varick St., New York 14, N. Y.
Eerd Wm. B. Eerdmans Publishing Co., 255 Jefferson Ave., S. E., Grand Rapids 3, Mich.
Gate Gateway Editions, Henry Regnery Co., 14 E. Jackson Blvd., Chicago 4, Ill.
GB Galaxy Books, Oxford University Press, Inc., 417 Fifth Ave., New York 16, N. Y.
Haf Hafner Library of World Classics, Hafner Publishing Co., 31 E. 10th St., New York 3, N. Y.
Im Doubleday Image Books, 575 Madison Ave., New York 22, N. Y.
Lib The Liberal Arts Press, Inc., 153 W. 72nd St., New York 23, N. Y.
Ment Mentor Books. New American Library of World Literature, Inc., 501 Madison Ave., New York 22, N. Y.
Mer Meridian Books, Inc., 12 E. 22nd St., New York 10, N. Y.
Muhl Muhlenberg Press, 2900 Queen Lane, Philadelphia 29, Pa.
Open The Open Court Publishing Co., La Salle, Ill.
PB Pocket Books, Inc., 630 Fifth Ave., New York 20, N. Y.
Pen Penguin Books, Inc., 3300 Clipper Mill Rd., Baltimore 11, Md.
Refl Reflection Books, Association Press, 291 Broadway, New York 7, N. Y.
Riv-Ed Riverside Editions, Houghton Mifflin Co., 2 Park St., Boston 7, Mass.
Torch Harper Torchbooks, Harper & Brothers, 49 E. 33rd St., New York 16, N. Y.
Ungar Frederick Ungar Publishing Co., 131 E. 23rd St., New York 10, N. Y.
WSP Washington Square Press, Inc., 630 Fifth Ave., New York 20, N. Y.

INDEX OF BIBLICAL REFERENCES

OLD TESTAMENT

NEW TESTAMENT

GENERAL INDEX

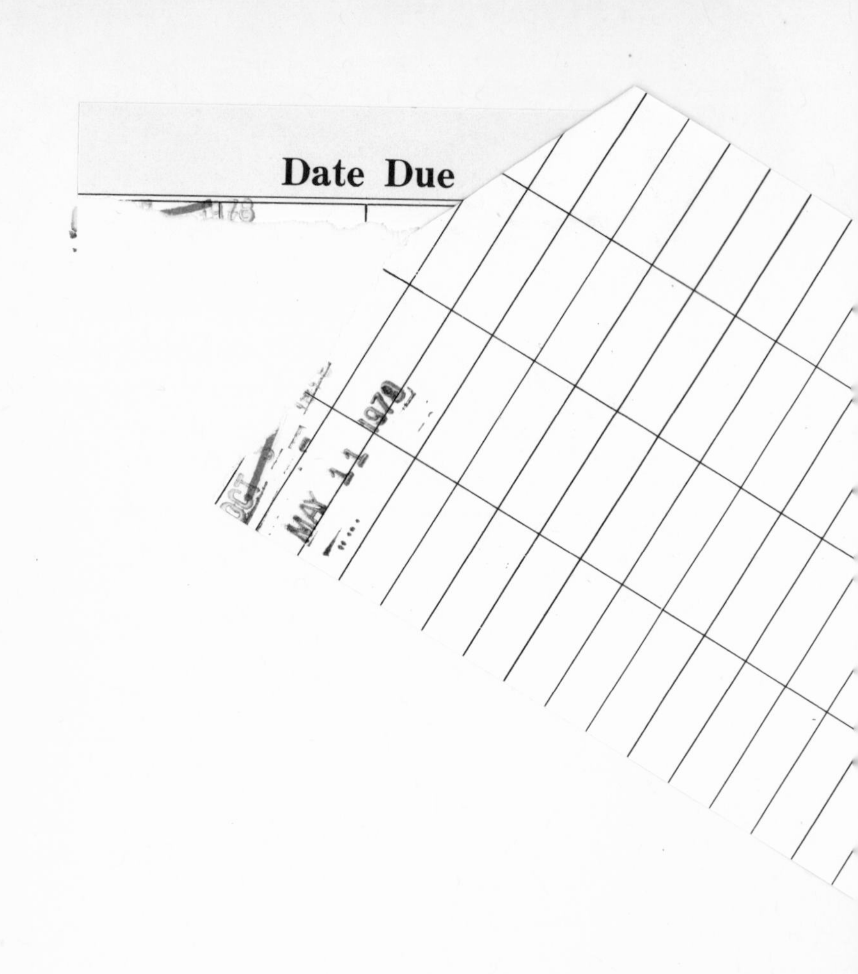
Date Due
MAY 11 1979